BEYOND CUBAN WATERS

BEYOND CUBAN WATERS

ÁFRICA, *LA YUMA*, AND THE
ISLAND'S GLOBAL IMAGINATION

Paul Ryer

Vanderbilt University Press | Nashville

This book is printed on acid-free paper.
Manufactured in the United States of America

This book was made possible in part
by financial assistance from the
RUTH LANDES MEMORIAL RESEARCH FUND,
a program of the Reed Foundation.

Library of Congress Cataloging-in-Publication Data on file
LC control number 2016030964
LC classification number F1760 .R94 2016
Dewey classification number 972.91—dc23
LC record available at *lccn.loc.gov/2016030964*

ISBN 978-0-8265-2118-7 (hardcover)
ISBN 978-0-8265-2119-4 (paperback)
ISBN 978-0-8265-2120-0 (ebook)

for Kelly

Contents

Acknowledgments

Although it is impossible to acknowledge every important impact on this project, I must begin with my father, Joseph Ryer, whose decision to sail with my sister and me to Haiti and the Caribbean from 1979 to 1981 set the stage for my anthropological consciousness and commitments. I have also been fortunate to have had a number of special teachers, including Mrs. Lambert, Mrs. Dailey, and Mr. Stoval. David Edwards and Deborah Gewertz redefine collegiate mentorship, and words are inadequate to thank either of them. At the University of Chicago, many colleagues and classmates contributed invaluable critiques, comments, and informal support, including especially Paul Silverstein, Kimbra Smith, Frank Romagosa, Daniel Wall, Keith Brown, Anne-Maria Makhulu, Frank Bechter, David Altshuler, Christopher Nelson, Matthew Hull, Hylton White, Krisztina Fehérváry, Robin Derby, Emily Vogt, and Greg Beckett. Among the faculty of the department, Marshall Sahlins, Andy Apter, Jean Comaroff, Susan Gal, John Kelly, James Fernandez, R. T. Smith, Stephan Palmié, and, most particularly, Michel-Rolph Trouillot taught me, step-by-step, to become a professional anthropologist.

The Ruth Landes Memorial Research Fund of the Reed Foundation, the University of Chicago, the Trustees of Amherst College, the John D. and Catherine T. MacArthur Foundation, Mount Holyoke College, and the University of California provided essential field research support. Beatriz Riefkohl, Josh Beck, and the staff of the University of Chicago's Center for Latin American Studies provided invaluable support during the difficult initial years of the project. My studies in Cuba also could not have succeeded without the extraordinary assistance of my parents, Marianne and Dean Lewis, who not only repeatedly brought assorted supplies, mail, and tax forms to Havana and a steady flow of books, articles, stories, and their own Cuban visitors back to the United States over the years, but also provided a quiet writing space in their attic.

Lynn Morgan and Debbora Battaglia were fantastic colleagues and mentors at Mount Holyoke College and beyond. The University of California provided a warm welcome and a welcome refuge, with special thanks to Amalia Cabezas, Deborah Wong, Jonathan Ritter, David Biggs, and Hong-Anh Ly. The staff and all my colleagues in the Department of Anthropology have been incredibly supportive. Particular thanks are due to Christina Schwenkel, Sally Ness, Susan Ossman, Robin Nelson, Derick Fay, T. S. Harvey, Karl Taube, Yolanda Moses, Christine Gailey, and Sang-Hee Lee, who each in different ways have made me a better scholar and anthropologist. Heartfelt thanks also to Felipe Vélez and Iván Noel Pérez for proofreading the text, to Eli Bortz and the editorial team at Vanderbilt University Press for their tremendous patience and faith in this project, and to the anonymous reviewers whose careful and insightful readings have greatly improved the argument and lucidity of the book.

It is such a gift to have a marvelous cohort of fellow ethnographers and students of contemporary Cuban life, especially including: Nadine Fernandez, Mona Rosendahl, Robin Moore, Audrey Charlton, Nancy Stout, Thomas Carter, Nancy Burke, Matthew Hill, Denni Blum, Kristina Wirtz, Ivor Miller, Kenneth Routon, Kaifa Roland, Michael Mason, David Forrest, Ariana Hernández Reguant, Katherine Hagedorn, Laurie Frederik, Shawn Wells, Sean Brotherton, Anna Cristina Pertierra, Noelle Stout, Jafari S. Allen, Benjamin Eastman, João Felipe Gonçalves, Teresa Maribel Sanchez, Hannah Garth, Mrinalini Tankha, and Laura-Zoe Humphreys. Too many Cubans to name individually put up with my questions and idiosyncrasies and shared their lives with breathtaking generosity, goodwill, and grace. Among them, special thanks to Lina, Rolando, Fernando, María Elena, Eladio, Verna, Mario and Sara, Fonsy, Zeida, Aymara, Mario and Marta, and especially Iván Noel Pérez, as well as Gregory Biniowsky, John Kim, René Flinn, and many, many others. The lessons they have taught me go far beyond the academic contents of this text, and I carry them with me every day.

Last but not least, Kelly, Liam, Martin, and Timothy have suffered through the writing of this book more than anyone and, although innocent of its inevitable shortcomings, are full partners in its accomplishment.

En aquellos últimos años, Esteban había asistido al desarrollo, en sí misma, de una propensión crítica—enojosa, a veces, por cuanto le vedaba el goce de ciertos entusiasmos inmediatos, compartidos por lo más—que se negaba a dejarse llevar por un criterio generalizado. Cuando la Revolución le era presentada como un acontecimiento sublime, sin taras ni fallas, la Revolución se le hacía vulnerable y torcida. Pero ante un monárquico la hubiera defendido con los mismos argumentos que lo exasperaban cuando salían de boca de un Collot d'Herbois. Aborrecía la desaforada demagogia del Pére Duchesne, tanto como las monsergas apocalípticas de los emigrados. Se sentía cura frente a los anticuras; anticura frente a los curas; monárquico cuando le decían que todos los reyes—¡un Jaime de Escocia, un Enrique IV, un Carlos de Suecia, dígame usted!—habían sido unos degenerados; antimonárquico cuando oía alabar a ciertos Borbones de España. "Soy un discutidor—admitía, recordando lo que Víctor le había dicho unos días antes—Pero discutidor conmigo mismo, que es peor."

Alejo Carpentier, El siglo de las luces

During these last years Esteban had witnessed the development within himself of a critical propensity—annoying at times, inasmuch as it deprived him of the pleasure of certain spontaneous enthusiasms, shared by the majority— which refused to allow itself to be guided by any general criterion. When the Revolution was offered to him as a sublime event, without blemish or fault, the Revolution thereby became warped and vulnerable. Yet to a monarchist he would have defended it with the same arguments which exasperated him when they came from the lips of Collot d'Herbois. He abominated the outrageous demagogy of the "Père Duchesne" as much as he did the apocalyptic ravings of the émigrés. When he was with anti-clericals he became a priest, and with priests he became anti-clerical; he was a monarchist when he was told that all kings—James of Scotland, Henry the Fourth, Charles of Sweden forsooth!— had been degenerate, and an anti-monarchist, when he heard some of the Spanish Bourbons being praised. "I'm too fond of arguing," he admitted, remembering what Victor had said to him a few days before, "but I argue with myself, which is worse."

Alejo Carpentier, *Explosion in a Cathedral*
(translated by John Sturrock)

AN ANTILLEAN ARCHIPELAGO

I first met Michel-Rolph Trouillot at a party in Chicago, shortly after concluding field research in Cuba.[1] He was new to the university, and I was full of enthusiasm for Cuba and thrilled to have the opportunity to engage with one of the great Caribbeanist thinkers of our time. At some point in the conversation, he asked me to characterize changes in the racial dynamics of contemporary Cuba in the context of an economic crisis and yet an enduring socialist state dedicated to Marxist models of equality. In answering, I began to retell an aphorism commonly heard in Cuba, in which a young white woman tells her mother she's met and is about to marry a black man. "No!" says the mom. "But he's a doctor," says the daughter. At this point Rolph leaned forward and finished the story for me: "'Ah then, he's not black, he's mulatto!' 'And Mom, he has a car.' 'No no no, then he's white!' the story concludes," Rolph said animatedly. "I heard this exact story all the time growing up in Haiti."

This recollected conversation highlights a central concern of this book: What wider patterns and connections are overlooked when we specialists focus strictly on Cuba as a culture or an island unto itself? What are the enduring cultural legacies of Cuban colonial and plantation history, as well as a half century of state socialism, and how do those articulate with other socialisms as well as wider regional and transnational realities? Not only is the Republic of Cuba in actuality an archipelago that includes two of the largest Caribbean islands and many smaller cays, but it is an archipelago within an Antilles of archipelagos with deeply global ties. Surely it is worthwhile to look out across the Caribbean and beyond, to see which stories are familiar enough for others to finish. And then, perhaps, some of what really is particular to contemporary Cuba might come into clearer focus as well. Indeed, there is no lack of things distinctively Cuban! Although I had relatively substantial Caribbean and Latin American experience before moving to Cuba, the revolutionary republic's differences were often so overwhelming that they might be best framed by an earlier contrapuntal conversation:

> A month after I had arrived in Havana to begin fieldwork, I bumped into Marina Majoli, a researcher I had previously met in Chicago, where she had been an exchange scholar. From our first meeting, Marina provided much-appreciated orientation for my planned project, but since my actual arrival, she had been on a family visit in Europe. The daughter of Italian diplomats, she was raised in Canada but had committed the past thirty years to the revolutionary process and to her Cuban partner. I was glad to see a familiar, sympathetic face.
>
> "Hello, Marina! I finally got here! How are you, and how was Italy?"
>
> "Hi Paul, bienvenido, good to see you. I'm fine. Italy was . . ." She looks flustered. "It was crazy, chaos. Nothing there makes any sense. I am so happy to be back—even though things here are difficult, at least everything in Cuba is logical."

Struggling bureaucratically, linguistically, and with a range of incomprehensible everyday practices, at that moment very little in Cuba seemed logical to me. In fact, ordinary things were becoming less and less intelligible: Why did Cubans go to work, when their pay was twelve to twenty dollars per month, and they could easily earn more in a single transaction in the hard-currency economy? How could it be that no one seemed malnourished, when the monthly food ration would last no more than a week? How did people stay decently dressed when there had been no clothing allowance in years? How could nearly every job be for the state? In the face of generations of political conflict with the United States, how and why did young people know so much about Hollywood? How could the visually striking racial integration of every neighborhood (indeed, of nearly every family) be reconciled with ubiquitous, vociferous race-based distinctions and discriminations?[2] In a moment, Marina's offhand comment made the case for long-term ethnographic practice: clearly, making sense of Cuba would be a long process.

The tension between strong regional similarities and insular nationalist distinctiveness has long occupied Caribbeanist scholarship, from Sidney

Mintz's (1971, 2010) seminal insight that the plantation system is the key to Caribbean regularities, to Antonio Benítez-Rojo's rhizome-inspired rendering of the paradox by which a "Haitian or a Martinican feels closer to France than to Jamaica, and a Puerto Rican identifies better with the United States than with Surinam" and yet they all share a common rhythm (1992, 37),[3] as well as many other scholars' historical and anthropological work (e.g., Trouillot 1992). In attempting to make sense of the distinctive—and distinctively state socialist—features of contemporary Cuba evident in my conversation with Marina Majoli, then, this book aims to link an emerging scholarly conversation about post-Soviet Cuba to wider Caribbean and diasporic trends. If Cuba has something to add to understanding "Caribbeanness," surely it would also be unwise to read as merely "Cuban" a story told as often in Port-au-Prince as in Havana. It is my contention that like the interplay of "global" and "local," the two readings are recursive and mutually enriching.

* * *

This is a semiotically oriented, ethnographically rooted study of everyday Cuban geographic imaginations about the world and Cuba's place in it, working from within the republic and its diasporas. After locating the project within its contemporary ethnographic context, I will first consider a vernacular mapping of the capitalist world by Cubans residing within the socialist republic by examining the rise and fall of the space of what I call *La Yuma* and its uppermost brands, symbols, and goods. Closely examined, these imported goods have particular local meanings far beyond the common politicized interpretation: rather, I argue that they both index and constitute emergent transnational remittance circuits, and making sense of them calls for methodological innovation as well as careful cultural interpretation. But there is another vernacular Cuban sense of elsewhere very much at odds with La Yuma in the post-Soviet era: that of *África*, often framed in Marxist evolutionist terms that seem irreducibly racist to a North American ear. And in a context in which, as we will see, the national:foreign boundary is profound (Roland 2011), we can also interrogate wider boundaries and borders by paying particular attention to those hardest to classify. Thus, I will consider Cuban-educated African students—often long-term residents who have adopted many revolutionary Cuban cultural practices—who offer a distinctive window into hyphenated Cubanness and shed a particular light on the interplay of racial and national boundaries in Cuba; Verena Stolcke's (formerly Verena Martinez-Alier) notion of "classificatory embarrassment" is particularly apt here (Stolcke [1974] 1989, 1043). Moving then from these geographies of elsewhere to Cuban notions of Cubanness (*cubanía* or *cubanidad*[4]) and focusing primarily on illustrative everyday usages and silences, I argue that these categories are not shaped as they would be in North America and that ultimately the ostensibly national classification, Cuban, is racialized as mixed or *mulato* precisely in counterpoint to these already examined imagined elsewheres.[5] Finally, I investigate the ways that migration transforms both signs and symbols of belonging, and in following migrants into diaspora, I trace the mapping and remapping of Cuban and foreign goods and fashions—in the process, the Cuban geographic imagination can be seen in a new way.

Thus, in this introductory chapter I situate the project in terms of its context in space and time, authorial and political positioning and methods, locate it in a context of dueling surveillances, and review emerging themes of its recent ethnographic research.[6] The first chapter considers the appropriation, idealization, and domestication (by both younger Cubans and African students) of symbols and goods from the United States and then looks ethnographically at Cuba's distinctively Caribbean socialist parallel economy. The second chapter outlines popular Cuban ideologies of África, both in interviews in the wake of massive internationalist experience and in observations of Cubans' interactions with African students long residing on the island. In Chapter 3, I consider ethnographic data on official and popular distinctions drawn by Cubans themselves to delimit contemporary national and racial classifications and identities—that is, who or what it means to be or become "Cuban." Chapter 4 examines changes and continuities in the meaning of styles, symbols, boundaries, and identities under conditions of diaspora and migration or serial migration (Ossman 2013). Finally, with the weight of the presented ethnographic and historical material and remapped geography of imagination, the book reconsiders the received paradigms of where and how to locate this socialist but not utopian society.

Positioning the Work: Space, Time, and Author

With the collapse of state socialism in Europe and eventually the fall of the Soviet Union itself in the early 1990s, Cuba suffered a massive crisis euphemistically referred to as the "Special Period in Times of Peace." As mentioned in virtually every scholarly work on Cuba written since, exchange with the Soviet Bloc COMECON nations, which had accounted for 83 percent of Cuba's external trade (Pérez-López 1995, 124), dried up; by the most conservative estimates, the economy shrank 35 to 50 percent (Centeno and Font 1997; Mujal-León 2011). Fuel, food, clothing, consumer goods, and spare parts went from scarce to nonexistent. Desperate to staunch the hemorrhage, Cuban officials sought new procedures, contacts, and theories—even from the so-called "enemy"—of potential use in saving their struggling system. In this context, the University of Havana established a scholarly exchange with the University of Chicago—largely underwritten by the John D. and Catherine T. MacArthur Foundation—in hopes of adapting the theories of the Chicago School of Economics to salvage still-existing socialism. By the strangest of ironies, then, it was the long-departed Milton Friedman and the "Chicago Boys" who opened the initial space for this project.

Without wishing to be unduly autobiographical, I feel it is important to locate the study briefly both in terms of my own initial interest in Cuba and in terms of the immediate Cuban research context. This is not so much due to a desire to find my authorial position on every page, but rather because these factors mark some of the distinctive conditions of the production of this knowledge (Verdery 1996, 4–9; Taylor 2010). As a young teenager in the late 1970s and early 1980s, I was homeschooled and lived in the Bahamas, Haiti, the Dominican Republic, and St. Croix, US Virgin Islands, while my alternatively oriented parents taught sailing and practiced back-to-the-sea subsistence living. In St. Croix, especially, we lived in a trailer park with Cruzan, Trinidadian, Antiguan, and Haitian neighbors and friends for two years. The point here is not some aporetic claim to ethnographic authority about the region—I've never set foot in Jamaica or Trinidad, for instance—but rather, simply to sketch the background to my Antillean archipelagic interest. In any case, most important of all were the three months spent on the northwest coast of Haiti, where the material conditions, malnutrition, and struggles of the people there in the face of a military well-armed by the United States was overwhelming.[7] In those Cold War days, Cuba was inaccessible but of considerable intellectual and political interest: in the 1980s I began to read about the provisions made by the Cuban government for the basic needs of its population (food, health, education) and to compare that to the staggering violence and inequalities of supposedly "democratic" Caribbean and Latin American nations.[8] In that context, Cuba—a country I had not visited at that point—became something of an ideal type for me, full of glowing statistics (Cole 1980a, 1980b; Benjamin, Collins, and Scott 1984) contrasting it to the imperialism of the United States and the poverty, hunger, sexism, and racism endemic to the US-dominated circum-Caribbean. Naïve as this certainly was, such typologizing was the common condition of most of the era's scholars and scholarship on Cuba, and it is noteworthy in an attempt to locate my own "cognitive mapping" as an ethnographer (Hernández-Reguant 2005, 303).

As the Cold War ended, I traveled and lived for another year studying fisheries development projects in the Caribbean and in Central America—including semesters living in small fishing communities in Belize and Grenada—before going to Chicago to study anthropology. By that time, the old idealizations of an Edenic Cuba were being challenged by equally lop-sided reports of massive deprivation, discontent, and the imminent, inevitable overthrow of Castro (e.g., Oppenheimer 1992). Nevertheless, with the new possibilities brought by the above-mentioned exchange program, Cuba promised to be an interesting site from which to evaluate regional alternatives, and there seemed to be a need to add ethnographic depth to a literature too dominated by etic (outside) black and white binarisms produced by off-island scholars. I first went to Havana during the rafting crisis of 1994,[9] established a number of academic contacts, and, after obtaining a Ruth Landes research grant from the Research Institute for the Study of Man, moved to Cuba for dissertation research, unluckily arriving in Havana in the wake of President Clinton's 1995 "Track Two" initiative, which called for increased academic and cultural exchange with Cuba explicitly as a means of destabilizing Castro's government. While the new policy probably did help in obtaining a US license to conduct research in Cuba,[10] it predictably and understandably put the Cuban state on the defensive with regard to visiting US-based academics, and I was left in limbo as a prearranged affiliation with the Center for African and Middle Eastern Studies (CEAMO) did not materialize.[11] Instead, I enrolled as a student at the University of Havana and was granted D-2 residency for the duration of my field stay, eventually affiliating with a master's-level program in Cuban, Caribbean, and Latin American studies in the Department of Modern History. This affiliation as a long-term graduate student resident and accompanying ID papers (*carné de identidad*) allowed me access to a wide range of scholars and resources including historical records and archives.[12] Classes were interesting, not only for their formal content but also for their form, for learning where the proper boundaries of criticism and disagreement were and to what extent and on what grounds students would or could challenge each other or their professors. Why did certain seemingly obscure debates generate enthusiasm while others did not? What were the possible meanings of silences? In any case, I learned the doxa of Cuban academic discourse at the University of Havana.

Simultaneously, I moved in—on a blind recommendation from CEAMO staff—with a Cuban family with which I am still in close contact today. The household, located on the twelfth floor of a high-rise built for the workers of a state-owned bus factory, consisted of a middle-aged woman and assorted sons, grandsons, wives, girlfriends, and other family members. Living in this complex—racially mixed like any Cuban neighborhood (or extended family)—taught me much about daily life, the struggles for goods and services (electricity, gas, water, a working elevator, etc.), and strategies for procuring essentials, beginning with food and clothing. This became a primary de facto site for observing daily manifestations of gender roles and racial and national consciousness among ordinary Cubans. Meanwhile, I gradually developed close friendships with a number of university classmates; with a couple who ran a private restaurant; with doctors, optometrists, biologists, and other professionals; and with Cubans of Iberian, African, Canarian, Chinese, and West Indian descent, as well as with students from South Africa, Mozambique, and the Western Sahara. Through these and many other sources I found people to interview. Often, interviewees led to more interviewees; it was never difficult to find a Cuban to talk to, although it was often difficult for people—especially higher-status or Party members—to express themselves freely on tape, and consequently many of my interviews were recorded in field notes alone (Weinreb 2009). Interviews with African and Arabic students were somewhat different: on the one hand, we had a common resident foreignness, which facilitated a certain camaraderie and at times a shared perspective on both positive and negative aspects of Cuban society. At the same time, my own nationality often both intrigued and threatened other resident foreigners. To counter this, I balanced breadth for depth, mixing more numerous general interviews and casual acquaintances with fewer close friendships.[13]

Aside from an obligatory return to the United States during summer vacation, I lived in this context in Havana for one year and then traveled to Santiago de Cuba and throughout the island before settling into a small apartment in Havana for an additional six months. Living on my own provided more space to think, but at the same time, I was finally faced with all the domestic tasks that had before been done cooperatively—acquiring my own food and navigating the parallel market chief among them. The amount of time and effort this required, even with a relatively plentiful supply of hard currency (convertible Cuban pesos, or CUC), was truly instructive (see Verdery 1992). During this latter stage, I held two smaller grants before returning to the United States in June 1997. Although juggling work and family obligations, I have traveled to Cuba at least a dozen times since then, including short ten-day visits, month-long research trips, and several gigs as educational study group leader, most recently in November 2017. These trips have added tremendous longitudinal breadth to my work, particularly in fast-changing areas such as youth fashion, and, of course, there are now telephones, email, Facebook, and other links that have greatly enhanced continued or expanded contact. Like other ethnographers of contemporary Cuba, many of my closest friends and informants have since gone into diaspora and are now scattered across the globe, but here too the Internet has not only allowed continued communication but, as we will see, fostered new communities as well.

A few other aspects of my position as an ethnographer are relevant here, not simply in terms of a reflexive anthropology but, more immediately, in terms of the kinds of racial, national, and gender identities ascribed to me *by Cubans*. I am speaking about local or "native" categories here, a context in which my identity—as I construe it, or as it is constructed in North America—is largely irrelevant.[14] There is no doubt that the gender, racial, and national categories into which Cubans placed me directly conditioned my daily interactions, data, and conclusions. Always labeled male and white in terms of gender and race,[15] in some contexts I "passed" for Cuban. More commonly, however, especially early on, before learning to move, dress, and react more like a Cuban—and almost inevitably in areas frequented by tourists—I was presumed to be foreign. Hustlers in Cuba often try to begin a conversation guessing a foreigner's nationality, and in my case, they most frequently guessed French, Spanish, or Argentinean. Because of the relative scarcity of Yankees at that time, and the popular perception that all North Americans are blue-eyed blondes, only rarely have I been identified as a North American.[16] In fact, given Cuba's immigration history, virtually any phenotype can conceivably be "Cuban." Thus, a very blonde-haired, blue-eyed Canadian friend of mine with a gift for accents and many years of practice, who lives, dresses, and moves like any Cuban of his age, is always assumed to be Cuban—to the point that he often has difficulty proving that he is not. The issue of spotting nationality becomes even more complicated when one considers the strategy, common among lighter-skinned Cubans, of "passing" for foreigners; in counterpoint to such narratives, darker-complexioned Cubans occasionally and somewhat ambivalently told stories of being mistaken for African students (see Chapters 2 and 3).

Before turning to the central themes of current Cuba-related research and its Caribbean ties, the next section explores a broader pattern enveloping it—a prevalent if episodic atmosphere of conspiracy and surveillance. This account of what I see as a striking cultural modality of contemporary Cuba is only here a sketch, designed to be overtaken shortly by a more in-depth examination of the major topics described above. Although not itself necessarily a *topic* of study, the conspiracy mode is no less a *condition* of my project than any already identified. While the conspiracy mode is certainly not unique to Cuba, it has distinctive local meanings that, in turn, inform conditions for research in Cuba that are unlike those encountered anywhere else in the region.

States of Surveillance

"Americans," once wrote Joan Didion, reporting on an incredulous, baffled critique of US society by the Cuban exile enclave in Miami, "are a people who could live and die without ever understanding those nuances of conspiracy and allegiance on which, in the Cuban view, the world turn[s]" (1987, 78; Lydia Martin, "Spy Culture Takes Toll on Exiles' Psyche," *Miami Herald*, February 8, 2006). Similarly within the Republic of Cuba itself, hardly a day passed during my time in Havana without some whiff of intrigue and machination, whether over the delayed arrival of the monthly egg ration or the deaths of Che Guevara and Camilo Cienfuegos, or even in the form of the quite possibly related explanation of the assassination of JFK as the doing of mobsters and Cuban-American bandits (e.g., Allard 2012). Indeed, there is so much putative conspiracy surrounding Cuba, on either side of the Straits of Florida, that these theories cannot be adequately analyzed simply in terms of their announced aims or internal logic. Rather, they must be considered discursively, as forming a historically traceable pattern. Although this is not the place for an extended exegesis (for more detail, see Ryer 2006, 2015), the very ubiquity of the genre in Cuba demands some attention.[17] In turn, this analysis will perhaps contextualize my own and other researchers' experiences of surveillance as relevant and realistic rather than paranormal or paranoid.

In his introduction to *Paranoia within Reason*, anthropologist George Marcus took the Cold War to be the condition of the conspiracy theory (1999, 2–3). While I would agree that baldly binary Cold War viewpoints eminently suit the absolute (true:false) claims of conspiracy, and while it is indisputable that the Straits of Florida demarcate one of the last fronts of that war, I would argue that the colonial-era Cuban tradition of conspiration and imperial intrigue precedes the superpowers by at least a century, involving the British, Spanish, and American great powers on at least two occasions—for example, the conspiracy known as La Escalera (Paquette 1988) and the conspiracy over the destruction of the USS *Maine*. Many Cubans to this day believe that the *Maine* was deliberately blown up in Havana's harbor by the Yankees themselves as a pretext for intervention just as Cuban forces were on the point of victory over Spain. I have heard racialized variants of the theory circulating in Havana that indicate that the white officers of the *Maine* were not coincidentally ashore while the black crewmen were all left aboard as sacrifices to Yankee imperialism. Such narratives predate the Cold War or the Cuban Revolution of 1959 and, although certainly responsive to contemporary conditions, have percolated in Cuba for over a century. Some have wondered whether the destruction of the *Maine* really marks a meaningful moment in the larger course of history, or whether the Spanish-Cuban-American War was in any case inevitable. Others have argued that an accident—perhaps a coal bunker fire—sank the ship. These debates continue today (Castañeda 1925; Santovenia y Echaide 1928; Weems 1958; Rickover 1976; Samuels and Samuels 1995; L. Pérez 1998b; Remesal 1998).

In any case, clearly the context at stake in conspiracy is not simply the Cold War as Marcus argued, but, more generally, the clash of empires indifferent to the realities of a local (in this case Cuban) constituency. I propose, then, that conspiracy theories characteristically analyze the hidden workings of such empires by an intimately affected, disenfranchised, and critical community of its local spectators presumed to be of the same *moral community* as the conspiracy theorist. These criticisms may or may not eventually be sustainable, but in circulation they are necessarily inconclusive, nefarious, and—unlike mere rumor—agentive and evoke the capricious misuse of legitimate authority in a situation of limited available information.[18] In revolutionary Cuba, such stories circulate in both civilian conversations and state-controlled media. In such narratives, the Cuban state presents itself and the Cuban people as indistinguishable, as the unitary victim of external conspiracy and aggression. Often able to marshal overwhelming evidence to support its arguments, the state has been consistent in this mode of presentation since the era of the Bay of Pigs Invasion and the Cuban Missile Crisis. The CIA's many acts of sabotage against Cuba and assassination attempts against Castro in the 1960s are no longer denied, even by the US government.[19] In fact, there are museums full of the sordid detritus of Yankee counterrevolutionary conspiracies against the revolutionary state.

There is also the more immediate context of ethnography and espionage to which I would now like to return. From the beginning of my professional interest in Cuba, it was clear that it would be impossible to prove that I was not an agent of the CIA—or, for that matter, not a communist infiltrator. In Havana, I may have been suspected of the former; in Miami, I've been accused of the latter. However doomed to inadequacy, my general approach was to disclose fully my identity, goals, and willingness to abide by the stated laws and regulations relevant to my situation.[20] In fact, neither government ever formally questioned me, but from the beginning of my time in Havana, I often had a sense of being on stage. It is difficult to know where reality ends and imagination begins.[21] Now a good friend, the neighbor who helped me find and move into the household I stayed with was the former head of Cuba's counterintelligence mission in Panama—he is described in detail in an influential but now discredited book (Oppenheimer 1992, chapter 5). Whether retired or not, he certainly kept an eye on me in addition to providing first-rate daily advice. I did not have a telephone, but expatriates and colleagues who did widely believed their phones to be bugged. More palpably, along with each piece of mail that arrived from the United States during my time in Havana, I received a postal notice (fig. 1). In each case, the original letter had been ripped open and then carefully enclosed with this notice in a heat-sealed cellophane wrapper. Even much more recently I have encountered traces of surveillance: as the coeditor of the blog *EthnoCuba* (*ethno-cuba.ucr.edu*), I grew accustomed to visits from both Communist Party of Cuba (Partido Comunista de Cuba, *pcc.cu*) and US Department of Defense servers. One of my posts in 2009 even elicited a response from someone at *pcc.cu*, although, as a colleague commented, even that could have been

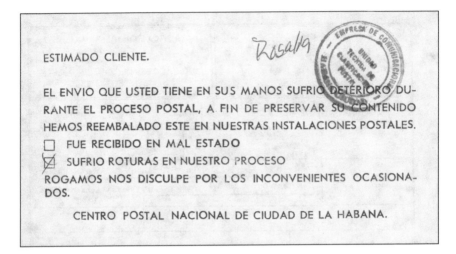

Figure 1. This postal notice is an example of the documentation I received along with each piece of mail that arrived from the United States. In each case, the original letter had been ripped open along the flap and was carefully enclosed with the following note in a transparent cellophane wrapper, which had been heat-sealed. The text reads: "Esteemed Client, The mail which you have in your hands suffered deterioration during the postal process. Towards the goal of preserving its contents, we have rewrapped it in our postal installations. It suffered rips in our processing (checked). We beg your pardon for the inconveniences occasioned. National Postal Center of the City of Havana."

a forged address.[22] Other evidence of surveillance on the part of the Cuban state was anecdotal, but I never met a Cuban who doubted that their government knew about me and what I was doing. If the topic came up, it was generally mentioned quite matter-of-factly or casually, not at all with the sense of horror or police-state oppression of the North American imagination.[23]

The longer-term question of the placement and politicization of Cuba-related research since the 1959 Revolution also has two sides.[24] On the Cuban side, the fate of the Oscar and Ruth Lewis team is pivotal. As described in the preface to their three-volume study, the Lewises went to Cuba in 1969 with the personal authorization of Fidel Castro in order to conduct a massive three-year study (their team included Oscar, Ruth, seven non-Cuban staff people, ten Cuban assistants, and auxiliary drivers, domestics, and other helpers). Although they were trained anthropologists, "using the techniques of tape-recorded autobiographies, the study would, in effect, be an oral history of contemporary Cuba as well as of the Cuban Revolution" (Lewis, Lewis, and Rigdon 1977, xii). From the beginning, they faced the suspicion of CIA backing and by the time their research was abruptly terminated by high-level Cuban authorities in June 1970, they were under intense surveillance (Lewis, Lewis, and Rigdon 1977, xiii, xix, xxvi; also see Butterworth 1980, xix). The bulk of the interviews, questionnaires, and transcripts still in Cuba were impounded. In a speech two years later, Raúl Castro referred to Oscar Lewis as a secret agent; ironically, the three volumes eventually published (using materials previously removed to the United States) present a distinctly positive picture of the revolution and its social accomplishments. Explaining the abrupt termination of the study, Ruth Lewis invokes the failure of the 1970 *zafra* (sugar harvest), the combination of increased external criticism and internal economic setbacks in Cuba at that time, and, especially, "the sensitive nature of our research [which] played a large part in the sudden end of the project" (Lewis, Lewis, and Rigdon 1977, xxv, xxvii; also see Verdery 1996, 7, 24). In his review essay, Maurice Halperin (1978) presents a more detailed and critical view of these events (see also Hernández-Reguant 2005).

The harassment, intimidation, and obstruction carried out by the US government against Fernando Coronil, then a graduate student in anthropology at the University of Chicago, is an equally sobering case. Since he presents his situation so eloquently, and as it is an important counterpoint to that of the Lewis team, I will reproduce Coronil's account at length here:

> Before undertaking this [Venezuela-related] research, I had carried out fieldwork in Cuba for a year on a project which was truncated by Cuban policy shifts. For a number of reasons I decided not to write about Cuba but to turn to the analysis of nationalist ideology and state power in Venezuela. However, on my return to the United States I was detained, excluded from entry on the ground that I was a subversive agent, denied information about the charges, and after several months ordered to leave the country "within forty-eight hours." As a result of a chance encounter in which family ties and political connections crossed, a well-connected lawyer obtained the suspension of my deportation (after it was mailed!) and undertook my defense.
>
> My defense involved a Kafkaesque "trial." Accused of being a subversive agent but refused information about the charges on the grounds that revealing it would endanger the security of the U.S. government, I

had to prepare my defense by imagining what could be construed as my guilt and countering it with a narrative supported by as much evidence as I could provide. An essential part of this defense involved producing an account of my life from my childhood up to that moment. This account had to be backed by letters from official and public figures, as well as by police and intelligence reports from the United States and Venezuela. As part of this process, I obtained the support of the then-President of Venezuela, Rafael Caldera (my father was his family's physician), who asked his ambassador in Washington to represent my case vis-à-vis U.S. authorities.

Nevertheless, my situation remained unchanged. After more than a year in the United States trying to resolve my case by legal or political means but without succeeding in securing even a hearing, Julie Skurski and I decided to return to Venezuela in order to carry out our new projects. When I began my work on the structures of political and economic power, however, I learned that my case was an object of rumor and gossip within these circles and that I had been under close surveillance since before my detention in Miami. My inability to prove my innocence, despite the considerable support I had received, proved my guilt. The mistrust, rumors, and surveillance which constrained my research also helped me understand how power creates reality by its effects.

The evidence I have since obtained (including documents through the Freedom of Information Act) suggests that I had unknowingly become entangled in a complex web of power that linked President Nixon's attempt to curtail U.S. dissidence and Latin American dissent to rivalries in Venezuela among different political leaders. At the end of 1978, during Carter's presidency, the case against me was unexpectedly dropped just as it had started with a letter that offered no explanation. (Coronil 1997, xv–xvi)

The adage that opposites are alike in all respects but one was never more apt than in these two cases. Lest the reader be infected by the paranoia regarding research in Cuba, however, consider an often-repeated aphorism appropriate to contemporary conditions: *"El que hizo la ley, hizo la trampa"* (literally "He who invented the law, invented the loophole," reminding us here that the apparent immobility of conspiracy and control is offset by the fluidities of everyday practice). As one Cuban intelligence officer—a close friend of my retired neighbor and of another North American anthropologist—put it to me: "as long as you are honest, and fair, we [an unspecified "we," to be sure, but meaning state security] will be happy." Learning to negotiate such complexities made Havana an interesting site for research, to say the least.

While the anthropological study of revolutionary Cuba repeatedly brushes up against the permeating surveillance described here, it would be wildly inaccurate to present conspiring states as the sole frame for research in and of Cuban culture. Indeed, in a certain sense, ethnographic writing on Cuba began with the diary of Christopher Columbus, which initiated a genre of travel writing about the archipelago that continues to this day.[25] Such writings, as with the Cuban colonial archive writ large, can often be productively mined for observations and details that locate and contextualize otherwise incongruous contemporary events and practices. More immediately, long before the revolution shut down academic departments of anthropology in the early 1960s as bourgeois deadwood, Cuban anthropology had received international recognition, largely thanks to one foundational figure.

Fernando Ortiz and the Roots and Routes of Cuban Anthropology

Within Cuban academic circles today, three men are often credited as "discoverers" of Cuba. Of these, Christopher Columbus is the first, and Alexander von Humboldt (Humboldt and Thrasher 1856) the second. But the usual deployment of the description is to denote the status and esteem held for the *tercer descubridor*,[26] Cuban-born Fernando Ortiz (1881–1969), who, over a prolific career as a writer and public intellectual, dedicated himself to the study of Cuban culture—an interest sparked, ironically, during his studies in Spain:

> It is a paradox that African Cuba was first discovered in Europe. Around 1900, while Fernando Ortiz was studying law in Madrid, excited by the wonders of criminology and the underworld of the Spanish prisons, he saw the *íremes* for the first time in his life. He was immediately asked by his Spanish friends and colleagues to tell them the story behind those masks. But he could say very little about a ritual and people he did not know. So the polymath set to work, and the literary method of Ortiz

became a virtual anthropology. It was virtual because he drew a map of Africa without having ever been to Africa and because his approach to things Cuban took shape elsewhere. At the Museo de Ultramar, he started looking with new eyes at his island. . . . And it all started in Madrid. (di Leo 2005, 52)

Ortiz wrote about an incredible range of topics, from indigenous Cuban cultures, the symbolic place of the hurricane, and the role of Spanish and African festivals in Cuban daily life, to his often-cited work on African influences in Cuban music and performance, the art of Wifredo Lam, the incorporation of African words into Cuban speech, and, most famously, the counterpoint of tobacco and sugar as the defining commodities of Cuban life. Richly historical, passionate, and lyrically written, over and over Ortiz's often problematic opus traces long-running patterns that later ethnographers stumble on as if for the first time—often with little more than a nod to several hallmark Ortizian concepts.

The first of these, Ortiz's notion of *ajiaco*, has been invariably cited, often marked as analogous to the North American "melting pot" and similar metaphors throughout the hemisphere. He proposed the *ajiaco*—a popular Cuban stew—as representative of the Cuban mixture of peoples and cultures, the "pot" being the island/archipelago of Cuba and the ingredients of the stew (pig, fish, plátanos, yucca, malanga, boniato, and other meats and tubers) arriving from Europe and Africa or found in America. Frequently added to, with some still-identifiable fragments now boiled, irreversibly, in an always changing broth, the *ajiaco* is more than the sum of its parts, uniquely "Cuban," and gives each component some of its own unique flavor. The argument that Cuban culture was not simply the sum of Spanish and African influences, but rather something new unto itself was a recurrent theme in Ortiz's work. "Transculturation" is another Ortizian neologism which is still cited time and again in both Cuban and non-Cuban writings about Cuban culture. Like the mention of the honorary doctorate bestowed on Ortiz by Columbia University, the putative validation of the term by the famous anthropologist Bronislaw Malinowski in his introduction to *Cuban Counterpoint* (Ortiz 1995a) may function locally to confirm Ortiz's stature in and his engagement with a global discipline. But at the same time, the de facto neglect of Ortiz's work within that wider discipline is itself telling (see Coronil in Ortiz 1995a, ix–lvi; Gonçalves 2014). This may have to do with structures of disciplinary power, as Coronil argues, but it may also reflect the reality that, as Robin Moore has pointed out, even the later opinions of don Fernando "are replete with troublesome ideological implications" (1994, 47). Or as Marc Perry puts it, Ortiz's work obfuscates the power dynamics of the Cuba he is investigating (2004, 100). In any case, most of Ortiz's studies are in some sense concerned with the development of an unproblematized national identity. In *Los negros curros* (1995b), for instance, Ortiz postulates profound differences between the *ñáñigos* and the *curros*, although both were ostensibly marginal "Afro-Cuban" groups of Havana. While the *ñáñigos* (and their secret society, the *abakuá*) were culturally West African, the *curros*, Ortiz argues, arriving principally from Seville, were thoroughly Spanish in orientation and culture:

> In the body of the curros—although in all cases Creoles and never Africans—there is always the shadow of Africa, but in their soul there is the light of Spain. The spirit of the ñáñigos, however, is the blackness of Africa, even after more than a century since arriving in Cuba and in the thousands of initiates, who today are not—in the great majority— blacks, but rather mulattos or whites, who may even have been born in or emigrated from Spain. (Ortiz 1995b, 7)

In addition to demonstrating his own color scales here, in his presentation of data distinguishing these (among other) groups, Ortiz leaves largely unexamined whatever hybridities and complexities might underlie his constitutive categories "Spain" and "Africa"—essentialized categories that, as we will see, are still deployed in Cuban vernaculars today.

There is a certain irony in the way the Cuban academy has enshrined the discoverer while burying the discovery of Cuban culture,[27] and it has everything to do with publicly permissible ideologies in an evolutionist modernist Marxist socialist state. Thus, Ortiz's major works have been assiduously reprinted; his house has been partly restored as the Fundación Fernando Ortiz, headed by Miguel Barnet; there are frequent lecture series and programs on Ortiz; and his work is widely studied at the university level. But meanwhile, until relatively recently, the vehicle of the discovery, in the form of the discipline of anthropology (or ethnology), has fared indifferently under the revolution. As mentioned, academic departments of anthropology were closed in the early 1960s as irrelevant to scientific socialism, and contacts of the sort that Ortiz had maintained with Western scholars were greatly curtailed. What did survive was a nationalist archaeology, a certain amount of internationalist exchange with the Soviet Bloc and with leftist African states in the 1970s and 1980s, and an underfunded Soviet-trained corps of folklorists and ethnologists (see Hernández-Reguant 2005).[28] In general, published work tended to be folkloric oral histories or survey-based studies (see, for instance, Barnet and Montejo 1968; Guanche Pérez 1983; López Valdés 1985; Núñez Jiménez 1985; Menéndez 1990; Bolívar Aróstegui 1994; Barreal Fernández 1998). Only since the economic crisis of the 1990s has this changed: there is now a journal of Cuban anthropology, *Catauro*, produced by the Fundación Fernando Ortiz, and an online journal, *Batey*,[29] as well as an emerging and thriving group of Cuban ethnographers working within the republic (Castellanos 2003; Couceiro Rodríguez 2009; Loyola Moya 2012; Rangel Rivero 2012).

Ethnographic Research in Revolutionary Cuba

> Anthropological field work in socialist Cuba was a profoundly unique experience for us, although some of the differences were subtle and not immediately perceived. . . . I can say flatly that there was not a single important aspect of the field work that was not affected in some degree by the great societal changes in Cuba, above all by the ubiquitous presence of the state. . . . With the government as the source of all goods and services, we were unavoidably dependent upon them for material things such as food and housing. Almost everything had to be done through the proper channels, a process involving a good deal of bureaucratic red tape. (Lewis, Lewis, and Rigdon 1977, xiii–xiv)

In considering the culture of surveillance in Cuba, I have already mentioned the foreshortened research of Oscar and Ruth Lewis. Beginning in 1969 and operating with a large team, the Lewises' project, by their own account an oral history rather than an ethnographically based study, grew out of the fundamental assumptions of the notorious "culture of poverty" school so strongly associated with Oscar Lewis. Indeed, as the culture of poverty was theorized as a recurrent feature of capitalist economies, socialist Cuba was expected to differ from Puerto Rico or Mexico. Despite the possibilities raised by their long-term residence in Havana while conducting their research, the

Lewis team, it bears noting, could not live in close contact with Cuban families or neighborhoods (see Lewis, Lewis, and Rigdon 1977, xiv–xv). Even in the face of the early termination of the project, the confiscation of many materials and interview tapes, and Oscar Lewis's death some months later, the team produced three thick and descriptive volumes resulting from the study as well as Douglas Butterworth's (1980) related monograph.

Aside from the Lewis team's work, there were several attempts to conduct sustained anthropological research in revolutionary Cuba in the 1960s and 1970s, most notably by Verena Stolcke and by Fernando Coronil. I have already referred to the difficulties originating in both Cuban and US government policies that forced Coronil to abandon his Cuba-related research (1997, xv). In the preface to her classic study, *Marriage, Class and Colour in Nineteenth-Century Cuba*—a work to which I am deeply indebted and about which I will have more to say elsewhere in this book—Stolcke describes her attempt to study current Cuban family organization and notes that "bureaucratic reasons" obliged her to redirect her study to a historical examination of family structure utilizing documents within the National Archive in Havana (Martinez-Alier 1974, vii–ix). With large-scale or long-term research projects so curtailed during the heyday of the revolution, the little anthropological literature produced (e.g., Cole 1980a, 1980b; Safa 1995) invariably relied on short visits, the continued goodwill of state officials and state-employed researchers, and statistics produced by the Cuban government, rather than on sustained ethnographic observation. The result: despite some politically charged curiosity, revolutionary Cuba remained a footnote and question mark for Western anthropology and inaccessible by in-depth ethnographic methods until the latter half of the 1980s, when Yvonne Daniel and Mona Rosendahl separately conducted studies. Out of necessity, Berkeley-trained Daniel's study focused exclusively on folkloric rather than popular dance: "I danced seven hours a day, six days a week, for most of one year" in affiliation with the National Folkloric company (1995, 23; also see 1991; 2005; 2011). In contrast, an anthropologist from politically neutral Sweden, Mona Rosendahl, was able to conduct more open-ended fieldwork in a municipality in eastern Cuba from 1988 to 1990 during the final years of the Soviet era.[30] Setting out to provide "an ethnographic analysis of socialist political ideology in Palmera and the processes of creating, recreating, denouncing, strengthening, questioning, and enforcing it" (1997, 5), Rosendahl alternately considers official ideology and its popular reception, paying particular attention to gender and reciprocity. As with earlier studies, however, very little attention is paid to official or vernacular racial divisions and virtually none to national classification or ideologies.

With the collapse of the Soviet Bloc and the retrenchments of the resulting economic crisis, which hit bottom in 1993, the Cuban state was forced to open the republic to tourism as a ready source of hard currency and concurrently began to accept Western students and researchers as long-term residents and ceased to tightly control their movement or residential arrangements. Just like that, long-term ethnographic observation was possible, and a new cohort first trickled, then flooded, into the country. The metaphor of the seven blind men—each busy describing his own small part of an elephant—may be apt. If the field is light-years ahead of where it was in the 1970s or 1980s, this is largely because it is hard to overstate how limited North American and European social scientists' knowledge about Cuba was even just twenty years ago. For instance, in their comprehensive comparative study of race in the Americas, Whitten and Torres talk about a total lack of knowledge about Cuban racial dynamics, even in the 1990s (1998, 12). Relative to that era, research today is both more nuanced and broadly grounded, and the growing scholarship of everyday life and experience in Cuba is exhilarating. But if, as Clifford Geertz (1973) warned us, cultural analysis is always incomplete, that is particularly true here. To return to the metaphor, what we ethnographers have mostly done thus far, it seems to me, is describe parts of the elephant in isolation: Cuban religious systems, racial patterns, cultural production, gender and sports, health and medicine, diasporas, etc. Even here, there is more work to be done. But beyond that, where did this elephant come from? What are its family and social networks like? In the end, how is Cuba alike and how is it different from other Caribbean, Latin American, post-colonial, or (post)socialist places? A few colleagues (Routon 2005; Gonçalves 2012; Madrid and Moore 2013) have wrestled with such questions, particularly Ariana Hernández-Reguant in "Cuba's Alternative Geographies" (2005) an essay that looks comprehensively at the cartographic renderings of Cuba by both Cuban and foreign anthropologists and intellectuals over the last century. Helpful as it is, however, that essay focused on intellectuals' mappings; in essence, this book provides not an alternate, but an additional mapping at the level of everyday, vernacular discourse. Certainly, as we will see, maps travel; ideas about the world, concepts like the *ajiaco*, sink into the street, the common sense of the *calle*. But not everything travels, and, as we will also see, the everyday still has a lot to show us.

So here I want to briefly note a number of clusters of contemporary ethnographic work in "greater Cuba"—that is, within the Republic of Cuba and its diasporas—and point to links with wider Caribbean work. Of course, I will also refer to particular works as relevant throughout the text. The first major topic, race, has been the subject of recent ethnographies by Nadine Fernandez (2010) and Kaifa Roland (2011) as well as a number of other ethnographic pieces that tackle the meanings of race in contemporary Cuba (N. Fernandez 2006; Hansing 2006; Roland 2006; Vaughan 2006; Allen 2007, 2009, 2011, 2012; Perry 2008; Queeley 2010a, 2010b). Taken together, this work provides a footing for thinking about how race operates in a socialist system that ostensibly eliminated it along with class by eliminating private control of the means of production (Marx and Engels 1970). Clearly, Cuba's last half century of state socialist theory and practice regarding race is distinctive in inter-American perspective! But also distinct, in Caribbean terms, is Cuba's particular racial composition: with literally millions of self-identified "white" Cubans, it seems to me that that unmarked category calls for further scrutiny than it has thus far received. As I will argue in Chapter 3, whiteness in Cuba may be unmarked, but it is certainly neither a self-evident category nor unrelated to a global geographic imagination.

Gender and sexuality, the second nexus, is central to the work of Noelle Stout (2014) and Jafari Allen (2011), but several other scholars' work on Cuban baseball (Carter 2008b; Kelly 2006; Eastman 2008) is very much about gender in a postcolonial, Caribbean context, with interesting comparisons between Cuban *peñas* and the Surinamese *winkel* studied by Gary Brana-Shute (1989) in the 1970s (see also Carter 2002). There is also a substantial conversation about sexuality, particularly in relation to encounters with tourists and other foreigners (e.g., Hodge 2001; Forrest 2002; Perry 2004, 2009; Allen 2007; Pertierra 2008; Stout 2008; Härkönen 2014a; Daigle 2015). More than most researchers, Amalia Cabezas (2009) does situate these aspects of Cuba in the wider Caribbean, in what Mark Padilla (2007) elegantly has called the "Caribbean Pleasure Industry," marked by a region-wide movement from an agricultural to tourist mode of production (also see Lumsden 1996; Freeman 2000; Bejel 2001; Black 2001; Curtis 2009; Jaffe 2010). Possibly the most extensive cluster of ethnographically rooted work in Cuba today examines so-called "Afro-Cuban" religion—that is, African-inspired

Cuban religious practice (Hagedorn 2001; Mason 2002; Palmié 2002, 2013; Brown 2003; Wirtz 2004, 2007, 2009; Hearn 2008; I. Miller 2009; Ochoa 2010; Routon 2010; Holbraad 2012a, 2012b; Beliso-De Jesús 2014).[31] Taken together, these diverse volumes represent some of the best work on Cuba today, but I wonder why, apart from brief treatments by Wirtz and Hearn, there is virtually no sustained attention here to Christian revivals of the kind commonly studied elsewhere in the Caribbean (e.g., Olwig 1990; Corse 2007). The boundary between Catholic and African-inspired practice is, of course, famously complicated, but what of the million or more Cuban Protestant and Evangelical practitioners? Surely there is a space here for additional work to round out the ethnographic picture of contemporary Cuban religious practices.

The next cluster of work, on consumption, really rests on recent volumes by Amelia R. Weinreb (2009) and Ana Cristina Pertierra (2011) (also see Gordy 2006; Sunderland and Denny 2007; Carter 2008a; Pertierra 2008, 2009; A. Porter 2008; Simoni 2008). What this work shares—understandably, given the savage economic crisis of 1990s Cuba during which the nation's economy shrank by about a third—is a premise of scarcity; Hanna Garth (2012) and Adriana Premat (2009, 2012) have written about food in this context as well. And yet, anthropologically speaking, it has long been recognised that scarcity is not simply an objective lack of goods, but rather a *relation* (Sahlins 1972), and indeed, there is much relevant ethnographic work on consumption from elsewhere in the Caribbean (e.g., D. Miller 1998; Browne and Salter 2004). Samuel Martínez (2007) makes a particularly interesting contribution, starting with Bataillian premises (Bataille and Stoekl 1985; Bataille 1988) to argue that even among the poorest Haitian sugarcane workers in the Dominican Republic, there is *excess* as well as scarcity. In Cuba as well there is both, as we can see in Hernández-Reguant's (2004, 2006) work on the celebration of conspicuous consumption in Cuban *timba* music in the later 1990s, and here, then, is another area of recursivity between Cuba and the wider region. There is a small but growing nucleus of fieldwork being done on Cuban diasporas and "reaspiras" (Behar 2009, 2013; Flores 2009; Carter 2011; Berg 2012).[32] Since the 1990s, anthropologists have been interested in migrant circuits and networks and working to adapt and develop appropriate multisited, mobile research methods (Gupta and Ferguson 2008). Such work certainly poses a challenge to research in what we might call "greater Cuba" as it does elsewhere. There is also, of course, a rich literature about diaspora and exile by Cuban-American academics (e.g., O'Reilly Herrera 2001; Pérez Firmat 2012). Given that massive migrations are the Antillean norm—where more than half of Grenada's population lives in North America or the United Kingdom and where remittances are a central pillar of national economies from Haiti to Honduras and now Cuba as well—here too there is value to looking across the water, to reading and pondering the work of Caribbeanist scholars—McAlister (2002); Strachan (2002); K. Clarke and Thomas (2006); Gregory (2007); Flores (2009); and Rahier, Hintzen, and Smith (2010), among others. Importantly, as I argue in considering the lives of Cuban-educated African students in Chapter 4, Cuban migration, like migration in the rest of the Caribbean, is multidirectional, not just out-migration as is generally presumed.

Another concentration of recent research focuses on Cuban cultural production—on music, dance, theater, film, arts, literature, urban design, etc., again foregrounding ethnographically grounded work (R. Moore 1997, 2006, 2010; Daniel 2005, 2011; Hernández-Reguant 2009, 2012; Frederik 2012; also see Vazquez 2013; Wirtz 2014).[33] There have also been shorter publications on landscape (Gropas 2006, 2007), cinema (Humphreys 2012), and urban planning (Hill 2007, 2012; Del Real and Pertierra 2008; Tanaka 2011). And finally, the topic of health care and medicine in Cuba has garnered a cluster of ethnographic investigations (Hirschfeld 2007; Whiteford and Branch 2008; Brotherton 2012; Burke 2013; also see Andaya 2014). As is often remarked, and too-often politicized, the Cuban health care system is indeed distinct from a regional perspective and, like its education system (Blum 2011), certainly reflects the organizational structure of the socialist state. But, I believe, there is still room to think even more broadly about "health" in this regard. For instance, having experienced hurricanes in St. Croix, in Haiti, and in Cuba, the distinctiveness of Cuba civil defense measures and their efficacy compared to measures elsewhere in the region, or even the United States, is stunning. This, it seems to me, is a difference worthy of much more investigation, for not only does it illustrate what is indeed particular to Cuba, but also what is possible more broadly.

* * *

This chapter began with my conversations with Michel-Rolph Trouillot and Marina Majoli in order to set out a dilemma. That Rolph could "finish the story" for me in a way few North American scholars could, illustrates how fundamentally, how fiercely, Cuba is indeed part of the Caribbean region and how its "family resemblance" to other Caribbean nations (Trouillot 1992, 35) as well as its place in the Atlantic and wider world is both profound and profoundly historical. Surely Sidney Mintz has taught us as much (Mintz 1986; Mintz and Price 1992). At the same time, however, the dislocations described in the conversation with Marina point not only to a particular, distinctive cultural logic in need of ethnographic unpacking, but also a distinctively *state socialist* particularity. I argue—and believe that the evidence of this book supports this argument—that contemporary Cuba is permeated with and often most intelligible in light of distinctive state socialist patterns (Verdery 1996), patterns that, among other things, have fundamentally shaped the anthropological study of Cuba over the past fifty years by forbidding, controlling, channeling, and surveilling the work accomplished. Nevertheless, since the mid-1990s, an ethnographic renaissance has pushed forward the old Ortizian paradigms of Cuban culture, shedding light on old theoretical questions and raising new ones. If today's ethnographers of Cuba are still like the proverbial blind men describing the elephant of Cuban culture, discovering its shape by the resistance it offers à la a Peircean "secondness," we have at least seen some major areas of developing research, which I have here divided heuristically. Clearly there is more to explore and wider links to be studied, but just as clearly, core topics for this work include socialism, state bureaucracy, surveillance; the economic and social crisis of the Special Period and resulting everyday struggles of *luchando, inventando,* and *resolviendo*; the reproduction and transformation of racism and racial identities; cubanidad, tourism and national:foreign boundaries; Cuban religion/religious revival; reciprocity, *socios,* and *sociolismo*; gender divisions and sexuality; socialist theory; and the transformation of production, distribution, and consumption. While the following chapters will focus on the vernacular emplotment of the Republic in a regional and global geography, they will also all remain embedded in the specific ethnographic patterns here introduced.

CHAPTER 1

THE RISE AND DECLINE OF *LA YUMA*

The Caribbean story as I read it is less an invitation to search for modernity in various times and places—a useful yet secondary enterprise—than an exhortation to change the terms of the debate. What needs to be analyzed further, better, and differently is the relation between the geography of management and the geography of imagination that together underpinned the development of world capitalism and the legitimacy of the West as the universal unmarked.

Michel-Rolph Trouillot, *Global Transformations: Anthropology and the Modern World*

Beginning with a seemingly simple popular term, *La Yuma*, this chapter interrogates one Cuban vernacular space of privileged foreignness. This chapter's focus on Cuban commonsense ideas about the boundaries between Cuba and the unmarked, whiter, richer foreignness of Europe and North America and the once and future place occupied by the Soviet Union's "lo bolo" along with the following chapter's exploration of *África* as another imagined space that marks a different shore of cubanidad, I propose, are part of a worldwide Cuban geography of the imagination.[1] In this imagined geography, the foreign is largely stripped of the impurities of home, and the Cuban:foreign boundary does indeed effectively constitute a new form of racial distinction (Roland 2011). Relying less on interviews than on observations and more on bodily style than on verbal ideologies, here I work through the lens of Western material goods and symbols that connote capitalism. The value of the commodities and the meaning of the metaphor have changed rapidly over the past two decades, and I argue that these changes index Cuba's painful reintegration into a not-new world economic order, specifically as symbols of a new remittance economy. However, even the humblest product—a pair of socks, a "Tommy" T-shirt—may be locally sought out in ways unanticipated from an outside perspective. Only after foregrounding such agentive desires of ordinary Cubans do I move to consider micropractices and macrostructures of the contemporary socioeconomic context. For despite the encroaching US dollar, Cuba's economy retains elements of a centralized command structure and is hardly "postsocialist." While also evident in events such as the state's distinctive civil defense against hurricanes, contemporary Cuban state socialist particularity is best illustrated, I argue, through an ethnographic examination of the parallel economy, which is officially invisible yet omnipresent in daily life. Although, rather than negating Cuba's Caribbean context or history, this examination will also, in fact, begin to suggest answers to many of the questions posed at the beginning of this book. If this balancing act seems unconventional, it is nevertheless a deliberate attempt to avoid the twin perils of pathologizing and pitying. Celebrating the ways Cubans pursue, appropriate, and reinterpret the goods and symbols of La Yuma does not deny the staggering inequalities of global capitalism or the severe experience of scarcity in fin de siècle Cuba, but it does localize the global and presents Cubans as subjects, rather than objects, of desire.

The Rise of *La Yuma*

In Havana, two possible origins for the vernacular Cuban term *La Yuma* are commonly proposed by those interested in the topic. Often, it is believed to derive from a 1957 American Western, *3:10 to Yuma*, and thus to refer literally to Yuma, Arizona—infamous in the United States, ironically, for its prison. The film, based on an eponymous Elmore Leonard short story and directed by Delmer Daves, starring Van Heflin, Glenn Ford, Felicia Farr, and Richard Joeskel, recounts the struggle of a stubborn farmer with a captured but still powerful robber baron as they both wait for a train that will deliver them to the US legal system. It apparently was extensively screened and widely popular in Cuba just before an era dominated by a genre of Soviet war movies, which seem to have been considerably less popular as entertainment. In such a context, this theory suggests, *3:10 to Yuma* had enough recognition, or captured enough of the Cuban imagination, to come to denote the United States (Daves [1957] 1993; also see Dopico 2004; Roland 2011, 65).

Another widely and often concurrently cited theory proposes that *Yuma* is simply derived from a mispronunciation of "US man" or of "United States." Common Cuban linguistic patterns, such as an elided "s" would seem to support this thesis. In either case, it is clear that as a spatial term, La Yuma's primary and original referent is the United States. In this context it is a singular feminine noun. It can also refer to a person or people from La Yuma:[2] I was *el yuma* or *un yuma*; a North American woman could be *una* or *la yuma*; and a group (or the total nation of people) would be *los yumas*. Clearly, the meanings ascribed to the term have a historical trajectory: it seems to have become increasingly popular, first with increased US-Cuba contact during the "blue-jean revolution" of the Carter administration (1978–79) and then especially in the Special Period following the end of the Soviet era. Since the millennium and the post-Chavista special relationship with Venezuela and ALBA (Bolivarian Alliance for the Americas) and the related stabilization of the now hybrid, dual-currency state socialist system, the term has declined in popularity and changed in tone. As I will argue below, it is probably no coincidence that the term was most prevalent during the period that Western goods first became widely (if unevenly) available, disrupting the previous uniformity of material culture under socialism, which Nadine Fernandez (1996, 44) succinctly described just before the 1993 legalization of the US dollar: "Every store has the same items, just as in every Cuban household you can find the same model of T.V., the same dishes, the same pots, the same glasses, the same sheets, the same knickknacks, and the same plastic flowers" (also see Veenis 1999, 91; Patico and Caldwell 2002, 285; Sunderland and Denny 2007; A. Porter 2008; Weinreb 2009; Pertierra 2011).

In any case, depending on context and intonation, the designation of a person as a *yuma* may be factual, envious, or critical—perhaps because it bespeaks more familiarity than conventional or official terms such as *Americano* or *estadounidense*.[3] Although not vulgar per se, and despite frequent intellectual analysis of its charter, the term has been distinctly more common on the street (and especially among men) than in the academy, and my self-referential use of the term was most warmly received in non-intellectual circles. Finally, while ostensibly apolitical, in its heyday in the 1990s it would have been very surprising to hear the term La Yuma used by a Party official or in the state media—which referred instead to the United States and its citizens as *los EE UU, los Estados Unidos, los yanquis, los imperialistas, los norteamericanos, los gringos*, and so on. With so many readily available official terms, why, then, should another have emerged in popular discourse?

I propose that La Yuma does have distinct meanings easily lost in translation, for it does not simply denote the geographic space as known to those of us who actually live in the United States. In the mid-1990s, perhaps the most common and compelling context for the term was encapsulated in a standard articulation of surprise, "*¡Asere, qué cosa más yuma!*" ("What a most *yuma* thing, buddy!"). Other common variations included: "*¡No, comp'ay, eso está yuma, yuma!*" ("Damn, compadre, that is *yuma, yuma!*"); "*¡Eso está yumático!*" ("That's *yumatic!*"); or even occasionally "*¡Eso está yumatiquísimo!*" ("That is most *yumatic!*"). This was often heard when faced with evidence for some new technological item such as a CD player, color TV, even a cruise missile. In such contexts, La Yuma was powerful, marvelous, and generally admirable (for the quality, beauty, or efficacy of its stuff, not its politics). Furthermore—as I would invariably be reprimanded for pointing out that the color TV "from La Yuma" had actually been made in Korea—by the turn of the millennium, the word no longer referred strictly to the fifty states, but rather to all the developed world, including especially the United States, Canada, Western Europe, and Japan, but also to South Korea, parts of South America, and all other sites with an abundance of such goods. La Yuma, then, quintessentially *excludes* Cuba,[4] the nations of the former Soviet Bloc, Africa, and the third world in general. Initially, during the Cold War, the closest contrasting term to *yuma* would have been *bolo* or *bola*. Literally "ball" or "ninepin," *bolo* was a popular referent to Russians and to the Soviet Bloc.[5] Just as "*yuma*" could refer to a place, to its goods, or to the people from that place, one might hear "*bolo*" or "*bola*" as a reference to a Russian man or woman and less frequently, and somewhat impersonally, to their place of origin. In such contexts, what we might call the popular discourse of *lo bolo* was largely affectionate, although perhaps with a trace of irony and sense of cultural distance or difference, in which Cuba was of the West and *los bolos* of the East. Most commonly, however, the term would be deployed as an adjective marking the goods or products of the Soviet Union or the socialist world, from popular *muñequitos rusos* (Russian, Polish, or popular Socialist-world cartoons), to goods such as Selena shortwave radio receivers or Russian washing machines. Such goods were seen as the shoddy, inefficient, and ugly—if serviceable—products of the colorless socialist "Second World," and any history of Cold War Cuban vernaculars would need to further explore "*lo bolo*" as the antonym of "la yuma."

In an ethnography of *post-Soviet* Cuba, however, the vernacular geographic imaginary that best came to contrast to La Yuma after the Russians went home and their goods stopped flowing is "África," in no small measure owing to the popular associations of that continent with backwardness, socialism, and scarcity, as I will demonstrate in the following chapter (also see Mbembe 2001). In any case, in counterpoint to Cockaigne La Yuma and its marvelous goods, the Soviet Bloc was strongly associated in this vernacular discourse with shoddy, rough, or crude goods, and, at the level of material culture, the inimitable word *chapucería* (literally "shoddiness") summed up an entire geopolitical critique of the shortcomings of state socialism and the rejection of ideologies of postcolonial solidarity. In contrast, for many if not most Cubans, La Yuma was at least initially an idealized land of milk, honey, and capitalism and, at that time, a reference for the sunniest side of the States. In the words of one Cuban scholar:

> La Yuma would always be associated with: Madonna; Coca-Cola;
> McDonalds; the Oscars; Michael Jackson; New York's skyscrapers; Bill
> Gates; etc.—the so-called "American Dream" or "American way of life"
> and its uppermost symbols. Never would La Yuma be associated with:
> south side Chicago—or Liberty City, Miami; crime and drugs; homelessness; U.S. imperialism; racism; etc.—for those who have a-critically
> and even unconsciously accepted yuma ideology, this would be only
> part of the official state discourse, or, to put it crudely, of the "communist propaganda." (Iván Noel Pérez, personal communication, 1998)

Pérez's words here are very much akin to Alexei Yurchak's extended description of the circulation of Western cultural symbols and forms of imagination in the later years of the Soviet Union—a phenomenon that he calls the "Imaginary West" (2006, chapter 5). Indeed, in its Special Period heyday, Cuban discourse about La Yuma also bore striking similarities to the discourse of "the normal" in late socialist and early postsocialist Europe, as documented by Fehérváry (2013), Rausing (2004), Veenis (1999), and Yurchak (2006). If at first "the material world . . . had sparkled so brightly on the other side of the Wall" for East Germans (Veenis 1999, 84), and the West provided a standard for equating "normal" with "civilized" (Fehérváry 2002, 390), then the "normal" was rooted in tastes, desires, and an idealization of Western life developed under state socialism. People "used it to refer to things that were clearly extraordinary in their local context, but were imagined to be part of average lifestyles in Western Europe or the United States" (Fehérváry 2013, 27). More generally, of course, *yuma* discourse also reflects wider Caribbean and Global South aspirations, such as those evident in the hopes of Dominican sex workers to find a westerner to marry and take them to "La Gloria" (Cabezas 1999, 108), and one can find analogous scales of value throughout the Caribbean (e.g., D. Miller 1997, 335–36; but also see Mazzarella 2003, 50). However, the Cuban background of a centralized, state-dominated economic system, political barriers to the completion of a "transnational migrant circuit" (Rouse 1991), limited or nonexistent advertising for these *yuma* goods (Hernández-Reguant 2002), and the fact of a rapid reintroduction to a hard-currency economy seems a distinctive mixture of late-socialist longing and Caribbean-rooted material culture.

Any well-dressed foreigner, including *comunitarios*,[6] Africans, or South Americans, has at least the potential to be a *yuma*. Importantly, the typical or default images associated with La Yuma also disproportionately involve "whiteness," and in a sense, *yumanidad* itself (or *cosas más yuma*) whitens and cleans: *yumas* who are phenotypically "white" come from places that by default confer the right sort of genealogy. Even *yumas* who are not white in Cuban terms become a shade or two lighter for displaying *yumanidad*. Raymond Smith (1988) and others have long described similar phenomena elsewhere in the Caribbean; this is a context in which Cubans of whatever color will often retell the "joke" with which I began my conversation with Professor Trouillot in the Introduction, about the young white woman marrying a black doctor with a car (also cited by Roland 2011, 35–36). In effect, markers from La Yuma can partly erase or shift normal racial, age, or other distinctions—thus, Kaifa Roland, an African-American anthropologist in Cuba, described herself as a *yuma morena* (2004, 52, 133). There are exceptions, of course, (such as students and other poor foreigners), and thus, *yumanidad* is marked contextually by a whole range of signs and symbols. Expensive, well-fitting, or difficult-to-obtain clothing; jewelry; a good watch; a smartphone; a rented Japanese automobile (rather than a Russian lada); a camera or video camera: such goods mark *los yumas*.

The Brands of *Yumanidad*

Of course, with the decline of state socialist power, legalization of the US dollar in 1993, post-Soviet growth in international tourism, and an unevenly distributed assistance from family abroad, many Cubans of both genders and across the full racial spectrum as well as Africans and other resident foreigners increasingly have been able to acquire such goods. This does not quite make them *yumas*—by their passports, they were and are still unmistakably Cuban[7]—or from the third world, but it did (and still does) indicate relatively high status to display such *cosas más yuma*, and thus certain *yuma* goods have come into great demand. There are far too many *yuma* signifiers in Cuba today to list them comprehensively, so I will principally focus on three central, groundbreaking ones: Nike, the US flag, and the Oscars. Perhaps not surprisingly, each of these in some manner approaches the position of what Daniel Miller famously called a "meta-symbol" (1998, 170). As Miller argued when looking at the meanings given to Coca-Cola in Trinidad, the values accorded global brands are largely perspectival and thus must be closely interrogated. What is in New York a "soft drink," in Port of Spain is a "sweet drink," signifying entirely different things. In the Cuban case, many of the most popular symbols are associated both with the original epicenter of La Yuma, the United States, and also more broadly with representations of an imagined cosmopolitan, capitalist world (see Hernández-Reguant 2002, 302–3; Foster 2008).

Occasionally seen on the island as early as the late 1970s, especially among those unusual families with opportunities to travel to Europe, by the latter half of the 1990s, no *marca* (brand name) was more sought-out by young Cubans than Nike. One woman I interviewed spent one month's wages, at that time eight US dollars, for a pair of socks bearing the Nike logo and then complained that she had to share them with her two big-footed brothers. Unlike its also-desirable competitors, Nike is a US-based brand and therefore legally prohibited by the US government from selling its goods in Cuba.[8] Thus, Nike apparel has had to be hand imported by family or friends visiting from Miami or elsewhere or made on the island itself. For example, an artisan in Havana, licensed for self-employment, sells leather belts he has handcrafted. A close examination shows belts he has embossed "Nike" with its logo. I have seen island-made Nike belts, T-shirts, hats, and shoes in addition to assorted imported articles.[9] From the 1990s onward, displaying the "swoosh," I would argue, did not solely represent one's economic power (Reebok cost just as much), but was simultaneously a tangible display of one's connectedness to the very heartland of La Yuma, to a cosmopolitan world beyond the island, as well as a display of one's power to not only overcome the scarcities represented by wearing the three-dollar

Chinese sneakers available in state shops, but also to outwit even the US government's own "blockade," as the trade embargo is known. This is clearly a Cuban analog of the continental "socialist consumer strategy in which objects for interior decorating were valued according to the mode by which they were acquired" (Fehérváry 2002, 387; also see Berdahl 1999, chapter 4; Pertierra 2011, 82, 161).

Although elsewhere it may be Rolexes rather than swooshes, Cuba is certainly not the only place with an industry dedicated to imitative branding (Lin 2011; Nakassis 2013). Still, the logic of such *marca*-copying practices cannot be accurately understood without careful attention to the meaningful local context. For example, after an international track meet, one of the Cuban athletes, dressed in the regulation Adidas tracksuit and shoes, took off his shoes to stretch. There was the swoosh, painted on the soles of his socks. That specific location makes little sense in relation to the international brand, but it is a significant site of power in some Cuban religious practices (Todd Ramón Ochoa, personal communication, 2000).

Let me be clear: there is nothing static or ahistorical about popular Cuban deployments of North American cultural products. On the contrary, these styles change so quickly that they are good markers of a given moment, and French and North American tastes were established on the island long before state socialism arrived.[10] Luis Pérez argues that this process began with the end of Spanish rule in 1898: "Products designed for the U.S. market projected into the Cuban market new concepts of gender relations, sexual modalities, and standards of beauty not simply as cultural types by as commodity related, accessible as an act of consumption. . . . U.S. products were appropriated to facilitate social integration and self-definition" (1999, 306). By the 1930s, he argues, a "dazzling display of consumer goods [brought] the appearance of abundance within reach." Although he tends to overlook European influences much noted by North American travel writers of the early twentieth century (the popularity of French automobiles, for instance, in Hergesheimer [1927, 3]; also see Irene Wright's description of Cuban fashions circa 1910, in Jenkins [2010]), Pérez notes that at that time such progress, civilization, and modernity implicitly underlined "the rejection of Africa in the formulation of Cuban," and "what conferred value on nationality was derived from association with modernity in its material forms" (1999, 325–26). In any event, by the eve of the revolution, North American consumer goods—from automobiles to air conditioners, from telephones to toasters and fans, from furniture and furnishings of all kinds to apparel—if not owned by all, were widely incorporated into daily usage (L. Pérez 1999, 347).

As even this brief prerevolutionary review suggests, then, Cuba came to state socialism from a different commodity history and aesthetic sensibility than other socialist societies of the twentieth century. Nevertheless, from the 1960s through the 1980s, Cuba shared a pan-socialist experience of the paucity and uniformity of material culture cited above (N. Fernandez 1996, 44). Although her models have recently been under attack as overdetermined (Thelen 2011; Verdery and Dunn 2011), Verdery's sketch of the differing logics of capitalism and socialism does help frame the distinctive context of the material culture of the classic socialist era in Cuba—which, to a great degree, does fit within the notion of an "economy of scarcity" (Kornai 1980; Lampland 1995; but also see Fehérváry 2009) resulting from hoarding and centralized budget planning:

> Socialism's inner drive was to accumulate not profits, like capitalist ones, but distributable resources. [Consequently] most valuable of all to the socialist bureaucracy was to get its hands not just on resources but on resources that generated other usable resources, resources that were themselves further productive. . . . Thus, if capitalism's inner logic rests on accumulating surplus value, the inner logic of socialism was to accumulate means of production. . . . In other words, what was rational in socialism differed from capitalist rationality. Both are stupid in their own way, but differently so.
>
> Socialism's redistributive emphasis leads to one of the great paradoxes of a paternalist regime claiming to satisfy needs. Having constantly to amass means of production so as to enhance redistributive power caused Party leaders to prefer heavy industry . . . at the expense of consumer industry. . . . In short, these systems had a basic tension between what was necessary to legitimate them—redistributing things to the masses—and what was necessary to their power—accumulating things at the center. (Verdery 1996, 25–26)

Thus, consumption was in theory a privilege of socialist citizens, but in practice a systemically neglected—if aroused—right, and the definition and satisfaction of "needs" became a political contest often separating ordinary citizens from state planners. Unlike in a capitalist, market-oriented system driven to find buyers for goods to produce profit (surplus value), in a socialist economy "as long as the food offered was edible or the clothes available covered you and kept you warm, that should be sufficient" (Verdery 1996, 28; also see Medvedev 2007). The economic crisis of the early 1990s compounded such experienced consumer neglect and material scarcity to the point of desperation: in those years one could literally walk for miles and miles, passing only empty window displays in Havana's commercial districts. It is against that background that *yuma* goods first arrived in Cuba in substantial quantities in the mid-1990s, as socialist trade agreements withered and the economic crisis forced the legalization of the US dollar.

Two decades ago, Nikes were an unmistakable sign of one's foreignness: "Havana knew me by my shoes," begins Tom Miller's 1992 travel account.

> Everyone looked at [my Air Nikes] as if they were laced with gold. . . . "What is it with my sneakers?" "They're Nikes, aren't they? [said Gustavo]. That's how we can spot you as a foreigner. The tennies we get here?" He exhaled a horse's neigh. "They're thin, they don't give you any support, and they fall apart in three months. They come from China and you have to wait a year to get another pair—if they have them in stock."
> (1996, 3–4)

Perhaps not coincidentally, Nike is also leisure wear; compare this to Rosendahl's late 1980s report regarding *bolo* footwear:

> Pancho, an old farmer who worked as an agricultural worker, was once complaining to his work-mates and a man from the local union about the lack of consumer goods. "It's getting worse and worse," he said. "Now there are no shoes at all in the shops, and the only shoes I have are these," he said, showing his heavy, worn boots. "Before we did not want to buy *botas rusas* (Russian boots) because they were so badly made, but now I would gladly buy them if there were any. It is terrible, this. I have to have shoes. I could go to work without trousers," he said laughing, "but not without shoes. That is impossible. And there are no files or machetes either. How can we work?" (1997, 125)

Both Tom Miller and Rosendahl's accounts reflect that era's discursive association of *chapucería* with socialist goods—locally familiar goods that raised what William Mazzarella has elsewhere called the "specter of provinciality" (2003, 48). By the late 1990s, however, Russian work boots had largely given way to Nikes and other hard-currency *yuma* brands and goods—again, items not available through official channels or the state-issued ration book, but acquired through connections and kin living abroad. With this transition, the theme of leisure takes precedence over a long-sanctioned emphasis on utility and agricultural production. Thus, for instance, in youth baseball leagues, players often wear Nike shoes, swing Easton bats, and field with Wilson or Rawlings gloves. These are all US-made products obtained (despite the US embargo) through family connections (Carter 2000, 295–96). Further underscoring the Nike phenomenon at the millennium, Thomas Carter described a national broadcast of boxing matches from the Kid Chocolate Gymnasium in Havana. Between rounds, the camera operators would focus their lenses on a mural:

> The mural consists of a basketball, volleyball, and a pair of white tennis shoes. The tennis shoes have a telltale, internationally recognized swoosh, the corporate logo of Nike, painted on their sides. No name is painted there for none is needed. The government has no agreement with Nike.
> . . . The symbolic swoosh also happens to contradict the state's ideals of how one achieves athletic excellence: for love of country rather than corporate sponsorship. (2000, 298–99)

In short, it would be no exaggeration to claim that in the 1990s, the US dollar was welcomed back to Cuba with a swoosh.

To round out this picture of the recommodificatory moment, I would like to describe two other popular deployments of *yuma* symbols in post-Soviet Cuba: the use of the US flag pattern and of the Oscars. The on-island backdrop to the fashionable flag, of course, is the state's intensive, decades-long use of both the Cuban and US flags and flag-derived motifs to symbolize resistance and aggression, independence and imperialism (e.g., Dawson 2001, 28–29; Cushing 2003; Muñiz 2003). The Cuban and US flags both contain stripes and stars and are red, white, and blue, but the white Cuban star is on a red background with blue stripes, rather than a white star on a blue background, making it easily evident to anyone who cares that the "Stars and Stripes" is the symbolic referent of these patterns.[11] At first, wearing the Yankee flag as a bodysuit, a shirt, or a scarf—see Figures 1.1, 1.2, 1.3, and 1.4—seems

Figure 1.1 US flag in fashion, Matanzas, 1999

Figure 1.2 Cienfuegos cyclist, 2017

Figure 1.3 Wagoneer, Trinidad, Cuba, 2017

Figure 1.4 Welcome back, Union Jack

a strongly political statement or a marker of a resistant subculture (Hebdige 1979). This is certainly how it was portrayed in the 1996 Miami film *Bitter Sugar* (Ichaso 1996), and how it is presented in recent US media portrayals of Cuban daily life, particularly following the Obama-Castro rapproachement of December 2014 (Ryer 2014). But for most Cubans, it has been first and foremost a fashion, functioning as a political statement only for some, or only secondarily so (see Hunt 1998; Ryer 2000b; Howard LaFranchi, *Christian Science Monitor*, October 15, 1997). For instance, one evening in 1997, I made dinner for a good friend who was an active member of the UJC (Young Communists' League). She arrived late but amused. "Paul, you wouldn't believe why I'm so late. My *reunión* (local Party meeting) went on and on and on, while we debated whether it was appropriate for *militantes* to wear Yankee flag Lycra, or whether we should ban it, at least from marches and *reuniones*." She started laughing, and could barely finish the story: "Some colleagues wanted to ban it, but after several *militantes* suggested that wearing the flag of the enemy on one's butt was hardly an unambiguous endorsement, the proposed ban turned into a 'recommendation.'"[12] That this style was at that time foremost a fashion was confirmed by many friends and informants, including some after their subsequent emigration and others whose politics were no secret to me. As with Nike, this fashion peaked in the late 1990s, and like Nike at that time, the flag fashion was certainly not available in either peso or hard-currency state-run stores on the island. Rather, each article had to be hand-imported from abroad—often by visiting relatives. In 2002, I met two cousins in the town of Trinidad: one girl was visiting from Florida and her island cousin was wearing a gift from the United States—a shirt with a star clearly patterned after the US flag. This, then, is an ethnographically critical relationship: *what is at stake locally is not a political symbol so much as a symbol marking an enviable status in an emerging remittance economy.* After all, it is precisely apparel with the US flag that is the fashion least likely to openly appear in state shops; such styles are only available when hand-imported by family or friends in Florida or elsewhere in the diaspora.[13] Although less common now than a few years ago, the fashion has proven remarkably durable and is still visible today—most recently, as the background to a superimposed image of Barack Obama

However striking such symbolic deployments may be in a still-socialist state, it is important to note that their massive and uncritical deployment does *not* mean that Cuban nationalism has disappeared. Thus, my Stars and Stripes–clad friends could nevertheless walk with Fidel Castro in their

Nikes when he famously traded his combat boots for his own pair of Nikes, marching to bring Elián back to the *patria* in 2000 or more recently to free the Five Heroes. Put another way, these young Cubans (and resident Africans) see no contradiction between displaying symbols of America/La Yuma and retaining their cubanidad.

The other related popular phenomenon I would like to note here is the status value of the Oscars.[14] Until my first Oscar night in Cuba in 1996, I had never paid much attention to that event, and I certainly did not intend to then. Only belatedly, after a pattern of comments and questions from my family and friends about the Oscars and where (or whether) I was going to watch, did I realize that this was something important to many young Cubans. By the next year, I understood it better: not only did the event show-case favorite North American actors in full regalia, and not only were Cuban films (e.g., Gutiérrez Alea and Tabio 1994a, 1994b) and Cuban or Cuban-American actors (like Andy Garcia and Cameron Diaz) often eagerly awaited on stage or on screen, but the Oscars were adamantly *not* broadcast on either state channel. And so it was something of a feat in the mid- to late 1990s for Cuban nationals to actually see the show: one needed access either to an illicit satellite feed or to one of the cable-equipped hotels generally reserved for foreigners. One émigré friend's brother in Havana called him on Oscar night for an update—calling for the first time ever, without so much as a prefatory salutation or inquiry into the details of his new life in La Yuma. Again, the intensity of interest seems bound to a context in which familiarity with the pageant marks access to an imagined wider, cosmopolitan world of hard currency and capitalism—to what I am calling La Yuma. Officially, the Cuban government maintains a critical stance toward such a spectacle of excess as Oscars night. However, it is worth unpacking the layers of such critiques. Consider, for instance, the book *¿Quién le pone el cascabel al Oscar?* (J. García 1999). Ostensibly, this book, published by one of the state presses, presents a critical examination of Hollywood and the Oscar ceremonies from an orthodox Marxist perspective. Thus, the title of the book—literally "Who puts the bell on Oscar?"—asks who will be brave enough to critique the spec-tacle. In practice, however, the book sold not for its prefatory critical essay, but for its cover, for the bulk of the text (composed of comprehensive lists of Oscar winners by year and category), and for the frequent stills from Oscar-winning films. The book was, in fact, an almanac and ode wrapped in a cri-tique, and it was certainly attractive to young Cubans on the former rather than the latter grounds. And while access is now easier, as Anna Cristina Pertierra describes in her Santiago de Cuba–based ethnography (2011, 224), the Oscars remain an important touchstone in Cuban youth culture.

The Domestication of La Yuma

By 1997, when socialist Cuba's first shopping mall opened and as the hit sounds of Cuban timba disseminated North American hip-hop rhythms and new attitudes toward capitalist consumption (Gordy 2006; Hernández-Reguant 2006), a new look had begun to rival Nike's popularity on the streets of Havana: the signature red, white, and blue blocks of Tommy Hilfiger were hot and hard to come by.[15] As with Nike and the Stars and Stripes, Hilfiger wear initially had to be hand-imported by tourists or from Miami, and *michi-michi* versions of the *marca* "Tommy" soon appeared.[16] When Livan Hernández won the World Series MVP that fall, teal Marlins caps were briefly *de moda*. A couple of years later, Nike and Hilfiger brands were widely distributed among young Cubans, and there was a clamor for FUBU and New York Yankees insignia. By 2002, Baby Phat jeans were hip, and Nike was old hat, and by the middle of the decade, the phrase "jardines de La Yuma" (gardens of La Yuma) came into use to describe Cuban tourist zones such as Old Havana and Varadero beach (Thomas Carter, personal communication). In 2008, it was Mango, Dolce & Gabbana, Converse and Puma sneakers, Jordache. In 2013, one still saw all these styles, including now-venerable Nike, Yankees, FUBU, and many more, while, as in Miami and beyond, the Union Jack has made a comeback. Noting the undeniable links to the North American hip-hop movement, Sujatha Fernandes has argued that young Cubans' adoption of the rap-associated brands Hilfiger and FUBU is a political statement and a "gesture of defiance" aimed at Cuban hierarchies: "Cuban rap audiences use their clothing, and their adoption of American slang such as 'aight' and 'mothafuka' as a way of distinguishing themselves as a group and highlighting their identity as young black Cubans" (2006, 128; also see Fedorak 2009). As with the flag fashion-as-resistance hypothesis, this interpretation is the most readily available one; it is not, however, an adequate explanation. Consider, for example, a couple I encountered at their daughter's baptism in a packed church service in Centro Habana—the young mother in a nice dress, the young father in a Hilfiger T-shirt. He was not making a political statement or marking himself as a "young, black Cuban"; he was dressed to celebrate an important occasion. At that time, FUBU and Tommy were as popular with *blancos* as *negros*, and young Cubans of whatever color (as well as resident Cuban-educated African students; see Chapter 2) may or may not have been fans of rap music and hip-hop style.[17] Certainly in some contexts these *marcas* do signal defiance of Cuban aesthetic, political, and racial hierarchies, and, arguably, with economic restratification a more militant hip-hop nationalism has taken root in Havana. But, as Barthes once put it, "meaning is like a grace that has descended upon the object" (1983, 65); imported brands may also cross (or create) boundaries in ways unanticipated or unrecognizable in global or etic perspective. Reduction to "resistance" is both unedifying and misleading, as is the unmarked presumption that Cuba can be divided into white and black—eliding the problematic of *mestizaje* examined in Chapter 3. As Alexei Yurchak argued in regards to late Soviet youth: "The act of the reproduction of form with the reinterpretation of meaning . . . cannot be reduced to resistance, opportunism, or dissimulation" (2003, 504).

Thus, I want to make a different argument than "style as resistance." Yes, defiance is an element of the dynamic, and certainly the initial allure of Western goods in this era has been replaced by more heterogeneous and ironic appropriations, but, arguably, what is also happening is the Cubanization of *yumanidad*—of *yuma*-ness. For instance, the 2003 documentary *Cuban Hip Hop All Stars* (Alafia 2004; also see Pérez-Rey 2004) showcased imported rhythms and movements and New York Yankees gear as popularized by 50 Cent and other North American rappers, but it also made clear that the imported styles had as much to do with placing new Cuban rap movements in relation to other Cuban music genres as with signifying the United States or the Cuban state. Here again, as with the Nike-soled socks, imported goods or cultural styles attach to and are transformed by specific and irreducible local meanings and histories. The popularity of New York Yankees insignia, for instance, evokes much more than a current association with global hip-hop culture (see West-Durán 2004, 25; also see Eastman 2008; Perry 2009). Not only have the New York Yankees long had a disproportionate number of fans on the island—think of Santiago in Hemingway's *The Old Man and the Sea* (1952), for instance—but it also did not go popularly unnoticed at that time that the team's starting pitchers Orlando "El Duque" Hernández and José Contreras were Cuban. Thus, the Yankees' success becomes a point of nationalist pride; to my chagrin, there must be fifty New York Yankees

Figure 1.5 Yankees logo, Havana, 2004

logos visible for each Red Sox insignia in Cuba (fig. 1.5). The Red Sox offered Contreras more money, but there was little doubt he would sign with New York—by Cuban national consensus, the proving ground par excellence for evaluating the international value of elite Cuban players. Similar domestications are apparent in the already-noted pride with which Cuban participation and triumph in the Oscars and Grammys are celebrated. Many times I have heard the argument that jazz was actually originally Cuban music, picked up and exported by an African-American military band from New Orleans stationed in Santiago de Cuba during the 1898–1902 US occupation.[18] Even Coca-Cola is nationalized in this vernacular; I cannot count the number of times I—a Yankee interlocutor to be sure—was reminded that this quintessential symbol of corporate Americana was headed by a Cuban CEO, Roberto Goizueta, who had arrived in the United States with virtually nothing but an entrepreneurial spirit (see Greising 1998; Foster 2008).[19] The Cubanization of Coke! We are almost back to the underwater narratives that put Cuba at the center of conspiracies, only here it is a celebration of a place on the US stage. There is as much appropriation, domestication, and reascription of meaning as there is "resistance" here.

* * *

If the United States continues as epicenter of La Yuma today, its emotional capital and aesthetic conduit is, without question, Miami. Certainly there are other stylistic influences—notably from increasing numbers of European tourists and diasporic Cubans in Spain and Italy—but the dominant styles come from Miami's working-class neighborhoods of Hialeah and Little Havana. Miami's fashions, of course, are embedded in a larger US scene, but suffice it to say that the city is the principal mediator of contemporary Cuban couture.[20] Thus, the path of the popularity of a Tommy T-shirt for a Cuban-educated Sudanese woman, as described in Chapter 4, runs from the double alienation of US popular culture through Cuban Miami to Cuba circa 1997 and then on to a dancehall in Alberta. And thus, contrary to the tired tropes of North American travel writers who feel transported back in time by the old cars and crumbling streets of Havana, there is absolutely nothing time-less, static, or frozen about contemporary Cuban fashions or culture. Vibrant, dynamic, and appropriative would be better descriptors.[21]

But by the same token, neither is La Yuma the hyperreal America of a European intellectual (e.g., Eco 1986; Baudrillard 1989; Hardt and Negri 2000, 4.2); it rests on very different points of access and travel, divergent interests and ironies, post-colonial experiences and expectations. Especially as the CUC (or convertible, hard-currency peso) takes an ever-firmer hold of daily life, La Yuma increasingly resembles the intimately ambivalent metro-politan migrant magnet *América* of the wider circum-Caribbean. Indeed, the very term *yuma* is gradually fading from everyday speech, often replaced by the more dismissive *pepe* (Roland 2011, 99); one can see a dynamic here very akin to those described by Mark Padilla in the *Caribbean Pleasure Industry* (2007) or the Gmelches' work in Barbados (Gmelch 2003; Gmelch and Gmelch 2012). But—at least until very recent reforms take hold—the migrant circuit in Cuba is incomplete, more of an escape route than trans-national loop: on a monthly salary of twenty US dollars, travel is dear indeed. Thus, for the recommodificatory moment that La Yuma marks, the closest comparisons are still with eastern Europe. Not that this is an exact match either: the economic changes are parallel, although without an accompanying political change in Cuba—perhaps because socialism never conflicted with

Cuban nationalism quite the way it did in small states in the shadow of the Soviet Union. But as in postsocialist Europe, a more discriminating and simultaneously blasé attitude toward now abundant (but prohibitively expensive) *yuma*/Western goods is increasingly apparent and often tinged with bitterness. Krisztina Fehérváry's description of Hungary in the 1990s is apt here:

> The sudden shift in Hungary's geopolitical status combined with the abundance and availability of [Western] commodities for cash created confusion about how people were to respond to them. While it was necessary to mark success in the postsocialist world with status goods, it was no longer appropriate to express delight with a commodity simply for its western origins or inventive design; on the contrary, normalizing or even denigrating such goods was a way of demonstrating one's active participation in and knowledge about a transformed social and economic order. (2002, 378)

Thus, not entirely unlike the Caucan peasants famously faced with the transition to commodified exchange (Taussig 1980), (post)socialist citizens in Europe and Cuba have eventually faced the paradox of desire for *and* disappointment in such goods (Patico and Caldwell 2002; Fehérváry 2012, 635). It is in this context of more abundant commodities, still-scarce convertible currency, and deepening social stratification that there is clear evidence of increasing anti-foreign sentiment and nostalgia for past socialist social networks and solidarity.[22] Not surprisingly given these dynamics,[23] La Yuma as a spatial term is less and less frequently heard, and now *yuma* is often enough of an insult to more plausibly filter back into the state-sponsored public lexicon of gringos, Yankees and imperialists; plausibly, the recent rise of nostalgia for the Soviet Union documented by Loss (2013) is inversely linked to declining popular enthusiasm for La Yuma.

By the mid-2000s the belt makers in the artisanal markets of Havana had a wider selection of handmade *marcas* than one could find in the 1990s: Levi, Fila, Adidas, Tommy, Wisconsin, and Nike. But they also had a newer, equally large selection of Cuban themes. I asked one craftsman which belts were the most popular, and he replied, "The ones that say Cuba." I asked which were most popular for Cubans, and he said, "Oh, these others: Tommy, Levi, Fila . . . The [Cuba-themed belts] are for foreigners" (Ryer, field notes, June 2004). In other words, while Cuban belts were on the table by that time, at the level of national style and material culture, the foreign:Cuban division was still a great gulf, and the allure of the foreign still outweighed the value of the local—unless it was for sale. But today in 2018, one would be hard-pressed to find any *michi-michi yuma* brands in these shops. Not that young people have entirely stopped wearing them, but certainly the remittance circuits have matured and demand for the latest hot brand from abroad is perhaps not so pressing. Thus, the presence or absence of Nike or Hilfiger does not really mark the boundary of a racial group in the narrow sense Fernandes proposed; there may be a loose generational divide, but younger Cuban women and men of every color tend to value and desire these brands and styles. At the same time, *yuma* brands do, still, denote a renewed racial boundary in the writ large sense that I argue throughout the book, wherein "Cuban" itself, resting on a crucial Cuban:foreign distinction (see Roland 2011), becomes imagined as a mixed racial category somewhere between the whiteness of the North and the blackness of Africa. Recurring distinction though it is, the various chapters of this book illustrate in different ways how little hesitation—or how little contradiction—there is in everyday Cuba in associating oneself with the styles and symbols of *lo extranjero*, the foreign—as long as it is the prosperous sort of foreign and not the largely silenced poverty of socialism, África, and the third world. In that sense, as Patico and Caldwell argue, "postsocialist consumption helps reveal the inner workings of an entire range of relationships and institutions in transformation. The interface of state socialism and global capitalism has produced shifting structures of rights, obligations, authority, and freedoms. Yet the 'exit from socialism' is far from unitary or complete, nor is it truly a radical departure from the past" (2002, 291; also see Gonçalves 2013).

With the riot of *yuma* goods now available to those with CUCs and friends abroad, the island certainly no longer has a classic "economy of scarcity." But in the Cuban case, it is only a partial change: moving from a geography of imagination to a geography of management, the rest of this chapter will consider some enduring and distinctive elements of state socialist macrostructures and micropractices that stand out from, and yet at times echo, wider Caribbean patterns. I have organized it in this somewhat counterintuitive way so as to not unduly subordinate symbolic agency to political economy. What theory of consumption or material utility, after all, has the power of thick description in explaining the meaning or intensity of a cultural preference for Coke over Pepsi, the Oscars over a Miss Universe pageant, or Nike sneakers over Reebok?

Everyday Economics of a Caribbean Socialist System

While the following chapter will better illustrate just how deeply Western Cuban self-consciousness is, after more than a half century of ideological polarization, virtually all academic work on Cuba carries a strong political charge. Mention the island's literacy rate, infant mortality statistics, or the number of Olympic medals won, and one is reiterating a pro-revolutionary political line. Conversely, to cite the average monthly salary as twenty US dollars without further context is to line up with anti-revolutionary claims. What makes Cuba particularly difficult to interpret? Might an ethnographic approach productively reframe such typical polarized, quantitatively oriented geographies of management? Keeping in mind that formal quantitative methods are particularly inadequate in Cuba, I believe there are good grounds to think so, of course, and thus I come back again to the relation between management and imagination.[24] More specifically, I have been implying, without reifying difference or overlooking continuities and overlaps between systems, past and present, not only that ideologies of La Yuma inform and animate the daily survival strategies and practices of many Cubans, but also that there are locally distinctive elements to the Cuban everyday (think back to the CIA parable cited at the beginning of this book). In any case, the following cases are intended to be illustrative, rather than definitive. Not intending to imply that Cuban society is organized from its economy upward, I am exploring here some of the striking features of that economic system as it is experienced in daily life as another element of the puzzle that is Cuba today.

The Parallel Economy, Case 1: The Optometrist

I once knew a now-deceased optometrist, then age about thirty, living in Havana. A long-time supporter of the revolution who served in Angola for two years, he was a gentle man, observant, intelligent, and unpretentious, with a household of four—himself, his wife, and two children—principally dependent on his salary to make ends meet. They lived in a relatively spacious two-bedroom apartment. Raised and trained by the revolution, with twenty years of experience in the eye care profession, my friend was paid 240 Cuban pesos per month.[25]

To begin to understand the significance of this typical professional salary, one must consider both the cost of living and the prices of basic goods. All education and health care is free, although school supplies and many medicines are now only available in dollars. Rent is paid, in pesos, at 10 percent of one's monthly wage. Utilities (cooking gas, electric, water, phone) are also paid in pesos and proportionate to a peso salary. Household heating is not necessary. A limited amount of food, rationed by the government, is sold in pesos.[26] Neither clothing nor footwear has been available in pesos since about 1990. Transportation is generally by bicycle or bus, or car.

In my friend's case, after paying rent and utilities and buying what rationed or subsidized food there is to be had, he was left with no more than one hundred pesos (five US dollars) per month from his salary to find two to three weeks' worth of food for four people, plus clothing, soap, and whatever other immediate expenses they might have. To meet these needs, there were several options. Firstly, there were now-legal private farmers' markets, which sell in Cuban pesos: CUP$5.00/lb. for rice, CUP$30.00/lb. for pork, CUP$15.00 for a pineapple. A decent selection of food was (and still is) available in dollar stores (originally for diplomats and tourists) at international prices (e.g., US$2.40/liter for cooking oil; US$1.00/lb. for pasta). And there is the *mercado negro*, the black market, which could provide nearly anything, also in dollars: US$1.00/lb. for chicken; US$1.00 for ten eggs; powdered milk at US$1.00/lb.; cheese at US$1.00 to $3.00/lb., etc.). Clothing is available, in dollars, at prices comparable to international prices for cheap, mass-produced clothing and footwear.

In other words, it was perhaps calorically possible for my friend to support himself, but impossible to also feed or clothe his family. And yet neither he nor any other Cuban appeared to be starving or naked.[27] At the birthday party of his son, there was enough cake and macaroni to feed thirty people and gifts including some new shirts, a baseball hat, and several toys—perhaps an outlay of forty to fifty US dollars, or about three months' salary. Noting my surprise at such extravagance, my friend took me aside to solve the puzzle.

"It is impossible on eight pesos a day, no?" My thoughts exactly, I nod.

"Well, you know I work in the [optometry] clinic on Reina, right? I give exams, make lenses, and do fittings. Well, I have a *socio* who also makes glasses, and his clinic is nearby.[28] So, when people come to my clinic, I send them to him. He sends people to me."

I am confused, and say so.

"Humm. . . . Look, the state owns the clinics, right? And they send us the materials to make glasses, right? So, although I'm not supposed to, I could make them at home, if I had the materials. I know how to do it. So, when the clinic receives a shipment . . . [He uses a characteristic gesture for stealing.] People come into the clinic, they need new glasses, I tell them there is no material to make them, they insist, and I recommend they go to a *particular*, to my friend's house.[29] He does the same for me, and so I do the work at home after-hours and charge a few dollars per pair." At last I understand. Take skills and materials from one's state job to moonlight for enough dollars to survive, with an occasional birthday party thrown in.

"Look," he said, "it pains me to have to tell you this, since I do not like it. I am not a crook. But what am I to do? How else would I feed my family?"

The optometrist's story is one simple example of one of the most common ways of "making do" for many professionals—for plumbers, electricians, and dentists, as well as optometrists. As virtually all materials are imported and distributed by the state, theft, filching, or "borrowing" from the state is systemic. This case also begins to address one of the puzzles that initially mystified me: why do Cubans work? In many cases, a state job provides the sole opportunity to obtain valuable credentials, contacts, and materials to moonlight or barter. One secretary I knew told me that she kept her job (which paid about two-thirds of an optometrist's salary) solely in order to photocopy documents on the side, for ten cents per page (in hard currency, of course). Doctors take medicines home to sell or trade; day care workers sometimes sell powdered milk from their nurseries.[30] Contemporary public opinion, while not exactly approving, holds such measures as theft generally only when carried out on a large scale. Nevertheless, the cumulative macroeconomic effect (e.g., no toner, no milk, no medicine, no gasoline, etc.) is the reproduction of a vicious cycle of low productivity and low wages.

I include the information on costs of living and on prices to illustrate that, on the one hand, a relatively low cost of living (free health care and education, subsidized rent and utilities) guarantees that a high percentage of dollar income is disposable (again, see Jatar-Hausmann 1999 and Padrón Hernández 2012); on the other hand, even a top professional salary is inadequate. Every Cuban household must have some supplemental or alternate sources of income. In addition to parallel market activities, these sources of income frequently include remittances from family abroad; income earned while traveling abroad (musicians, athletes, doctors); tourist-sector gratuities in hard currency; and, in the countryside, domestic food production (e.g., of a pig). Also implicated here is a Cuban pattern of reciprocity most closely analyzed by Mona Rosendahl (1997) and Elise Andaya (2009)—again, a system of reciprocity akin to those described in other socialist systems (Yang 1994; Veenis 1999).

The Parallel Economy, Case 2: The Chicken King

A friend of a friend of mine is the manager of a state-owned fast-food place in Havana. Such a business draws a mixture of foreigners and Cubans with dollars. Like any dollar-based operation, it's the kind of place Cubans are lucky to work, because they can shortchange foreigners a nickel or more per transaction, which adds up quickly in relation to their official salaries of less than one US dollar a day. Plus, they can cut out a few French fries per serving and sell extra servings off the books; when the manager is out, hamburger patties shrink to half-size;[31] ice cream scoopers scoop hollow balls of ice cream and trade cartons of the resulting surplus on the black market. But Cubans, and resident foreigners, have learned to expect such schemes, to count their change and protest loudly as necessary. It is management, faced with the same necessities and peso salary as everyone else, that has the opportunity to really make a good living. The fast-food restaurant provides just one example.

As store manager, my friend's friend oversees resupply of the kitchen and knows when to expect food shipments. Knowing that on a given day he would receive one thousand frozen chickens, he called a contact and ordered two hundred chickens to be delivered on that same day and then was on hand to receive them and load them all into the deep freeze.[32] He now had twelve hundred chickens on hand, but only one thousand to account for in his inventory. Thus, proceeds from the next two hundred fried chicken sales could go straight into his pocket, and his books would balance perfectly. No one would be shortchanged. After paying his supplier, the dollar or more of value added to each of those two hundred raw chickens—labor, cooking oil, facilities, and location of the restaurant—was pure manager's profit.

Although the Chicken King's story provides a relatively large-scale and profitable example, the principle is applicable at various levels.[33] In restaurants and bars with a selection ostensibly limited to rice, beans, or rum, I learned to ask "What do you have *off* the menu?" Often, waiters or bartenders bring in their own supplies and make drinks or serve other foods to-order, at a price negotiated on the spot. Consider, then, the difficulties of control endemic to the system: not only do state planners have to guard against outright loss or theft of work time or supplies, but they have to watch out for unauthorized, off-the-books surpluses as well (also see Hill 2004, 164). It is also important to note here that, like the first case, this example is drawn from Havana, the urban capital of Cuba. It was generally more difficult for me to evaluate rural economic strategies, which perhaps involve a higher proportion of barter but which clearly both overlap with urban practices and often implicate the consuming city, as illustrated in the case of the Shrimp Train.

The Parallel Economy, Case 3: Shrimp Train to Havana

Traveling during the semester break, I needed to get from a town in the center of the island to Havana, and I wanted to pay in pesos, not dollars.[34] So I went to the train station, where after a normal ninety-minute wait in line at the ticket office, I was sourly told to put my name on a waiting list in the back corner. Somebody hissed at me then, in an inimitably Cuban manner, and I turned around. A woman who looked like a younger version of Sharon Stone was trying to get my attention. "Where are you going?" she asked.

"Havana, tomorrow" I said. "But I don't have a ticket."

"Me too. Me neither." she said. "Here's what you do. Just get a ticket to the nearest town, and once you're on the train they won't kick you off."

"OK." I said, pleased to discover *la mecánica* of this mode of transportation.[35]

The next morning, however, after another two-hour lineup, the sour ticket seller repeated her story. No tickets, not even to the next town. "Go over to that corner," she said, indicating I should sign the waiting list. Inquiring for the list in the appropriate area, I got nothing but blank looks, until somebody hissed at me.

"Need a ticket?" Speaking softly, a thirty-something *mulato* offered me a deal: five US dollars for a ticket all the way to Havana. He went off with my state-issued ID to talk to Ms. Sourface, leaving me with his "sister" and her two-year-old son.[36] Pretty soon she turned to me and asked me to watch the boy while she went to the bathroom. I agreed and for fifteen minutes, with the help of the hundred other adults sitting in the station, kept an eye on the boy. I was reveling in the Durkheimianness of the moment, in that (to me startling) confidence, trust, and social solidarity Cubans expect and receive from each other, when my ticket arrived.

"Five dollars," he said. "You can screw my sister for another five," he added.[37]

So much for Durkheimian moments, I thought, and excused myself somewhat awkwardly.

But I did get on board that train that evening. Twelve cars with one hundred seats each— not one of them empty. This train not only predated the revolution but did not seem to have been washed since. Who cared? A seat was a seat. Settling into the trip, however, I was bemused by continuing waves of commotion. First, there were groups of people moving about, loaded with heavy-looking boxes and duffel bags. Second, groups of conductors and occasional policemen swooped around here and there. Ms. Stone tapped me on the shoulder as I went exploring. "Looking for me?"

We started talking in a vestibule, just inches from the uncovered linkage shifting irregularly between cars. Her name was Niurka, and she had just graduated from university with a degree in economics. She had the usual interest in things foreign and shared the near-universal failure to correctly guess my nationality. "American," I said. Predictably, she was surprised and pleased, and predictably she had family in Miami.[38] Virtually every male passerby—including the captain of police, whom she seemed to know well—appeared smitten by this true blonde *cubana* and jealous of the foreigner she was flirting with.

"See those people?" she said.

Those clusters of heavily burdened people, maybe twenty or thirty of them in total, were still moving back and forth; I realized I recognized some of them.

"They're smuggling cheese. I don't do that, though. Too heavy. I'm smuggling shrimp, myself."

Niurka explained that the cheese smugglers were moving around the train looking for unoccupied seats—their own or of compatriots—in which they would sit briefly, pretending to sleep until the police went by, when they would reverse direction. All night long, twenty or thirty of them, with forty to sixty pounds of cheese each.[39] But, she said, shrimp was better. Niurka was smuggling shrimp, and she didn't have a ticket straight through. One of the major ports for the state-owned shrimp fleet was near her home town, and she could buy frozen shrimp for US$1.00/lb. Properly packaged in a leak-proof container, the shrimp could be sold for

twice that in Havana; her buyer would be ready when we arrived
at dawn. For a load of shrimp she risked a fine of one hundred US
dollars or more and made about fifteen US dollars after expenses,
including a three-dollar gift to her friend the policeman.[40]

"Do your parents know?"

"Yeah, they don't like it much, but . . . Well, I've only done it six
or seven times. I want to have my own money, you know, and I'm
doing my [national] service now so I don't make anything.[41] Hey,
remember about getting a ticket to the nearest town? Well, we passed
it. Warn me if you see a conductor."

"But you said they wouldn't kick you off the train!"

"No, they won't, if they don't catch you."

"You mean you don't have a seat?"

"No, well, my friends do, but why waste the extra twenty-three
pesos?"

""Tickets!" The conductor has come up from behind suddenly,
and while I put on my dumbest, slowest foreign accent, Niurka dis-
appears a moment and returns with a ticket—her friend's. Scowling
suspiciously, the conductor moves on and immediately a third friend
brushes by, returning the all-important ticket to the friend ahead.[42]
I'm not sure whether I'm in *Some Like It Hot* or on the *Midnight
Express*, but I am beginning to see some of Niurka's strategic motives
beyond the usual ones (e.g., curiosity, money, an exit visa) that
underlie many Cuban:foreign flirtations.

"You have a boyfriend, don't you?"

"Well . . . Yeah, more-or-less. But it's not very formal. What's
your phone number? I'll bring you some shrimp on my next trip."

By midnight the train smells like a seafood and cheese casserole,
but there is no food to be had. We pull into Santa Clara. Halfway
home, we'll be there by morning.

"Come on," says Niurka. "Let's get something to eat." I look out.
We're at an unlit siding, chain-link-fenced and desolate.

"Come on," she says, and jumps down.

Sure enough, somebody hisses at us. Some entrepreneurs are
furtively passing sandwiches through a hole cut in the fence. We

each buy two ham sandwiches for CUP$5.00 and stretch a moment. Suddenly, police jump out of cars ahead and behind and come running toward us. The vendors bolt; we climb aboard. As the train lurches forward, the police captain swings up, and Niurka hands him her second sandwich.

"Thanks," he said, "I didn't catch anybody tonight."

Despite all the excitement, I am getting tired, and I wish Niurka a good night.

"See you tomorrow," I say.

"Well, actually, you won't," she says, "but I'll call you next time I'm in Havana."

"What do you mean, I won't? See you at the station."

"No, well, see, there's kind of an unofficial stop just before the station, and I'll be getting off there."

Early in the morning, as light filters through my muddy window and we pull into the industrial outskirts of Havana, the train slows to a roll as slow as forward motion can be, before regathering steam. Singly and in pairs, then in waves, people are abandoning the train, bent under duffels and boxes of cheese and shrimp, leaving only a faint scent for the scores of inspectors waiting down the track.

She never did bring me those shrimp.

Although it was never entirely clear to what extent the thousand or more non-smugglers on the train were aware of the ongoing hustling, it does seem clear that the conductors and onboard police were deliberately not uncovering much smuggling, not to mention the possible "unofficial" stop that unloaded the cheeses and shrimp. By the nature of the parallel market, it is difficult to obtain quantifiably conclusive or comprehensive answers to most questions about such practices, which closely parallel those satirized and celebrated in the hit film *Guantanamera* (Gutiérrez Alea and Tabio 1994a). Whatever her reasons for confiding in me, Niurka was not only navigating the parallel market, but also consciously using her gender and her position in Cuba's racial and aesthetic spectrums.[43] One of her two fellow smugglers was a black man, possibly her boyfriend, who carefully kept a low profile, letting her do the flirtation and negotiation with policemen, conductors, and foreigners. As any of my black male Cuban friends would attest, traveling alone he would have been much more likely to be searched or harassed.

Again, these three cases are intended as illustrative vignettes of an economic system that, I argue, is still not entirely organized according to the patterns familiar to North Americans, nor at first glance, to the rest of the Caribbean. However, before leaving it at that, it would be worth giving a closer read to the economic anthropological literature of the Caribbean. For instance, Browne and Salter's *Creole Economics: Caribbean Cunning under the French Flag*, which focuses on informal economic activity in capitalist, contemporary Martinique, illustrates many parallels, particularly through the figure of the *débrouillard* (2004); a foray into Cuban history will similarly reveal deeply Caribbean roots of informal economic activity, as my professor Enrique Sosa once pointed out (Novás Calvo 1973; Serpa 1982). At the day, perhaps postsocialist and postcolonial realities are not so separable (Gonçalves 2012, 2013).

I propose, however, that one can extrapolate from such real-life economic examples to make a general proposition about the production, distribution, and consumption of goods in socialist Cuba. Consider oranges, for example. Valencia oranges are grown in abundance on the Isle of Youth, where they are harvested by Cuban workers (and, formerly, by African students as well). It is highly unlikely that these pickers themselves have a shortage of oranges at home. And the truckers who take the citrus to the port at Nueva Gerona might pop a sack or two in their cab to take home. The barge over to the main island is loaded high, but perhaps an unexpected percentage will have "spoiled" by the time the cargo arrives.[44] Similarly, the truckers who bring the remaining oranges to distribution centers in Havana may drop a sack or two off with a *socio* en route. And the workers who actually distribute produce in the city certainly siphon off a percentage for their families or special customers (who will then owe them a favor at the gas pump, bicycle shop, etc.), as I've already indicated. Thus, very few oranges may actually appear in the official market—an *apparent* shortage—but in fact, a lot of fruit has already been distributed.[45]

In other words, at each stage of the Cuban distribution process, while the *price* of oranges remains fixed, the *quantity* decreases. This continues to be distinct from the global capitalist system, in which at every stage of distribution from production to consumption, the price of oranges rises, and the quantity remains relatively constant. This model is an oversimplification, of course, and does not work as well for imported durable goods as for domestically produced, high-volume products and foodstuffs such as oranges, sugar, or potatoes. Nor have I been able to trace the complete route (from production to consumption) of an actual commodity in Cuba, and thus there is necessarily an extrapolative aspect to my model—an extrapolation that, needless to say, draws on interactions and cases such as the three presented here. However, despite its limitations, this model does help to explain one of the grand puzzles of Cuba with which I began this book: how it is that in a country with no apparent supply of food or clothing or money, no one ever appears malnourished, unclothed, or without recourse for an occasional birthday party.

* * *

If these microethnographic cases suggest that the structural economic logic of Cuba today is distinct in a regional perspective, they should not be read to imply that Cubans are anything but Western, modern, and Caribbean subjects. It is only that much of their actual activity best becomes visible with sustained, close-up observation. But simply solving the CIA's dilemma is, it seems to me, insufficient. This more accurate methodology may improve a geography of management, but without some sense of the desires and dreams that motive this activity, the entire intentionality of the productive process is subsumed to some sort of unexamined struggle for subsistence. To deny that the contemporary situation is experienced as a struggle by most Cuban citizens would be disingenuous indeed, but to fetishize "struggle" as sufficient or self-evident explanation is equally condescending and facile. Very often a sock is just a sock, but sometimes a sock may be a symbol of something worth a significant struggle, with irreducible local meanings best made intelligible ethnographically. In this chapter, I have explored La Yuma and will now turn to Cuban ideologies of África—specifically, as another element of a popular geography of the imagination that, I argue, significantly animates daily activity within the republic and also delineates the presumptive racialized borders of cubanidad.

CHAPTER 2

ÁFRICA IN REVOLUTIONARY CUBA

I f, as I am arguing, La Yuma is an originary, imagined elsewhere to Cuba's own putative hybridity and *mestizaje*, it is not the only such elsewhere. Having explored the space popularly associated with whiteness in the previous chapter, I will focus here on the character of that elsewhere commonly associated with blackness before turning to Cuban ideologies of *mestizaje* in Chapter 3. Toward this goal, I deploy *África*, the Spanish-language term for Africa, to gloss vernacular Cuban ideologies of and about that continent. Perhaps in the course of this investigation, we will discover that Achille Mbembe is right, and that "Africa as an idea, a concept, has historically served, and continues to serve, as a polemical argument for the West's desperate desire to assert its difference from the rest of the world" (2001, 2). From the first glance, it certainly seems that in Cuba, as in the rest of the West to which he refers, "narrative about Africa is always a pretext for a comment about something else, some other place, some other people" (3). Is this all there is? Or are there complicating qualities to Cuba's África? Is Cuba part of the West, or is it arguably more immediately "postcolonial" than Western republics such as those of the United States and Europe?[1] Also, how does Cuba's Marxist inflection of Western ideologies play out in África? And if the lament over the silencing of complex African realities and languages in lieu of essentialized images and constructions depends in part on the lack of in-depth study and experience (Mbembe 2001, 7), how might the massive scale and relatively sustained quality of postrevolutionary Cuban contact with Africa affect matters?

The first part of this chapter, then, traces the shape (and silences) of the contemporary popular category África in Cuba, beginning with the experience of Cuban *internacionalistas* in Africa and particularly examining the evolutionistic quality to their África. The encounter with resident Africans—and, in counterpoint, Arabs and West Indians—within the republic forms the second major part of the chapter. Critically examining "African" and "Cuban" identities in interaction and mixture, I elaborate ways in which the social space that African students occupy as black foreigners presented a potential classificatory challenge to the order of things within the republic and set the stage for understanding their complex relationship to *cubanía*, which will be explored in Chapter 4.

Ľ Internationale 1: Cubans in Africa

One Cuban in thirty, or about four hundred thousand out of twelve million people, has gone to Africa—the majority to Angola, but also to Ethiopia, Mozambique, and a score of other states—since the 1959 Revolution, which brought the internationalist ideals of state socialism to Cuba. While there are, of course, extensive historical, diplomatic, and cultural links between the Caribbean and Africa, the direction and scale of Cuban travel is noteworthy, even in a region where international travel is routine. In addition to soldiers who generally served in relatively regulated military bodies for two years each, thousands of Cuban doctors, teachers, engineers, diplomats, and scholars have traveled and worked in Africa and then returned to the Caribbean over the past half century. Modern Cuban-African internationalism took shape in the early 1960s with Cuba's limited support for anticolonial struggles in Algeria and the Congo (Guevara 2000). Larger-scale involvement, however, did not occur until the Ethiopian and, particularly, the Angolan conflicts in the 1970s, in which Cuban troops played a decisive role from the time of Operation Carlotta onward. With the resolution of the Angolan War and the end of Soviet aid in the 1990s, Cuban involvement with African states declined precipitously to the level of diplomats and delegations, although recently there has been a resurgence, and throughout sub-Saharan Africa there are still teams of Cuban agricultural engineers, sports trainers, and, especially, medical personnel.[2] In any case, the renewed focus on international medical aid in the twenty-first century is no longer Africa-centric: the most significant resurrection of *internacionalismo cubano* in recent years was "Plan Barrio Adentro"—the posting of some ten thousand Cuban medical personnel to Venezuela, arguably indirectly in a quid pro quo for subsidized oil and other support from the Chávez government.[3] There are also significant teams of Cuban doctors working in the aftermath of natural disasters in Central America, Pakistan, Haiti, and elsewhere. Indeed, media-savvy Fidel Castro put fifteen hundred physicians on standby to assist in Hurricane Katrina relief—an offer that, needless to say, was not accepted by the Bush administration. But in any case, even in the twenty-first century there are thousands of Cuban doctors working in twenty-one African states (Gleijeses 2002, 393; Silvia Barthelemy, "The People of Gambia Are Grateful for Cuban Cooperation," *Granma Internacional,* December 14, 2005; Almer 2011; Burke 2013).

Unfortunately, most of the literature of Cuban-African internationalism is either no more than policy-oriented chronology or burdened with extreme rhetorical biases.[4] For my purposes, two useful contrasting texts are those by anti-Castro Carlos Moore (1988) and by Piero Gleijeses, a political scientist sympathetic to the revolutionary government who was able to carry out years of research in Cuban and US archives, as well as interview many involved policy makers in Cuba, the United States, and Africa. But while it fills in numerous quantitative holes, even Gleijeses's scholarly, relatively balanced project revolves around themes and questions such as "was Cuba acting as a Soviet proxy?" (2002, 392)—that is, around matters of political leadership and heroic histories (Gleijeses, Risquet, and Remírez 2007). In some respects, literary scholar Christabelle Peters's recent book *Cuban Identity and the Angolan Experience* (2012) is much more daring. Based on analyses of Cuban films and literature dealing with the internationalist era, as well as a two-month journey through Cuba, Peters argues that Cuba's involvement in Africa, and specifically Angola, "gave birth to a new idealized image of what it meant to be Cuban" (7). Working over a much longer length of time, with interviews in the context of daily life as well as with *longue durée* images of Africa evident in Cuban history and archives (see the following chapter), I am honestly not quite so sanguine about radical change: as we will see, much of the Cuban-African encounter was interpreted through preexisting ideological and cultural lenses. Indeed, interviews from a recent PhD dissertation by anthropologist Marisabel Almer, "Remembering Angola: Cuban Internationalism, Transnational Spaces, and the Politics of Memories" (2011), are, like my own interviews here, replete with evidence of the renewal of long-term Cuban ideologies through the very processes of Cubans' experiences in Africa. My own focus here, of course, is instead on culturally meaningful implications of such a movement and is, in the first instance, based on interviews with returned *internacionalistas* in which I asked them to recall, reconstruct, and reflect on their experiences. The interviews were conducted with Cubans who had been teachers, students, journalists, soldiers, photographers, writers, translators, doctors, and dentists—in Mozambique, Angola, Ghana, Libya, South Africa, Tanzania, Ethiopia, Egypt, Congo, Nigeria, Zaire, Burkina Faso, and Benin, as well as Nicaragua, Syria, Yemen, and Saudi Arabia.

Interviewing *internacionalistas* of so many professions returned from so many different places in varying decades—to say nothing of personal inclinations or self-identifications—results in a veritable riot of data, much of which is self-contradictory—for example: "Africa did/did not affect me"; "Africans are beautiful/ugly"; "we accomplished something worthwhile/it was a waste of resources and lives." Just as I argue in the next chapter that it would be an error to shut out the cacophony of racial reference for some false sense of order, so too here patterns must be teased and tested, not forced, out of the ethnographic jumble. But taken together, the polyphonic perspectives do eventually give some sense of what is disputable and what is doxic. I begin this section on Cuban experiences in Africa, then, with an abridged interview, conducted in Spanish in Havana in 1997 with a white woman who had worked as a translator in the Congo. My first questions to her were "Where did you go?" and "Why did you go?"

Julia Sánchez

"I visited Angola, Nigeria, Zaire, Burkina-Faso, and Benin, but my main assignment was to go twice to the Congo, in 1977–78 for sixteen months and in 1980 for three more months. Both times I went as a translator, once for the Federation of Cuban Women (FMC) and once on a military mission [which we have agreed not to talk about]."

"Why? Well . . . I was born in Villa Clara, in a black neighborhood. From my earliest times, then, I had a lot of curiosity about an impenetrable black world: I was told African-derived stories as a child, I read a lot of African literature, and so I went to Africa with great pride and happiness. I have no regrets from internationalism, even now. I am not, by the way, a religious person." Julia answers thoughtfully, but with increasing animation. She continues without further questions.

"Before going to Africa, I had met Congolese students here at the university, but when I arrived to the Republic of Congo, no books—the Africa that I saw had nothing to do with what I expected from the books I had read beforehand, except perhaps in the writings of Congolese writer Henrie Lopes—I don't know if you know him? Anyway, neither did it have to do with the written or spoken stories of my childhood. . . . Perhaps it had more to do with the Congolese students I had known, who were from ultra-bourgeois families. But the reality was not much related to Cuban stories about Africa."

"Africans, Congolese, were very educated.[5] There were no fights; it was always tranquil. Children were always very respectful of their parents and adults. I saw little sign of religion in Africa— at least of the santería sort that I would have noticed and was keeping an eye out for. I remember certain tribal customs. . . . There was a lot of misery, and injustice between men and women in the villages. African women work a lot, men work less. Men have three, four wives, who at heart would rather not have to smile at their rival wives every morning."

"Would you return again?"

"I would love to go a third time, sincerely. Truly I would."

"Are you still in contact with friends there?"

"No. I wrote several times, but no response. Later I met one person I knew in Korea, an African woman with the FMC-equivalent organization there. But these weren't like my contacts with the people I lived with, that I grew to know and to love. I don't know what has become of them."

"What was the relation between Africans and Cubans of African descent?"

"Oh, Africans and *negros cubanos* have nothing to do—totally different, their *gestos* (gestures) are different. One could never mistake Cuban for African; Congolese were tall, beautiful people."

Because of this last, somewhat unusual comment, I asked Julia what she thought about racism in Cuba. Without missing a beat, she replied, "It seems to me that there is endogamy in all three [Cuban] groups—white, black, mulatto. Many *internacionalistas* acted more that way with the distance of being away from Cuba and in Africa."

"What changed when you returned?"

"I felt neither more nor less Cuban when I returned. . . . Yes, internationalism for sure meant that Cubans came back saying to their friends and families, 'you don't know what it is like to be really hungry,' and 'Cuba is not so bad after all.' But even before the Special Period, things here were changing, in terms of internationalist sentiment; there was less altruism, less of a sense of completing a mission out of solidarity—more hardly knew why they were going."

An exegesis of this conversation (and many others) would have to begin with the depth of socialist idealism, naiveté, and ignorance with which many Cubans set out for Africa. For at least this white Cuban, the "real" Africa, although unexpected, "had nothing to do with black Cubans" or their own impenetrable black world. Although Africa is self-consciously valorized in her description of Congolese people, one is reminded of Mbembe's critique of even sympathetic outsiders' attempts at solidarity: "The other sign, in the discourse of our times, under which African life is interpreted is that of intimacy. It is assumed that, although the African possesses a self-referring structure that makes him or her close to 'being human,' he or she belongs, up to a point, to a world we cannot penetrate. . . . In this perspective, Africa is essentially, for us, an object of experimentation" (2001, 2). Troublingly, despite the ostensible sympathy, África is more than an object of experimentation: it is also a renewed site for the reproduction of racial ideologies *within* Cuba.

Each internationalist had her or his own expressed reasons for going to Africa, such as "for the professional challenge," "to test myself," out of "humanitarian conviction," or sometimes "for the chance to travel." Sitting in an apartment full of mementos of Africa—masks, tapestries, animal skins—I posed the question to a self-identified *mulato* journalist returned from Angola, and he responded, "I wanted to demonstrate to my children that I had been in the midst of the hottest problems of the moment in which I was living" (Enrique Ibarra interview). Very commonly, interlocutors ascribed themselves one motive, and other less idealistic motives to the general population. Félix Pérez, a surgeon of Chinese descent (who insisted on driving me home after our interview), told me, "The motives for going on an international mission varied according to the person. In my case, I did it out of humanitarian conviction—that it might be good for the Angolan people. I think that Fidel has influenced us positively in this brotherhood with other peoples in the world." He was motivated, he added, by "almost a paternalistic sentiment that we must teach other peoples less fortunate than us, and this was my fundamental motivation.[6] For sure, other people traveled with a less altruistic sentiment—for example, if you are a doctor and do a mission, in that era you would be given an automobile.[7] If you did not go, you did not have a right to an automobile."

In nearly every interview and conversation with repatriated Cubans, I asked them what struck them the most strongly when they arrived in Africa and what they remembered most vividly. Across the spectrum, many who had gone to Angola commented about the terrible smell of Luanda, the poor sanitation and trash in an otherwise beautiful city. Some arrived right into active war zones; others were on civilian missions in calmer areas or times and traveled more freely. Many talked about their immediate health concerns—potable water, snakes, green flies, mosquito-borne diseases—as the biggest adjustment. Others recalled the initial shock: "Well, the entrance is a violent change. You spend fourteen or sixteen hours on an airplane and arrive at a country you don't know and begin to live in a new dynamic. In my case, it was also the first time I was in the army" (Juan González, interview). One very dark-skinned Cuban *internacionalista* who had been assigned a mission in Ghana told me the thing that surprised him most during his time in Africa was that he was often mistaken for an African American from the United States, but never for an African. Another typical comment: "One thing that really caught my attention was that in Angola, I did not see mulattos, which is one of the first signs of a cultural relation between races, no? Blacks and whites have to produce mulattos, but there were very, very few. The few I saw were generally people who had ascended [socially] and were racist against the blacks, on those below" (Juan González, interview).

Quite a number of accounts involved war atrocities as particularly vivid memories. For example, Félix Pérez, the Chinese-Cuban physician quoted earlier, recounted:

They were terrible, the things, they were like the horrors of Nazi fascism. Women arrived [to my hospital, in Luanda] with their wombs cut open, their husband's head put inside, and sutured up. Horrors—some that you can imagine, but then truckloads of civilians that had suffered the violence of Savimbi's guerillas would arrive. . . . I tell you, no war is justified, but there was justification for the defense of the Angolan people [from that]. . . . Of course, in all wars injustices are committed. The Angolan troops themselves committed injustices as well.

Certainly not every meaningful conversation was a formal or pre-planned interview: sitting in Céspedes Park in Santiago de Cuba during a semester break, I struck up a conversation with a thirty-one-year-old black cook named Fernando. It turns out he had been in Angola for four years (two tours); he described shooting a Unita guerilla and being wounded by a landmine, and he showed me the scars. I asked him what he thought about Africa, having been there and back, and he said he'd been very affected by the conditions there. "Even with the Special Period, Cuba is much better off than Africa; I wouldn't go again, but am not sorry I went either. In the end, I just tried to survive." Fernando really lit up at my mention of the television mini-series *Algo más que soñar* and repeated what I have heard others say—that it had done more to open up Cuban society for a discussion of the revolutionary "bourgeoisie" than any other show—even more than *Strawberry and Chocolate* (Gutiérrez Alea and Tabío 1994b) had for gay rights.[8]

A minority of internationalists rejected the notion that the experience had affected Cuban society in general or themselves in particular. Juan González, the white veteran of Angola quoted earlier, explained:

It seems to me that it was designed so that the Cubans in Angola were always within their military unit. There were no weekend passes or the like, and so relations between Cubans and Angolans were very limited. One lived within the base, and there was no motive to leave it or to get to know citizens of that country. We drank Cuban water and ate Cuban food and smoked Cuban cigars.

I tell you that in the time I was in Angola, I met no one by name and surname; I did not have extensive conversations. From a cultural point of view, I had no interchange—that is, I left nothing, and they gave me nothing. I don't have and did not leave friends there and have no one to write to. I got to know nobody, and I moved around more than most [other Cubans].

This statement attests to the limited value or weight that can be assigned to a cultural migration on the basis of scale alone. Note that military units, through which the majority of Cubans experienced Africa, had relatively limited cultural contact with Africans. As Trouillot put it: "in no way can we assume a simple correlation between the magnitude of events as they happened and their relevance for the generations that inherit them" (1995, 16). Here again, the experience ultimately seems to renew and solidify a priori ideologies and prejudices—often expressed most forcefully among *blancos* and *mulatos*, but among *negros cubanos* as well. In the end, straining for meaning out of the raw migration is perhaps better suited for a committed journalist and novelist like Gabriel García Márquez than for an anthropologist:

I arrived in Havana [as the first troops were returning from Angola]. Already at the airport I had the distinct feeling that something very profound had happened in the life of Cuba since I had last been there. The change was indefinable but quite evident in the people's mood as well as the spontaneity of things . . . : it touched the very heart of Cuban life. There was a new men's fashion for lightweight suits with short-sleeved jackets; Portuguese words had found their way into the latest slang; old African strains reappeared in new popular tunes. (1989, 59; also see Peters 2012, 78)

Numerous *internacionalistas*, like Julia Sánchez (cited earlier) and many soldiers (e.g., Fundora, in Geldof 1991) as well as famous novelists, strenuously disagreed with the notion that their efforts were without lasting import. They argued that they did develop close relationships, and they spoke passionately about how much the experience affected them; they gave their children Portuguese names or had children with Africans (see below). They said things like, "Yes, of course we had many relations with the Angolan people—with patients and their families—and the opinion we had was very positive" (Félix Pérez, interview). One African-Cuban journalist said to me:

What very much caught my attention was how the people were, and I said, "they look like us, but then I realized that it was us who were like them, for having suffered through a process of colonization. We are like the Angolans because we were the descendants of Africans and Angolans. . . . In general, I had Angolan friends, many Angolan friends, because as a journalist, that facilitated my work, and I was able to get to know great people who had many serious problems. Then, in the Special Period, I sometimes felt like an Angolan! I would love to go back to see the people I left, the young folks, to see what is happening in the lives of all my Angolan friends. (Enrique Ibarra, interview)

Indeed, it was more common for a conversation about África to trigger strong emotional responses in former *internacionalistas* than to trigger the overtly negating and seemingly indifferent attitude of Juan González. Early in my fieldwork, on a short trip into the countryside a few hours from Havana, I was presented to a relative of my host family who had served in the military in Angola. Now a truck driver, Luis, a *blanco cubano*, readily agreed to an interview, which he formalized by serving us both homemade rum in cups made from decapitated beer cans. Luis was in Angola from 1981 to 1982, arriving just days before a South African invasion. Gradually, as we talked, he became more emotional. He described the attempt to rescue thirty-two Cubans trapped in a town and the horrible deaths resulting. Sixteen were rescued. But, he said, "their [the South Africans'] equipment was better" and there were many deaths. Luis spoke eloquently and at length about the history and politics of the region—particularly about Savimbi, and the problems caused by imposed colonial borders.

In response to my question about what he thought about Angolans, or Africans, he paused and finally said only that "Angola doesn't have the level of development we have here." And he talked about how, for a long time after returning [to Cuba], whenever he heard a backfire of a car or such, he'd hit the ground, and he had trouble sleeping. Luis was clearly a keen observer, but did not seem like someone who normally talked about his feelings or dwelled on past experiences. He made no more comments about Africa as such, but was clearly glad to return to Cuba. He did comment on how young he and the other Cuban troops were and how much this war was a shock. Perhaps there is an implicit criticism in that; however, he also explicitly said, "Look, we did manage to accomplish something," referring to the containment of South African apartheid. By the end of the conversation, thinking about the friends he lost, Luis was quite agitated, his eyes watering, and he turned away,

combed his hair a moment, and said, "Look, let's not talk about this any-
more, it makes me uncomfortable to remember, and I have to go to work
now. I'll be back to visit tonight" (Luis Hernández, interview). The topic of
African internationalism repeatedly touched a nerve like this among veterans,
evoking strong if otherwise silent emotions and memories; I learned to take
care not to embarrass them—particularly men who had been in combat. I
also found that África was often wrapped in ideologies of development and
underdevelopment.[9] As Luis put it, "Africa does not have the level of development we have here." But is "development" discourse, with its notions of
linear progress, not a direct descendant of European evolutionistic ideologies
that most immediately trace back to the nineteenth century's stages of savagery, barbarism, and civilization?

África in Cuban Evolutionist Ideologies

In general, official media and popular speech seem much more synchronized
with respect to evolutionist ideologies than is the case with the racial beliefs
considered in the next chapter. More remains to be said, though, regarding
the ideological frames inherited and redeployed by both people and state.
Broadly put, the tension is between a Eurocentric, Marxist evolutionary
scheme (progressing from savagery to barbarism to civilization) and an anticolonial elevation of the Africanity of Cuba—which was famously referred
to by Fidel Castro as a Latin *African* nation (Casal 1989, 484)—to the status
of guardian of authentic Cubanness (e.g., R. Moore 1997).[10] For a review of
the *longue durée* of these discourses, see Ada Ferrer's work (e.g., her analysis of
Antonio Maceo's reconfiguration of colonial discourse in the famous protest
at Baraguá in 1878 [1999, 66]) as well as Aline Helg's work in tracing evolutionist ideologies into the twentieth century (e.g., "only through education,
training, and the legal marriage of the new generation of Afro-Cubans . . .
would [African] barbarian and savage practices" be eradicated [1995, 136]).

Thus, there are tensions within Cuban interpretive frameworks that
label African societies (and Africanity) as "primitive" or "backward," but
that simultaneously suppose the vitality of Cuban culture to spring not from
Europe, but from Cuba's kinship with and descent from Africa (e.g., the
"Surgical Genealogy" of Chapter 3; M. Moreno Fraginals [1983, 172–78]).
In Castro's words: "Many things bind us to Angola: the cause, common interests, policy, ideology. But we are also united by blood ties. And I mean this in

two ways: by the blood of our ancestors and the blood we have shed together on the battlefield. . . . We have fulfilled our elementary internationalist duty with Angola" (Castro Ruz 1981, 107).

While many Cubans are understandably proud of their role in turning back the clearest remnant of European colonialism in Africa, apartheid, Eurocentric—in this case Marxist—classifications of civil and savage society nevertheless prevail. In many officially published texts, modernist notions of progress and development predominate over "traditional culture," which is explicitly seen as obstructive. Take for example Gabriel García Márquez's assertion that "cultural conditions [in Angola were] closer to the Stone Age than to the twentieth century. . . . Age-old superstitions were a hindrance not only in everyday life, but in the conduct of the war" ([1977] 1981, 54).[11] These tensions of ideology, value, and interpretation reflect ambivalent identifications with European and African heritages.

At street level, in conversations with Cubans across the color spectrum, one is bombarded by such evolutionist presumptions. In the words of the Chinese-Cuban doctor and former internationalist mentioned earlier: "There are those who say that Angolans were barbarians, savages, because between sixty and seventy percent of the people live in tribes in the stage of advanced primitive communism, before reaching slavery, feudalism, and the rest" (Félix Pérez, interview). Often, the framework is unconscious, as was the case with a black veteran of the war in Angola who told me numerous jokes about Cubans outwitting African tribesmen and "cannibals." In other cases, my interview topic itself brought the ideology to the fore:

> Luanda is a very developed city. In general, the cities in Angola are developed, much more developed, I would say, than some zones in Cuba. But the people, how the people lived . . . the level was really very underdeveloped. I knew that the Angolans had 150 years of backwardness compared to us, because Cuba gained its independence in 1902 but slavery ended in 1889, while this only happened recently in Angola. Angola still had slavery-like conditions because for the Portuguese, for the colonizers, the Angolan was an animal with clothes. (Enrique Ibarra, interview)

Often, evolutionist ideology was interwoven with other things, such as views on Angolan women and gender relations:[12]

Robberies, assassinations, have to be seen in terms of their cultural primitivism—perhaps it is not correct to call them primitive from our point of view, perhaps the male-female relation in middle-class California is not the same as the typical machismo of an African tribe living in the stage of primitive communism. We see it as violence, and for them it is normal, just as a tribe of monkeys in which the dominant male expresses his control over the females of his troupe by showing his teeth and striking them. It cannot be said that that might be primitivism. It is simply another type of life. But I got to a point of loving them and understanding them [Angolan women]; I did not have sentiments of hate or disrespect, only of regret for all they had suffered, for the horrors they had been through. (Félix Pérez, interview)

Again, it is important to frame such sentiments in the context of decades of incessant study of Marx and talk in the Cuban media—in schools and text-books, Party meetings, marches, and speeches—about "development" and "underdevelopment." It is no coincidence that the single most famous film of the revolution, released in 1968, is titled *Memories of Underdevelopment* (Gutiérrez Alea 1968).

It seems paradoxical, of course, that Cubans would claim postcolonial kinship and solidarity with Africa and simultaneously presume Cuba's own higher status as more developed (not to mention aspire to further develop itself in accord with late socialist orthodoxy). With deep roots in the century-old *blanqueamiento* (whitening) campaigns, this contradiction extends well beyond the public pronouncements of politicians. It can be summarized, I believe, with a hegemonic proposition: that despite its problems and poverty, Cuba *is* Western.

There was a great abyss [between Cubans and Angolans], because whatever Cuban, however humble, is formed in this [Cuban] experi-ence. This is a country of the first world, although poor, but it is of the first world, of the West, even though we say the West is the United States. No, we are Westerners, so much so that he who comes from the most humble place in Cuba comes with a culture—four hundred years, five hundred years, or one hundred years as a nation. But one hundred solid years, so that Cuba did not have far to go. And then, Angola is a very poor country; it has a lot of natural resources: petroleum, uranium, diamonds, great rivers to produce electricity. But there was no one to take advantage of this because Angolans themselves continue divided in tribes. That is a cultural phenomenon that, I don't know—look, you could find a building like this one we are sitting in [a three-story walk-up], occupied by Angolans, and after the Portuguese left, instead of using the kitchen, they would light a fire right inside the house or on the terrace to cook very basic food. There was no development, they did not receive any influence of development. (Juan González, interview)

If Cuba is the West, the concept of "solidarity" seems false coin indeed. In Havana in August 1994, during the depths of the Special Period, I made the mistake of remarking to a Cuban intellectual, a *jabao* (see below) who was railing at the disintegration of his society, that the situation was bad, but not as bad as it could be. "Tell me," he challenged, "where is it worse?" "Well," I said, "I was in Haiti recently, and . . ." "Haiti!" he cut me off. "Haiti! Don't you see, we don't want to be compared to Haiti? We were supposed to be in the vanguard, to the level of Japan or France by now, and all you can come up with is Haiti? Please."[13] Notions of development, of course, are aspirational and relative, not fixed or static. But this is the point: these beliefs aspire to put as much ocean as possible between Cuba and its African postcolonial partners, even while blood ties are announced and solidarity sworn. From the perspective of such oft-expressed statements, rather than some shared "postcoloniality" or historically inferred kinship, one can see Mbembe's argument: Given the conflicting imperatives of Cuban ideologies, África cannot possibly be real. Rather, it only makes sense as part of an imagined geography against which Cubans can and do define themselves, their island, and their Cubanness.

Cuban internationalist travel adds a specific, immediate dimension to these tensions of development, underdevelopment, and national identity. One *mulato* veteran of the war in Angola, interviewed on the brink of the Special Period, spoke to the question of national identity in both Angola and in Cuba. In the process, he not only reproduced a common Cuban image of Africans as primitive and backward, but also described a change in his own sense of identity *as Cuban*:

They even eat mice. Have you ever seen anyone in this world eat mice? [. . .] And they consider [Angola] a rich country. "Well, if you're so rich why are you so hungry?" Well . . . I suppose it's national pride that makes you think your country is the best in the world because it's where you were born. As Martí said, "Our [Cuban] wine is bitter. Bitter though it may be, it's ours, isn't it?" I loved Cuba more after I went away. (Fundora, quoted in Geldof 1991, 82, 85)

On the one hand, revolutionary Cuba has been nationally self-defined in anticolonial, international solidarity with African states, but it is also, at least aspirationally, a "modern" nation precisely in counterpoint to Africa and to its own international projects there.[14] The issue here is complicated in part by the wide range of experiences and perspectives of internationalists, but also, in the post-Soviet era, by the linkages and associations between now largely silenced tropes: África, internationalism, and the Soviet Bloc. In the words of one self-identified *mulato* interviewee, a documentary filmmaker who spent two years in the Congo and Angola: "Africa? Who now can remember Africa? [Around 1990] we stopped talking about Poland, Hungary, and Bulgaria. Where is Bulgaria? It ceased to exist, just as Angola ceased to exist. Now, people try to forget about all that" (field notes, August 1994).[15] Despite such vocal, bitter silencing of África and the internationalist projects of the Soviet era, I argue that even if it is as a lack, an absence, or an undesirable alternative, *of course* Cubans strongly retain a well-developed geographical category for that continent. It is worth reiterating that for many Cubans, the predominant association with Africa is poverty: "When I got to the People's Republic of Angola, what really drew my attention was seeing so much poverty . . . you cannot conceive of how a human being could live as they do. You have to go there and see it, see how they live, almost like animals" (Fundora, quoted in Geldof 1991, 77). As we have seen, these associations are strongly embedded in a Western, Marxist evolutionism, and recurrent associations with Africa include backwardness, colonialism, and primitivism—even among those who speak most warmly of their experiences there.

Finally, interviews with returned *internacionalistas* brought out one other interesting pattern—the Cubans' own encounter with the possibility that they might have been seen as outsiders or colonizers by Africans: "For me, the biggest shock was to see some Angolans who did not care for the Cubans. For example, a young man said to me, 'it is true that the Portuguese were bad, and they beat people, but the Cubans do not pay, they do not give people money,' and that was true. The mentality of the Angolan and of the Cuban are very different in millions of situations" (Enrique Ibarra, interview; also see Fundora, in Geldof 1991, 85). Despite such occasional unease, Cuban-African internationalism clearly did not produce the kind of systemic crisis of popular confidence that, say, the United States experienced in Vietnam. There may be multiple reasons for this, including a measure of military success and an often-supportive world opinion, as well as a general association of colonialism with capitalist states, but surely one additional consideration is the steady flow of living African students who, from the 1970s on, have resided in the homeland. Not only have their residencies generally been enthusiastic (at least for those who persevered through their programs), but with respect to Cuban evolutionist frameworks, I will argue, these students have actively countered such ideologies with a self-presentation as professional, civilized people—just as have generations of upwardly mobile Cubans of color.

* * *

Before turning to the students, however, some further inquiry into the shape of África—of the Cuban image of the continent—is in order. To put the issue bluntly: how do other popular categories such as "Arab" and "Caribbean" (or less commonly "Antillean") bump up against África? Informed not only by mass media but also by *internacionalistas* returned from the Middle East, North Africa, and the circum-Caribbean as well as resident students of those regions, a consideration of *árabe* and *caribeño* reinforces the separation between actual African geography and its imaginative aspects. In the words of one student from the Western Sahara: "When Cubans discover we are not Cubans, but Arabs, they automatically think we each have an oil well. Literally, they think that you just plug a hose into a sand dune and get all covered in oil. They also think there is no water in our countries, which—look at me!—is contradicted by the evidence that there are people living who are from there" (Ibrahim Ali, interview).

I conducted a series of interviews with Cubans who had served in North Africa and the Middle East, including a married couple who had worked as medical specialists in Libya in the mid-1980s. Their notion of the distinction between Arab and African was certainly more detailed than the average Cuban's: they described many details of Arabic religion, language, dress, customs; the general reserve and strict gender separation of

Libyan society; limits on the consumption of alcohol. They spoke at length about their group's experience within the racial structure of Libyan and North African society, which was "not very black." As they explained: "Only recently have some Sudanese immigrated for work, while the majority of our group of Cuban medical personnel, especially the nurses, was black" (Caridad and Ramón Hernández, interview). Once, one of the doctors in their group, who was black and traveling in an embassy car, was detained, having been mistaken for a Sudanese subversive; they all had to stay inside for a few days until it was ironed out. In fact, the whites on the staff were occasionally, to their surprise, not believed to be Cuban at all (also see Fernández de Juan 1998).

The Western Sahara and Libya, in short, are viewed as Arabic rather than African. Thus, one could say that África's northern border is roughly the desert between the Arab world and black Africa. Just as in US vernacular, the literal outline of the continent is, of course, recognized, but just as in the United States as well, the *imagined* space stops short of the Sahara, precisely in relation to its association with blackness, primitiveness, and poverty. The Antilles present a different angle on Cuban geographies of blackness. Although Haiti is so close, so intertwined with Cuban history—without the Haitian Revolution, Cuba would look very, very different today, and one could find any number of parallels between the two revolutions as seminal events of their respective centuries, for their populations and the region at large—there is little interest in comparing the two republics. Despite Cubans' typically Caribbean popular interest in Caribbean history, and despite a substantive immigration of Haitian laborers in the twentieth century, in western Cuba's vernacular at least, Haiti has been largely silenced.[16] Or perhaps its erasure is indication that, in some way, the *longue durée* fear of Cuba becoming "another Haiti" described by historians (Helg 1995; Ferrer 1999) and the evolutionistic ideologies associating Haiti with a shameful primitiveness, have sustained long-running Cuban associations between Haiti and África. Other Caribbean nations, however, present a conundrum paralleling the development and underdevelopment of the region:

> Coming out of the Habana Libre I overheard a tall black man arguing with the guard at the door. He wasn't all that well-dressed and didn't speak Spanish well; the policeman was as suspicious, rude, and aggressive as he

would have been to a black Cuban national in a hotel zone, even after seeing the man's foreign passport. He was a student from Dominica, and the guard thought he was from the Dominican Republic. Hearing him repeatedly enunciate "Dominica" in [West Indian] English, I intervened, and as soon as we began to speak, in English, the policeman became much more civil and almost apologetic, and he was permitted into the hotel. (Ryer, field notes)

If this is all strictly an imagination about blackness, then what about the experience of African-Americans in contemporary Cuba? I would refer the reader to the work of Roland (2011), Alfonso-Wells (2004), Allen (2011), and Perry (2016) for firsthand accounts that demonstrate both nuanced interpretations and the common experience of color-based discrimination similar to that described here, particularly in tourist zones. In general, the experience of holders of passports from the industrialized nations, once their citizenship and prosperity is established, is very different from that of a poor student from Dominica. Even he, however, would be envied by many Cubans for his ability to come and go freely, to speak English, and to earn at least a modicum of exchangeable currency.

In short, as an imagined space in popular Cuban discourse, África is aligned with the Soviet era, with Cold War conflicts, with internationalist ideologies of that era, and with postcolonialism. The putative primitiveness of precolonial Africa partly offsets a general recognition that European colonialism and apartheid were problematic: "Well, the problem of black Africa is that Africa has an arbitrary division. The borders are arbitrary, made by the colonizing whites. Look at the map of Africa: the borders are practically in straight lines," says Juan González, drawing a grid with his hands. "And when you see this, you realize that we are talking about territories that are absurd." While the basic critique remains salient to occasional official roundtables and to Cuban academics, it is certainly no coincidence that the end of the Soviet era and disillusionment with state-sponsored *internacionalismo* coincided with the rapid decline of everyday speech about África in the early 1990s.

L'Internationale 2: Africans in Cuba

The complement of Cuban travel to Africa has been that of Africans to Cuba. Beginning with just a few university students in the 1960s and early

1970s, an estimated thirty thousand African students have taken up residence in Cuba, with the majority arriving in the late 1970s and 1980s to study alongside Cuban students on the appropriately named Isle of Youth.[17] Some fifty miles south of the main island of the republic, "La Isla" became a major site of international contact following the South African army's 1978 massacre of a Namibian refugee settlement in Angola. Surviving children were brought to the island to be educated and were soon joined by thousands more. Until the Special Period of the 1990s, students—most arriving at the age of twelve to twenty—from over thirty African and non-African states studied and worked alongside young Cubans on the Isle of Youth.[18] In its heyday, it held dozens of work-exchange secondary schools, supported by students' mostly agricultural labor, teaching trade or vocational skills to both Cuban and African students (Marshall 1987; Rojas 1987; Ferguson 1988; Jané 1988; M. Richmond 1991; Blum 2008, 2011). Instruction was in both Spanish and the dominant language of the students' respective national states. From here, after a number of years of study, the top students went on to study in Havana, while others returned to their home nations (Rich 1989, 407) or went into exile as political refugees (Berger 2001).[19] Keeping in mind that this is a study of Cuban ideologies and categories (including África), *not* an ethnography of African students in Cuba, the research methodology in this instance includes both interviews with students (from Angola, Mozambique, Ghana, Sudan, Tanzania, Congo, South Africa, Ethiopia, the Western Sahara, Zimbabwe, Mali, Nigeria, and Burkina Faso, as well as Dominica and other Latin American and European nations) and also, where possible, observations of African-Cuban daily life and interaction—of studying, shopping, eating, flirting, fighting, dancing, parallel economic activity, etc. While the combination of interview and observation was better grounded than the interview-only work with former *internacionalistas*, because of the practicalities of maintaining an affiliation (and visa), most of my interactions were confined to the vicinity of Havana, with shorter trips to eastern Cuba and the Isle of Youth.

Although relying too much on statistics may obscure rather than elucidate the cultural meanings of the categories I am examining (Trouillot 1995, 16–17), a bit more framing is in order here. Just like the international missions, the international education project has evolved since the Soviet era to focus on professional training, especially in medicine, and has shifted toward a tuition-charging system relying on the reputation of the Cuban educational system to attract paying foreign students—particularly from Latin America, Angola, the Western Sahara, and South Africa. For example, Havana's Latin American School of Medicine, inaugurated in 1999, has enrolled over ten thousand students from sixty-six Latin American *pueblos* and African countries. Of these, five hundred per year receive full scholarships; others pay up to five thousand US dollars per year in tuition. In the late 1990s, Cuba's long alliance with the African National Congress led to a renewed exchange with a South African state in need of medical personnel willing to work in poor black areas: roughly four hundred Cuban doctors were posted to South Africa and seventy new South African medical students were welcomed in Cuba (see Fidel Castro, *www.ain.cubaweb.cu/discursos/fide17.htm*). Among the estimated two to three thousand still studying throughout Cuba in the twenty-first century are the last few hundred students from the Western Sahara and three hundred Angolans (also see García Alonso 2006).[20]

* * *

> Miguel Alberto, you were saying that it is difficult to find some Cuban that did not have a family member, a friend, or at least a close acquaintance who had been in Angola. And I would tell you, too, that it is very difficult to find a Cuban family that does not know a foreign student in Cuba, because in some manner, whether at an intermediate or higher educational level, we [Cubans] have all had to have such relations with foreign students in the level at which we were studying." (Báez 2000)

I originally met Moses, a South African medical student who at the time had lived in Cuba for six years, at a cafeteria near the university. He was waiting in line ahead of me, asking about a table, and, despite his medical frock, seemed out of place.[21] We struck up a conversation and had lunch, and we soon became friends. As a South African, he was in an interesting position. Economically, his currency was worth quite a bit in Cuban terms, so unlike many students, he could afford the two-dollar lunch. Secondly, he had an explicit appreciation for the role that Cuba played in southern Africa. He had a Cuban girlfriend who wanted to go to South Africa with him, but he was ambivalent about the prospect. Moses preferred Spanish to English, after so long living and studying in Cuba; Xhosa was his native language. The following excerpt from my field notes records a quotidian incident that occurred the first time I visited his apartment.

Students in El Barrio

Moses lives in Flores [a residential area on the outskirts of Havana].
It is a huge apartment, the whole top floor, but, of course, no phone,
and an hour to the university by bike or a longer wait for the 264
or 230 bus. Anyway, I biked over in the afternoon to invite him
to a poker game next week, and a friend of his named Vusi was there,
with his Cuban wife (a *mulata*, not as dark-skinned as Vusi). Vusi has
been in Cuba for nine years, first on the Isle of Youth and has since
been in Santiago to study law, and his wife is from Santiago. He is
about to return home to South Africa for the first time and is very
excited. He will send for his wife later. I talked to Vusi at considerable
length. He does not yet have a job back home, but as there is considerable professional flight right now, he thinks it will work out pretty
well and is excited to see his brother and his parents, who are, he says,
now old. He's from the Transvaal.

It was around this point that a commotion started below;
someone knocked, and Moses went and opened the door, and we
could tell something was wrong, so Vusi's wife went down, then
quickly came and got him, then went out the back way. I went down
to see what was going on; a man was in the doorway speaking bel-
ligerently and trying to brush past Vusi to get upstairs. When I came
down too, he reluctantly backed out to the street. He had two friends
and a three-wheeled bicycle, all black Cubans, and there were three
of us foreign students. As far as I could make sense of the situation,
both from what he was saying and from Moses and Vusi afterward,
Moses knows the guy's sister and had loaned her ten dollars recently.
It was because of that that when the guy knocked and said "I'm
fulana's brother,"[22] Moses opened the door. It was clear that the guy
was on something strong; he was salivating excessively and not very
coherent, and he smelled of rum, at minimum. Anyway, he had so
many different stories, such as that Moses had given his sister a false
bill and that he needed my (visible) bicycle in exchange, etc.,[23] that it
was apparent he had been trying to force his way in for a strong-arm
robbery. He said, indeed, that he had expected Moses to be alone and

had never seen the other guy (Vusi), and I was clearly a puzzle. He left me relatively, but not entirely, unbothered.

Moses was flustered, and even made a simple grammatical mistake in Spanish (*una problema*) which he corrected at once, but it was unusual for him . . . perhaps also because we'd just been speaking in English. At one point during the dispute, or more accurately, harangue, he and Vusi switched into an African language, not Xhosa, but one that Moses later said was more common. At this, the Cuban stopped and caught his breath in confusion. He was shirtless and had a word tattooed on his chest but moved too much for me to read it. By this point, we were outside in front of Moses's house and various neighbors had started to pay attention. They were watching, ostensibly noncommittally but very publicly, and *fulano* was now more or less grandstanding. One white family gathered to watch from across the street, mostly women with one young man, but then a black mechanic neighbor drifted over toward Moses, casually but not coincidentally holding a large pipe wrench. The neighbor was accosted by the aggressive guy, who physically leaned into him; the mechanic tolerated almost full-body contact but avoided eye contact—seemingly in a nonconfrontational refusal to commit to his version of events. Another very big black man walked by and stopped and asked Moses if everything was okay. The two associates of the combatant had entirely backed off at this point and shortly loaded the guy on the bike and drove away. A couple of minutes later the police showed up, having been called by Vusi's wife, who told us that she had called, saying, "I'm from Santiago de Cuba, and there are some men who've been *tomando*,[24] who are bothering some foreign students," and she gave the approximate address. The police came surprisingly quickly, took a description, and went off to try to find the guys. Throughout the incident, Moses handled himself with restraint; perhaps nervous, he seemed stiffer and more formal than usual. Vusi was more fluid and somehow more Cuban in his form, though also with an obvious accent.

Later, Moses invited me to meet his friend Mary, a middle-aged white Cuban neighbor, who referred to him with evident affection as her "African son." In reference to the confrontation today, she described Moses as an innocent, and lectured him to be more careful opening the door, especially given the visibility of my bicycle. Vusi had said pretty much the same thing. We didn't stay long, as it was getting dark and I had a long bike ride home.

Interestingly, Moses's neighbors, of all colors, were immediately prepared to intervene in support of him and his guests (given the possible role of my bicycle). The question of nationality was irrelevant for the moment; Moses was a decent young man and a neighbor, and there was a palpable sense of concern for his well-being in this situation. At the same time, ignorant of the details, no one rushed to provoke the bellicose Cubans either. But clearly, if push came to shove, the local community had Moses's back, and those Cuban *tomados* would not be welcome to return. Moses's respectability and good relations with his neighbors led to a clear demonstration of the famous Cuban solidarity in action. While as we have seen, theft from the state may be tolerated, theft from individuals—irrespective of their nationality, color, or other details—is not okay. More than that, this story is an example of the fluid and spontaneous social warmth, engagement, and concern that permeates Cuban neighborhoods, enveloping resident foreigners as well as Cuban nationals.

On Being and Becoming African in Revolutionary Cuba

Internationalist education must be first situated in Cuba's attempt to revolutionize its own educational system. Very briefly: All schools were nationalized in 1961, and the successful, massive literacy campaign of the early 1960s deliberately brought well-educated young urbanites into contact with illiterate rural Cubans. As Fidel Castro put it "You are going to teach, but as you teach, you will also learn. [The campesinos] will teach you the 'why' of the Revolution better than any speech. They will show you what life has been like in the countryside" (quoted in Mesa-Lago 1971, 478). Rural internationalist schools in Cuba derive from converging histories. As Max Figueroa Araujo writes, after "a long effort . . . the basic secondary school in the countryside was organized and put into operation. The result was the combination of the ideas expounded by Martí with the theories of Marx on education, study, and work" (1976, 128). The "ideas expounded by Martí," of course, refers to the nationalist sentiments of the so-called father of the Cuban nation, José Martí.

Thus, the postrevolutionary internationalist school, like the revolution itself, is grounded in a history of Cuban nationalism as well as socialist ideology—although the influence of the US land-grant university system on Martí's thinking about education has been largely obscured.[25]

As noted, most Africans' initial experiences in Cuba were in such rural work-study schools on the Isle of Youth at the junior/high school level, surrounded by compatriots. By the time I began my fieldwork, much of that type of international education was being mothballed, and I did not, in any case, have easy access to the island due to the terms of my visa. However, most of the Africans I interviewed later, who were each engaged in extended studies at one of the universities on the main island, had stories about their time there. The majority indicated they had really enjoyed it as a "pre," that the hard work, such as cutting grass with a machete, was done by Cuban professionals, while the students picked or collected citrus and other crops. Just as among their Cuban contemporaries, there was disagreement between those who complained of being exploited and those who enjoyed the relative freedom of being away from home and in a new mix of peers. Of course, my interlocutors only included those who had successfully made the academic and personal adjustments necessary to continue on in the Cuban educational system.[26]

In some settings, such as the University of Oriente in Santiago de Cuba, all international students were housed together in a dormitory separated from Cuban students. In other cases, as at the University of Havana, some students lived in a dorm with Cuban *becados* (scholarship students), while others lived with Cuban families, and a few, like Moses, had their own apartments. Even in the more "separated" facilities, however, one did not feel a sense of quarantine; visiting the international dormitory in Santiago, I was struck not only by the range of African nationalities, as well as Haitian, Ecuadorian, and Nicaraguan students, but also by how their Cuban classmates, friends, and partners moved freely through the space. For example, my interviews with two Mozambican students to whom I had been referred were repeatedly interrupted by their children and the children's Cuban mothers, more as if we were in a multifamily apartment than a US-style dormitory.

At the time, the two economics students had one more year of study before they would return to Mozambique. The Cuban mother of the younger boy was not about to let him leave when his father returned to Mozambique,[27] and the distress of that future separation was a major focus of our conversation.

Just as the vast majority of *internacionalistas* were male, the majority of African students sent to Cuba were men, and most of them had established relationships—from casual liaisons to long-term marriages—with Cuban women. Indeed, in the context of explaining my interest in African students, one young white Cuban man commented with a mixture of bitterness and resignation that "of course the Africans love Cuba and want to stay here, because where else will they find so many white girls willing to sleep with them?" (field notes, 1997). This perception does not mesh easily with my observations. For example, in our interview, an Ethiopian veterinary student who had resided in Cuba for thirteen years without a visit home commented at some length and with satisfaction that his Cuban wife's color and features were similar to his own, very Ethiopian. Africans often had Cuban partners with complexions somewhat lighter than their own, but not to an extreme degree, and given the sheer number of Cubans of intermediate color, this was hardly a surprise. Of the African women I interviewed, a smaller proportion were involved with Cubans, but my sample size was small; in at least the case of one Tanzanian woman I knew well, she claimed that her studies and religious practices as a Muslim precluded dating Cuban men.

It is not easy to represent true love in an academic text, and certainly Nadine Fernandez (2010) is, deservedly, the authoritative resource on contemporary romance between Cubans, but I would like to make the claim that sincere romances are no less interesting or possible in Cuban-African relations than in intranational ones. As the guest speaker at an evening English-language class in Havana, I once asked students to speak about their favorite music. One self-described *mulata* surprised me by saying that her favorite music was African music. She clarified to say "Angolan music" and looked shyly at the man sitting beside her. She was a student at José Antonio Echeverría City University (CUJAE), Cuba's leading technical university.[28] I then spoke with her boyfriend, who was an Angolan student studying chemistry there as well. He was hoping to stay in Cuba after finishing his bachelor's degree and continue studying for a doctorate. In Cuban terms, he was a *prieto*, much blacker than she. It was clear that they were very much in love, and she was a big part of the reason he wanted to stay in Cuba.

Pan-Africanism, Made in Cuba

Revolutionary Cuba is the common reality into which all resident African students have been thrown: Cuban educational structures, socioeconomic conditions, language, racial and evolutionistic ideologies, prejudices, and so forth. Each foreign student, then, has had to develop a viable mode of being and transacting as part of his or her everyday. Very often, appreciative of the free educational opportunity afforded them and with a more dialogic or comparative perspective about Cuban society, they are more positive about Cuba, its state, and its prospects than are their Cuban classmates. While many may welcome the opportunity to land in Miami, just as would most young Cubans, this desire is tempered by a recurrent appreciation of the options available to them within the republic as well as by the limitations their *lack* of Cuban citizenship—with its special status under the US government's Cuban Adjustment Act (1966–2016)—placed on them in migrating to the United States. It is ironic, then, that these students typically strive to distinguish themselves from the Cuban norm in two distinct ways: through pan-African associations and through the adoption of the signs and styles of global capitalism. The remainder of this chapter and Chapter 4 will explore this paradox, which also carries echoes of the *yuma* material of the previous chapter. Let me look first at a visit with a student leader at CUJAE in 1997:

> Osmara introduced me to the African students' leader, a man named Roland from Burkina Faso, who arrived to the Isle of Youth in 1986 and is now in his fourth of five years at CUJAE. They then gave me a tour of the institute. The architecture is modern but not microbrigade shoddy. There are schools of tropical architecture, hydraulic engineering, mechanical engineering, chemistry, and so on. I was invited to a celebration and bonfire for May 21 and dance on the 22nd organized by the African Student Union to celebrate the day of the Organization of African States, May 25. Roland described pan-African sentiment as the rule of the day and proposed that African students could sometimes appreciate Cuba in a way that young Cubans couldn't. He showed me the African Student Union banner, with an outline of the continent in green, red, black, and yellow, a copy of their newsletter, and estimated that eighty percent of the Africans at CUJAE were active members. (Ryer, field notes)

This independent association is all the more striking for its rarity in a state where almost every social organization is government-sponsored. Of course, it is unlikely that an organization of temporary visa-holding scholarship students would pose much threat to the Cuban state, and that political reality underlined most of my tours and official interactions with African students and their Cuban guardians. I did, however, privately hear a similarly nuanced and unsolicited appreciation for Cuba's social system and, especially, its educational largesse relative to their home states, from many African students. The best evidence for the intensity and sincerity of such sentiments might be found online, in the statements of students who have since returned home or emigrated elsewhere.[29] There are many of these statements—for example: "How proudly the graduates return to their country to lose their names and be called 'the Fidelitos' or 'the crazy ones.' Most people call 'crazy' those who think and act differently. Their madness resides in serving their fellowman instead of swallowing him up that is so instilled in the consumer society" (Touré 2004; also see Alcántara 2013). In any case, it is in Cuba, with the tacit approval of the government, that a strongly pan-African esprit has been forged among resident Cuban-educated Africans. It is in Cuba that these students have come to know each other so well, studying, of course, but also helping each other navigate Cuban bureaucracies and ideologies together; it is in Cuba that recurrent celebrations such as the one mentioned above or the rallies for the Day of Africa and the liberation of the Five Heroes (e.g., Naranjo 2009) have become important to them (also see Kaba Akoriyea 2012, 227–28).[30] There are certainly personal or national variations in the reactions to Cuban society: the Ethiopians I interviewed dismissed Cuban racism more readily than did much darker-skinned Ghanaians, for instance. But overall, just as pan-Caribbean interactions are more common in New York or Toronto than on home islands, the shared Cuban experience seemed to enable a shared sense of identity as African and cosmopolitan, and this sense of identity accompanied their invariable resistance to the sort of evolutionistic reduction of Africa to a primitive, poor, black space that I explored earlier in this chapter.

Life in Cuba for resident African students was never easy. In addition to long-term separation from home and family, often with little or no communication for years at a time, the status of temporary residency presents certain challenges—including the need to maintain satisfactory academic progress and avoid any trouble with authorities as well as being ineligible to work—and has offered other, sometimes dubious, benefits. Resident status did allow access to both the *peso* and *divisa* (hard currency) economies; thus, for example, African students were always able to access the *diplotiendas* (diplomatic stores, now open to Cuban nationals as well) and enter tourist hotels and embassies at will. Residency papers generally authorized a limited food ration and student housing and even allowed one to buy and sell an automobile—an ownership privilege generally forbidden to Cuban nationals until very recently.

Thus, at the end of the Soviet era, many African students held liminal, if locally privileged, semitolerated, and shifting positions as middlemen and brokers: "another important source of black-market goods is foreign citizens residing in Cuba, who [had] access to the diplotiendas or technotiendas or receive[d] goods from abroad. . . . Russians, Bulgarians, and Africans residing in Cuba had a reputation for being particularly active in black-market activities" (Pérez-López 1995, 98). However, through at least the mid-1990s, such behavior was often socially scorned by the very Cubans who needed help accessing scarce goods and services: "[Africans] bought and sold, yes. They would go and buy large quantities of goods and then sell them. It was opportunism, it was unpleasant and made them unpopular." (Enrique Ibarra, interview). Even those with no personal reservations about plying the parallel market were often dismissive of African students in the racialized terms I will examine in the following chapter. I once asked a good friend, Julita, to introduce me to any African students she met in the course of running her small business. Making a sour face, she said that sometimes her boyfriend Juan knew some, that they were ugly and mostly interested in buying Adidas sneakers, but that she would introduce me to them when she could. Such negative attitudes and cutting aesthetic remarks—from a young white woman whose partner was a black Cuban, no less—were common during my fieldwork. However, they were certainly not universal. When I asked a zoologist, also *blanco*, if he knew any Africans, he described in detail having just been on a long bus ride with two beautiful, graceful African women and being utterly smitten by their attire, language, and regal bearing. Nevertheless, negative perceptions predominated, especially among lighter-skinned Cubans. A *mulato* academic in Havana to whom I mentioned an interest in visiting the Isle of Youth blurted out that I should not bother, that the African "monkeys" had absolutely destroyed the schools and hotels there, and there was nothing to see.

Convertirse en Yumas

What, then, would motivate foreigners to such low-status and risky activity as trading in the parallel market? For one thing, during the economic crisis of the Special Period, resident Africans, like Cuban citizens, simply could not survive on their official rations. But it was not just hunger that pushed them into the marketplace: I propose that the pull of possible prestige— associated with the sort of desirable *yuma* goods and symbols I have already described—contributed as well, particularly in the context of confronting negative evolutionist ideologies. Ironically, as the narrative below illustrates, these associations are with capitalism and with the United States rather than with Africa.

Passing for Yumas

After the *novella*, I walked to the bus stop on Línea, which was deserted until a group of six young people arrived. Although it was a warm night, the three young black men, perhaps in their early twenties, were wearing padded jackets with assorted arm patches, baggy jeans and nice sneakers—all imported, fashionable couture. The young women seemed somewhat younger and were wearing the sort of tight-fitting outfits typically worn to go out, but not provocative enough to mark them as *jineteras* (hustlers). With nothing else to do, I watched as one of the men tried to talk the women into accompanying them home. The women, ranging from *mulata* to *morena*, were conversing conspiratorially, evidently about their dates and their next move. While they whispered to each other, I was surprised to hear two of the guys speaking to each other in English, but could not place their accents or quite make sense of what they were saying.

"Where are you guys from?" I ask in Spanish, and offer them a cigarette. [I do not smoke, but have found the offer a great way to start conversations.]

"United States," one of the guys says indistinctly, after a short hesitation. I frequently encounter this sort of pause with Americans in Cuba illegally, so I wave it off.

"Hey, me too, I live in Chicago. Where are you from?" Instead of starting a conversation, this provokes consternation. The guy closest to me freezes, mumbles something, and looks embarrassed.

All three men seem suddenly uncomfortable and move to the other side of the bus stop. The girls have been watching, and the boldest now approaches me. "You're from La Yuma too?" she asks. I nod. I've just figured out what is happening, but it is too late. "So how come they don't want to talk with you?" I shrug noncommittally, but she too has figured it out.

"Come on, we're going," she says to the other women. "These assholes aren't Americans, they're a bunch of lying Africans [literally *africanos descarados*]. Let's go." One of the women glares at her date; the third looks pained, but walks away with her friends despite the guys' entreaties to stay and talk. My bus arrives just then, and no way am I going to miss it at this hour, so I climb aboard without ever finding out exactly where they were from—maybe Ghana?—but in any case, I can see that thanks to me their evening is ruined, and although I can't applaud the dissembling, I feel sorry for interfering all the way home.

The dissembling in question in this incident from my field notes in 1997 was, of course, the three Africans' strategy of presenting themselves as African-Americans to their Cuban dates. Fully understanding that citizens of the industrialized nations—with their linguistic abilities, attire, and cosmopolitanism—are preferred partners, they were seeking to transform their foreignness from that of the third world to the first world. Clearly, resident African students not only have worked as intermediaries for Cubans seeking Nike shoes and other prestige goods, but also often did and do value the same symbols and familiarity with American pop culture themselves (see Chapter 1 and Chapter 4). This stylistic association with African America, although not necessarily the extreme mimicry described above, is an effective and general strategy of self-presentation.

I went for dinner at the restored 1830, which is now clearly a *jinetera* haunt, unlike a few years ago when the food was bad and it was usually deserted.[31] Waiting in line at the bar's bathroom, I overheard two black Cuban women talking. The older, who was working as the bathroom monitor, was complaining, saying, "the worst are the blacks with the blacks." She clearly had been shortchanged a tip, but the other younger one interrupted with some interest: "Hey, isn't he African? He seems like it to me." At that moment, the man in question reappeared down the hallway, saying to the young woman as he approached, in English, "Hey, my nigger, what's up?" The younger woman immediately said to him, in Spanish, "Where are you from?" He got a bit prickly, answering, in Spanish, "I live here." "But where are you from?" she persists. "I live here. Do you want to see my ID?" "It's that my dad lives in Africa," she says. He softens noticeably, saying, "I'm Congolese—I'm from the Republic of Congo." She absolutely beams with delight, "Oh, my dad lives in the Congo, in Brazzaville!" I missed the rest, but the rapprochement was unmistakable, and it seemed like the beginning of a long conversation. (Ryer, field notes, June 2004)

While the young Cuban woman in this described encounter was probably *jineteando* [hustling], given the context, it was also evident that her interest in the Congo was sincere and familial. What was the Congolese man doing? Without further observation or interaction, I can only speculate, but from his speech and attire—a well-pressed white shirt and pants, imported dress shoes, a gold chain, and a good watch—his self-presentation was a careful image of hip-hop inflected prosperity. In the vernacular, if she was a *negra clara*, he would be a *prieto oscuro*; he was blacker, but neither his color nor nationality proved off-putting. To the contrary, his African *gestos* were what had caught her attention in the first place.

If these cases showcase the fluidity and frequent intimacy of Cuban-African interactions, they also illustrate the importance, to Africans as much as to Cubans, of the principle described by the aphorism of the black, car-owning doctor who becomes reracialized according to his personal and professional status (see the Introduction). In discussing the historical trajectory of Cuban categories in the next chapter, I will refer to Stolcke's ([1974] 1989) notion of classificatory embarrassment. She coined the term to refer to the trouble posed to a nineteenth-century Cuban labor order predicated on color, when Chinese laborers entered the system. Stolcke shows how the Chinese—often lighter-skinned than the Iberian-descended upper classes but with the labor status of black slaves—embarrassed the system, which was unable to assign them a legal color or determine whether they had the right to marry white Creoles. Borrowing her term, I propose that Africans in contemporary Cuba pose a potential classificatory embarrassment of their own. As we have seen, as foreigners, they automatically have an enviable mobility, both in the form of certain privileges afforded to them while residing in Cuba and in the form of their ability to leave the republic behind. But as blacks from a continent associated with poverty, primitivism, and stillborn socialist ideologies, they face additional hurdles in the search for respect. If they would face scorn as poor, black, badly dressed students, it is with success in the project of converting themselves into *yumas*—a project generally pursued by their Cuban peers as well—that these students embarrass the system, and the relative value of citizenship becomes most apparent.

* * *

Thus, the paradox of the coexisting yet seemingly contradictory strategies of "made-in-Cuba pan-Africanism" and "convertirse en yumas" [making oneself into a *yuma*] is, in the end, perfectly intelligible. These are twin responses to long-standing racist and evolutionistic ideologies that permeate Cuba as they do elsewhere. In the face of the projection of África as an imaginary space of poverty, blackness, socialism, and backwardness, and confronted with a widespread post-Soviet silencing of their continent, African students have responded with their own network of solidarity and celebration of pan-Africanism. At the same time, just like their Cuban peers, these students have found it important to distance themselves from the poverty and primitiveness associated with their home continent and color by skillfully navigating their local privileges as foreigners and deploying the signs and symbols of a prosperity commonly associated, in the same Cuban vernacular, with a very different, if equally imagined, space. To a certain degree, each of these elsewheres is familiar: La Yuma through the increased interaction with loved ones and diasporic remittance relationships and África through the fading memories and oral histories of *internacionalistas*. But in the end, Mbembe was right; África is not really a referent for the continent, but is rather one of the backdrops for a polemical argument about something else—in this case, for a presumptively hybrid, mixed, brown Cuban national identity.

CHAPTER 3

COLOR, *MESTIZAJE*, AND BELONGING IN CUBA

F undamentally, this chapter examines the interplay of race and place in
Cuba. To illustrate, I begin with an ethnographic moment that demonstrates some locally meaningful characteristics of racial and national identity
in Cuba that are often unanticipated and distinctive in relation to North
American expectations and are intelligibly Caribbean while being in many
ways distinctive, particularly in light of the atypically large percentage of the
population that self-identifies as "white." National discourse, I will argue, is
naturalized at all levels: both the Cuban state and ordinary Cuban people presume the reality of nations in general and of their nation in particular. Racial
discourse is more complex: while the state (as it is represented by its major
officials and as it propagates its positions through the various media which
it controls) has generally attempted to maintain an official silence about race
(except under certain conditions explored here), race is an incessant feature of
daily life and of popular speech and therefore merits more extensive consideration. I then raise the question of the nature of the category "Afro-Cuban,"
consider links between color classification and behavior, and briefly locate
these categories in Cuban history.

Whiteness and the National Concept in Popular Discourse

Although there is little debate in Cuba today about the category of "nation,"
what is left for debate are the precise *borders* of national identity (particularly *cubanidad* or *cubanía*, Cubanness) as well as the appropriate *value* of
different national identities (see my analysis of La Yuma in Chapter 1).
At the same time, however, the interwovenness of racial and national

discourses (and of their constitutive categories) should be evident from phrases like *"blanco cubano"* (*Cuban* white), *"El cubano es más que blanco, más que mulato, más que negro"* (The Cuban is more than white, more than mulatto, more than black), and *"El que no tiene de Congo, tiene de Carabalí"* (Literally: "He who is without blood from the Congo, has blood from Carabalí"—implying that all Cubans have some African ancestry). It has been argued that cubanidad is "for all intents and purposes, synonymous to *mestizaje* (race-mixture)" (Kutzinski 1993, 7). To begin, I want to ethnographically examine an important, too-easily overlooked frame for the commonsense color of "Cuba" today—the paradoxical relationship between "whiteness" and "Cubanness."

Intimate Ideologies: A Surgical Genealogy

At a party held in one of the more elegant neighborhoods of Havana, I was introduced to a Cuban surgeon. After a few minutes of prefatory conversation, and curious to discover a Yankee in his backyard, he asked me what I was doing in Cuba.

"I'm a graduate student in anthropology, enrolled in the history department at the University of Havana," I replied.

"That's very interesting. So what exactly do you do?"

"Well, I am interested in learning about Cuban culture, particularly in the influences of contemporary exchanges between Cuba and Africa . . ."

"Ah," he interrupted. "I was in Africa as chief of staff at a hospital in Luanda. And I can tell you, this is a very interesting topic, since Cuban culture is really African culture, we are profoundly African in our music, our mentality, our language. It would be very difficult to find a Cuban without African influences, without African blood . . ."

"Yes," I agreed, "I've often heard the saying '*El que no tiene de Congo, tiene de Carabalí.*'"[1]

The doctor looked both pleased and suddenly uncomfortable and leaned forward to clarify:

"Although not in my case," he adds. "*Mira.* My mother's family actually came from Portugal, and my father's grandparents were all from Spain." He then recited both his surnames, the surnames of his grandparents, and identified their region of origin in Spain as well.

"But you are Cuban, no?" I interjected. "I mean, you grew up here, the accent, the rhythm, you were saying that those are African, that Cuba is culturally African, and you are Cuban . . ."

"Well, *culturally*, yes, in that general sense, yes." But he very much wanted to move on to talk about other things.

I have had enough conversations like this one that eventually I could have finished it myself,[2] tracing the intricacies of an interlocutor's ancestry to Galicia, Andalucía, Sicily, France, Portugal, Ireland, or elsewhere. In other words, I propose that it exemplifies a social pattern, certainly not *unique* to Cuba but which to the best of my knowledge has not been described in the Cuban studies literature. It is a pattern wherein self-identified white Cubans exempt themselves from the presumed Africanity of Cuba through their own family genealogies.[3] An underlying assumption, of course, is the equation of "whiteness"—of racial purity—with European or North American ancestry. Many of those Cubans, then, who can identify some or all their ancestors as Spanish, Italian, Portuguese, English, Scandinavian, other European, or North American are prone to do so in certain contexts as sufficient proof of their own whiteness.[4] Such narratives are often mixed with a conspicuous silence about other (non-white) ancestors,[5] and construct an essential "elsewhere" of racial purity to contrast with the *mestizo* "here."

A second variant or type of tale that I also heard to the point of rote perhaps deserves separate treatment. It involves white Cubans' stories of "passing" as foreign in some venue such as a hotel or a dollar-only store from which Cuban nationals are or were ordinarily restricted (also see Roland 2011, 82). Several friends actively polished their Spanish, French, or Italian accents for such purposes. "Foreign" in these situations is distinct from the foreignness of African students. Here, "foreign" implies that these Cubans were mistaken for European or North American visitors and given free rein by hotel or shop security people. Thus, it asserts a social status with powerful—although changing—economic implications and fits neatly into Cuban cultural, aesthetic, and color hierarchies. There is much merit, in fact, to Kaifa Roland's (2004) assertion that *all* Cubans are effectively racialized as black vis-à-vis foreigners, who are in effect categorically white.

A third manner in which lighter-skinned Cubans often identified themselves and their families with foreignness was recounting and reiterating "white" physical traits within their family. I came to dread the presentation of pictures of someone's child with the enthusiastic: "*¡Mira! ¿Ves qué rubia es?*" (Look! See how blond she is?) Or, "See how straight his hair is? *¡Parece un americanito!*" (He looks like a little American boy!) "You couldn't tell the difference, could you?" (This last, obviously, was directed at me as a "native authority" on North American physiognomy). Other favored opportunities for racialized comparisons of this sort might be provided by an American movie, a fashion magazine, or in any spot where European or North American foreigners physically congregate.

While the openness with which African phenotypical features are devalued in everyday speech is often striking from a North American perspective, theorizations of nationality and color in Cuba must also carefully consider the equally open and difficult hypervaluation of "white" features illustrated here. Again, the point here is to re-mark the normally unmarked "white" category as a no less constructed part of the racial classification system than "black" or "mulatto" categories. In some sense, all these narrative variants involve a personal denial of one's Cubanness—cubanidad—in asserting one's whiteness. From this it might seem that Cubanness is a racialized national term associated with blackness. Certainly it is fair to say that many Cubans today are conscious of and proudly propose—at least abstractly—the Africanity of Cuban culture, an emphasis repeated and reflected in academic work from the time of Fernando Ortiz to the present.

However, as we have seen, in some regards the Cuban:African boundary challenges—or rather, adds a dimension to—such a conventional popular association. Although long-time residents in the republic, resident African and international students are generally black enough, as evident by their *gestos* (gestures or mannerisms), dress, accents, legal privileges, and passports, to lack cubanidad; they are *not* Cuban. Indeed, in today's Cuba, rather than being poor, backward, third world cousins, they are in some cases much more privileged than Cubans of whatever color or racial status and thus present a particular classificatory embarrassment (Stolcke [1974] 1989) to Cuban racial and national hierarchies. In any case, if it is correct to interpret white Cubans' stories of "passing" for foreign as evidence that "Cuban" has become racialized, that cubanidad has a color, nevertheless, the existence within the republic of black "foreigners" suggests that in the popular imagination, the ostensibly national category "Cuban" is integrated into a longer-run racialized classificatory discourse, not exactly as nationalizing blackness, but more precisely as "brown," an intermediate *mestizaje*—what the literary critic Vera Kutzinski called "perhaps the principal signifier of Cuba's national cultural identity" (1993, 7).

The problem, of course, is precisely that the concept of *mestizaje* implies a priori purities and "fixes" pure identities. As Stephan Palmié has noted in another Cuban context in relation to the presumption of initially separate "traditions" and "modernities," "the contrasts resulting from typological reconstructions . . . impart artificial closure to 'traditions' that should initially be approached as fuzzy sets of ideas and practices whose boundedness in social space needs to be established rather than presumed" (2002, 115). At the same time, this chapter reinforces the idea that there *are* racial and national boundaries in contemporary Cuba and that even as they are continually contested and re-established, those boundaries are not located or drawn by the precise logic that would be used elsewhere (in North America, for instance). Of course, semiotically speaking, partiality and arbitrariness are the conditions of possibility of classification. Consider Figure 3.1, the *Bohemia* cover showing twelve Cubans. Would a foreigner and Cuban group these people the same ways? How *do* we fairly characterize the racial system of contemporary Cuba? Again, an ethnographic example is a good starting point.

Black Canadian, Cuban White

Through another anthropologist, I was introduced to David, a principled, spare young man recently arrived in Cuba from Canada as part of his university studies. Although white by Cuban standards, Jamaica-descended David identifies himself as black. He was looking for a cheap apartment, and could I help? In fact, I did know someone, my neighbor Roberto, who made it his business to track down foreigners looking for private rooms.[6] I arranged for them to meet, and they went off to look at apartments.

That evening Roberto's wife came over, agitated, asking me to visit but warning me that Robertico was upset by that crazy foreigner.

I went to see, and indeed, he was pale and pacing, smoking and drinking some of his precious Johnny Walker. Roberto, by the way, although visibly with some African ancestry, unhesitantly identifies himself as white. He and David have similar complexions. Roberto's hair is somewhat straighter, but other Cubans consider his features somewhat more "African" than David's.

"Paul, that goddamn Canadian or Jamaican or whatever he is, what kind of people you turn up, these foreigners . . ." I shrug, as nonchalantly as possible, to distance myself from the as yet unexplained disaster.

"Listen, not only did he want a private apartment, with a telephone and everything, for nothing, he's too cheap to want to pay anything. He won't pay more than 125 Cuban pesos a month! So I take him to a couple of places, using up my own gasoline, and then he says he wants a place in Centro Habana."

Roberto takes a deep breath. "So I say to him, 'No, you don't want to live in Centro Habana, *hay muchos negros delincuentes* [there are many black delinquents] there.'[7] And he got mad and said I was being racist. Just for stating a fact. There are a lot of black delinquents in Centro Habana. He is the one who was being racist, identifying himself with trash like that. I didn't say that all blacks were delinquents, just that there are a lot of black delinquents in Centro Habana. How dare he call me a racist, when I have a black son, when I risked my life in Africa fighting for the rights of black people?!"

This everyday encounter is a good one to consider national and racial patterns partly because it is so rich in ironies and complexities. The immediate irony, in North American terms, is that Roberto himself would arguably be black; while in Cuban terms, David is white. Not black, not mulatto, but white. And my first surprise was my total ignorance until that moment—after months of close contact—of Roberto's second family, consisting of a black woman and their son.[8] In retrospect, it is clear that his previous failure to share this information (well-known to his white family as well as to colleagues and neighbors) had more to do with a concept of respect for them

Figure 3.1 *Bohemia* (International Edition)

and perhaps his perception that I was too narrow-minded to properly appreciate such conquests than it did with any ethically or racially based shame.

Although there were other moments when Roberto made unequivocally (either in Cuban or North American terms) racist remarks such as "Paul, *no andes con negros*" (Paul, don't hang around with blacks), his comments to David were so far within the bounds of acceptable Cuban racial discourse that he was sincerely shocked to be challenged on them (Perry 2004, 205). Again, our presumptive status as white foreigners within Cuba's racial, economic, and aesthetic spectrums is without question relevant, as outlined in the Introduction. But Roberto once told me that one of the things that most impressed him about Africa was the lack of racism there, and he meant it; in his own terms, Roberto is a firmly antiracist revolutionary.[9] This exchange with David surprised him; he probably assumed David would identify himself as white or perhaps as mulatto, but not as black, and *inconceivably* (given David's foreignness and soft-spoken, well-educated manner) with a bunch of hoodlums.[10]

I had the opportunity later to hear the same exchange from David's perspective, which followed a logic familiar to Anglo-Americans. He was equally, although more quietly, upset. David could not describe the association of "black" with "delinquent" as anything but racist, and a rather crude racism at that. He was aware that he could or would "pass" as white in Cuba but was all the more conscious of the devil's bargain made in passing and thereby accepting the divisions of the system. At minimum, the above ethnographic encounter demonstrates that there is certainly a clearly delineated racial consciousness in Cuba today but that the commonly presumed boundaries of racial groups in Cuba are *not* drawn in the same places or by the same ("one-drop") logic of North American convention. For the purpose of further unpacking and understanding Cuban complexities, I propose to begin with the following heuristic divisions between state and popular, and between national and racial discourses.[11] This division establishes four areas to be investigated, although not all are equally contested, and they are not evenly addressed here. I will start with the way that the Cuban state frames national and racial topics before looking at popular treatments of the same.

National Doxicities

In the Republic of Cuba, the reality and importance of nations, national classification, boundaries, and borders is unquestioned by the government, and in this acceptance the population at large largely concurs. Even within a Cuban academy preoccupied with its national identity, there is little critique of the concept of the nation either in the sense that it exists or in the sense that its impact is positive; what is contested is its proper form and boundaries (Carbonell 1961; Ibarra 1981; Sorín Zocolsky 1985; Fernández Retamar 1989; Ubieta Gómez 1993; Anonymous 1995; D. García 1995;

Torres-Cuevas 1995, 1996; Guanche Pérez 1996; Gay-Calbó 2000; Portuondo Zúñiga 2001). Despite the sheer volume of writing published by the state-controlled media, one could fairly argue that the underlying idea of national classification is doxic in contemporary Cuba.[12] Years ago, Benedict Anderson (1983) pointed out the irony of warfare between socialist nation-states ostensibly committed to universal revolution, and this tension is evident within the state-controlled media.

For example, consider the book *Humanism, Patriotism, and Internationalism in Cuban Students*, by Mónica Sorín Zocolsky, an Argentinian psychologist residing in Cuba. The work is fairly representative of official Cuban socialist treatments of nationalism: after separating out capitalist, individualistic notions of nationalism-as-power, dominance, and privilege, Sorín Zocolsky stresses the properly collective nature of socialist patriotism. "It is fundamental that . . . the child [learn to] perceive the strong links that exist between his daily conduct [regarding production, regarding study] and the destiny of his patria" (1985, 44).[13] Her operational definition of proper socialist patriotism includes:

- knowledge and love of the patria, its history, geography, and traditions
- sentiment of commitment regarding the destiny of the patria
- knowledge of, and intransigent hatred of, the enemy of the patria
- respect for the symbols of the patria
- identification with the heroes and martyrs of the patria and with its workers
- discipline
- love of work; an active position with regard to the job of constructing socialism (in study and work) (44)
- Her operational definition of appropriate internationalism includes:
- knowledge and respect of the various common and distinctive characteristics of humanity and its different nations
- a sense of love and identification with the proletarians [working people] of the world, independent of their nationality
- an active position of hatred toward the enemies of the [working] class, regardless of their nationality (47)

Beyond the propagandistic tone, note the slippage between the "Working Men of All Nations, Unite!!!" ideology of the *Communist Manifesto* and the enduring acceptance here of separate nationalities, *patrias*. As widely noted by scholars of virtually all other socialist state contexts, the *patria*, or nation, is presumed, accepted, and celebrated in Cuban socialist rhetoric—with the conventional nod to class sensitivity and international solidarity. However, the question of racial identity is treated differently: even into this century, nonnational racial groupings have been mostly suppressed in favor of, or in the name of, national unity.

State Discourse on Race 1: Silence at Home

Since the revolution, the Cuban state has charted an unusual course— carefully adhered to by mass media and public figures—around racial topics and issues. In terms of domestic policy, the state's strategy can be summed up as follows: for more than forty years, the state was ideologically dedicated to ending racial discrimination (along with all other social ills) via economic leveling rather than through any type of race-acknowledging or affirmative action programs; in recent years this has softened somewhat.[14] Implementation can be considered in three phases: the early consolidation of the revolution, the heyday of the revolution, and the post-Soviet era. Initially, in 1959, Fidel Castro shocked the nation with his call to end racial discrimination and with his revolutionary desegregating policies. With the establishment of state socialism, however, public discussion of racial questions became taboo, at least until the late 1990s. With the end of the Soviet era and the reorientation toward large-scale western tourism, racial topics have made a limited reappearance. However, of these three periods, the race silence of the second phase is unquestionably the dominant public ideology even today. In this section I examine the official or public domestic discourse and its silences. This will be followed by an examination of the Cuban state's treatment of race in an international perspective and ultimately in comparison to vigorous domestic popular discourse. Although I am concerned principally with racial classification here, it is worth keeping an eye on national terminology embedded within the described contexts.

A black Cuban exile, Carlos Moore (1988; 2008), was the first scholar to produce a detailed analysis of the official treatment of race in the initial moments of the revolution. As part of a work that evaluates nearly all events in Cuba since 1959 in terms of their utility to Fidel Castro's gaining and retaining power,[15] Moore argues that "the subject of race is opened . . . and quickly closed" by Castro himself in the first months of 1959. Then, "At no time between March 1959 and the Third Congress of the Cuban Communist

Party in February 1986, *twenty-seven years later*, did Castro or any of his top lieutenants attempt to open Cuba's racial Pandora's box again" (C. Moore 1988, 28; emphasis in original). Less polemical scholars have described the process as one in which racial segregation was abolished in the initial months of 1959, and then "racial discrimination moved out of the realm of public discourse" (N. Fernandez 1996, 125; 2010, 42, 79, 109; also see Pérez Sarduy and Stubbs 2000, 5; Fuente 2001). Before considering outside analyses of the rationale for the blanket of silence that descended over the topic in Cuba, let us look at the stated logic of this policy. The quotation, by José Felipe Carneado, is from the introduction to a book with the rather dubious (to North Americans) title of *The Black Problem in Cuba, and Its Definitive Solution* (Serviat 1986).

> Denouncing the anti-national objective of discrimination and racial prejudices, and after noting the ethnic and historical factors of the Cuban nation, *compañero* Fidel reaffirmed: "What the eternal enemies of Cuba and of this Revolution would have liked, is that we would have divided ourselves in a thousand pieces, and therefore, to be able to destroy us."[16]
>
> Thus he audaciously, firmly, valiantly set forth one of the great tasks of the national-liberating process: to eliminate racial discrimination in the workplace and in all the realms of Cuban life in order to definitively integrate the nation, to do away with one of the factors that kept it divided and weak in the face of its fierce enemies, from inside and out. (José Felipe Carneado, quoted in Serviat 1986, ix; my translation)

In tone, this is fairly typical Cuban Marxist revolutionary rhetoric. It also repeats a primary theme of Castro's speeches on the topic: any division between Cubans—racialized self-identification as well as racial segregation or discrimination—is described as a threat to the survival of the socialist nation, ringed by powerful enemies. As Nadine Fernandez argues, silence about race, then, became a key byproduct of state ideology and policy (2010, 71–72). If doxicity is difficult to document, pervasive silence is even harder to describe—especially amidst all the revolutionary noise, the billboards covered with revolutionary slogans, speeches filled with them, media saturated by exhortations: "Socialism or Death, *Patria* or Death, We Shall Overcome!"; "Until Victory Forever"; "100% Cuban." Too many to list, these are the aphorisms of José Martí, Che Guevara, Fidel Castro, the Party, and other revolutionaries worldwide. Most are appeals to revolution and nationalism: "The Cuban is more than white, more than mulatto, more than black" is one famous quote of Martí's, found on murals, in public lectures, endlessly repeated in articles and books (quoted in Ortiz 1941, 30). Nevertheless, although the state essentially rejected the logic of North American-style affirmative action, race-blind revolutionary policies, which effectively reduced "race" to "color," certainly did not have race-blind *effects*:

> There is clear consensus on the fact that the early redistributive measures of the Revolution (the two Agrarian Reform Laws, the Urban Reform Law, etc.) improved the status of blacks in particular, as they were overrepresented in the lowest [economic] sectors of the population. Revolutionary measures tending to equalize access to health and educational facilities (developing a massive public health system with preventative emphasis, elimination of private schools, expansion and improvement of the state school system, expansion of higher education and school facilities associated with the workplace) have had special impact upon blacks. However, the Cuban Revolutionary Government has been criticized because they have not enacted policies of "positive discrimination" or "affirmative action" to offset the residual differences in life chances, access to elite schools or top-level appointments which are the legacy of hundreds of years of oppression and discrimination.
>
> The Cuban Revolutionary Government's position has been clear on this issue. They see "positive discrimination" measures as contrary to the egalitarian goals of the Revolution insofar as they tend to make the color of the skin an issue. They have practiced some form of "positive discrimination" in terms of providing special facilities (i.e., rural communities) or programs (scholarships, etc.) to all members of a formerly disadvantaged group, but these examples have always involved all members of a formerly disadvantaged group, regardless of race. (Casal 1989, 480–81)

Filling out and updating this comparative perspective in careful, detailed, and judiciously organized work, the historian Alejandro de la Fuente has considered the statistical evidence available from Cuban census and other official documents and concludes that the revolution's race-blind strategy has indeed narrowed or eliminated the racial divide in terms of education, mortality, longevity, professional opportunity, and other statistical indices (1995,

131–68; Fuente 2001, part iv; also see Álvarez Ramírez 2013). Meanwhile, from an ethnographic perspective, N. Fernandez notes that the impact of the silence policy on individuals varied according to their generational position and was most beneficial for the generation that came of age during the 1960s (2010, chapter 2).

Like Fernandez and other researchers working in Cuba during the Special Period, I frequently heard commentaries at the street level about the ambiguities in the Cuban state's treatment of racial classification in terms of its mandatory identification papers for all citizens and resident foreigners (the *carné de identidad*).[17] Like prerevolutionary versions, newer *carné* now include spaces for skin color (minimally including *blanco/a*, *mulato/a*, and *negro/a*) as part of the physical description of the bearer, but the terms used are often haphazardly chosen (Alfonso-Wells 2004). Also striking to many visitors is the underrepresentation of black Cubans in the official media, and the persistence of publicly performed comedy routines including blackface and disparaging racial stereotypes (e.g., R. Moore 1997, 151; Frederik 2012). Looking both at conferences on race and at popular publications, N. Fernandez has argued in "The Changing Discourse on Race in Contemporary Cuba" that "the hegemonic silence on race has been fractured, and now race is slowly seeping into the domain of legitimate debate," (2001, 120) and more recent work from the republic bears this out (Fernández Robaina 2007; Anonymous 2012; Morales Domínguez, Prevost, and Nimtz 2013). However, what has come to be known as "the Zurbano affair," in which Cuban Roberto Zurbano was censured for an article he wrote for the *New York Times*—which had misleadingly retitled his work—illustrates the continuing complexities of public discourse on race in Cuba ("For Blacks in Cuba, the Revolution Hasn't Begun," March 23, 2013; see also West-Durán 2013; Luis 2014; Zurbano 2014). Thus, keeping in mind the enduring state control of mass media, I would note that the "new" debate on race reaches Cuban audiences unevenly. In light of this fact, my own approach is to still consider the state's silence on race as a domestic issue side by side with its public treatment of race in international perspective as a concrete reality.

State Discourse on Race 2: Regarding Race and Racism in the United States

Despite the domestic silence—frequently buttressed by authoritative reminders that "race" has no basis in biology—and the ascription of any racial consciousness remaining in Cuba to the lingering effects of capitalist colonization, race has in fact, under specific conditions, received periodic coverage in the Cuban mass media throughout the revolution. The following excerpts are from the main national daily newspaper, *Granma*, the "Official Organ of the Central Committee of the Communist Party of Cuba."[18] The excerpts are neither intended to be exhaustive, nor intended to make light of the reported events. Rather, they are illustrative of the manner in which the revolutionary Cuban state, while—as we've seen—stonewalling the topic domestically, has represented racism and race as ever-present realities of capitalism abroad. This particular set of articles and the accompanying editorial report on the extraordinary riots in Miami in May 1980 that followed the acquittal of four white policemen on trial for the beating death of a black man, Arthur McDuffie.[19]

The caption of the large front-page photograph reads: "The flames rise towards the sky in the northeast of Miami, announcing that the energies released in racial confrontations have not yet been suffocated. The black population was violently protesting the acquittal by a racist jury in Tampa of four white policemen who beat to death a black citizen for having run a red light." Two lines of bold-faced print read: "A stretch of more than three kilometers of one of the commercial streets of Miami destroyed by violent racial clashes. Losses of more than 100 million dollars reported. Damages considered more costly than those of the events of Watts and Detroit." The article's main text then reports on estimated damage compared to those recapitulated riots. In the "Reasons for the Protest" that follow, the paper adds ironically that, according to the Voice of America, the riots were not caused by the acquittal alone but were also in protest of the arrival of "thousands of Cubans" who might take away the jobs of the black population.

With additional photographs, the story continues on later pages, reporting on the casualty count, providing structural reasons for the riots, and adding some eyewitness accounts showing the inadequacy of medical care to a black man. The day's reporting on events in the United States concludes with a scathing editorial by Oscar Ferrer, "In the United States: One 'Justice' for Whites and Another for Blacks" (*Granma*, May 20, 1980; my translation). It is impossible not to share the outrage about these events and certainly not to deny the existence of racial problems of the United States. My intent here, however, is neither to defend the state of race relations in the United States nor even to suggest that the Cuban press is unduly biased. In fact, although its origin is occluded, much of the material reported by the paper was culled from the US media itself.[20] Obviously, this particular story is not an everyday event—but neither is it unprecedented: every such US race riot has been given full media attention in the Cuban press, and in such capitalist-world cases the reality of race is presumed. That the city in this case was Miami and that it occurred at the time of the Mariel boatlift, in Portes and Stepick's famous "year to remember," only adds to the drama. Certainly much of the coverage of race and race relations in the United States is more mundane. US, Latin American or European-made television documentaries, exposes, and news stories about race and racial discrimination are regularly rebroadcast and reprinted. "Two Black North Americans Were Unjustly Jailed for 17 Years," reads a representative headline in *Granma* on March 27, 1992. These stories are just the tip of the iceberg. North American perspectives on race relations are routinely evident in the numerous Hollywood movies shown weekly as mass entertainment on Cuban television. Books on the civil rights struggle such as *NOW: El movimiento negro en Estados Unidos* (Desnoes 1967) and *El pueblo negro de Estados Unidos: Raíces históricas de su lucha actual* (O'Reilly 1984) are published in Spanish and widely available; Angela Davis's autobiography has been translated and reprinted (Davis 1976).[21] Marc Perry notes the popularity of "Free Mumia!" shirts—one fashion statement certain to meet with official approval—within the Cuban hip-hop community (2004, 176, 208). Somewhat ironically, given the aforementioned underrepresentation of blacks in Cuba's own movie industry, the booklet "El racismo en el cine" analyzed the transmission of racist ideologies as a structural product of colonialism and capitalism (Calvo and Armengol 1978; also see Fuente 2001, 325). Novels, as well, figure in the broader cultural war vs. racism, imperialism, and colonialism (e.g., A. Clarke 1980). Again, the important point is the paradoxical contrast of the Cuban state media's commonsense treatment of race and racial struggles abroad—intended for domestic consumption—with the nearly complete silence of the state media on race or racism at home.[22]

What, then, should we make of the presented dichotomy within official discourse about race? What is the relevance of the national border to race or to the deployment of racial categories? Given that the reality of nation-states is not challenged and that the heavily deployed concept of "citizen" is not interrogated, a lot ultimately hinges on a distinction (important to the Cuban authorities) between socialist and capitalist states. Within that logic, what else, besides this political division, makes race a nonissue at home and yet a legitimate variable abroad? Especially since the collapse of the Soviet Bloc and the development of Western tourism to the island, the socialist:capitalist distinction is much less emphatic. Perhaps the lessening of this distinction is also related to the limited opening of state discourse to the topic of race (N. Fernandez 2001). But even if the opening is a partial one, the inter-weaving of racial and national discourse is increasingly evident.

Popular Racial Terms and Categories

Thus far in this chapter, I have considered some ethnographic material relating to racial consciousness as well as distinguished between state and popular discourse regarding race. I have not yet, however, provided a detailed account of everyday racial terms, categories, or their contemporary usage in practice.[23] Before attempting to assess the proper theoretical place or *meaning* of basic categories (not to mention practices), the first task of this section is to present an approximate lexicon of racial terms. As will become clear, in vernacular usage, Cuban racial descriptors are numerous, subtle, fluid, and overlapping—yet at the same time, they are consistent enough for a breath-takingly fine-toothed social evaluation. To demonstrate the basic terrain, I will first reproduce terms I have personally encountered in popular use in Havana between 1994 and 2017.[24]

Classification of Persons

blanco – overall term for whites, with skin color from very fair through wheat-colored.

blanco lechoso – person with milky white skin. According to sev-eral informants, there are hardly any Cubans in this category, because it is only possible for *blancos* with no suntan.

albino/a – literally "albino." Indicates a person with white-blonde hair, white-white skin, or even a very fair-skinned person with red hair and freckles.

blanco blanco – very blonde person, or a "truly" white person.

rubio/a – literally "blonde," but often by extension indicates, again, a "truly" white person.

castaño – literally "chestnut-colored." Indicates a person with fair skin and dark brown hair.

trigueño/a – literally "wheat-colored." Indicates a person with olive-white skin and dark but straight ("good") hair.

blanco cubano – "Cuban white," as opposed to "really" white. Implies an underlying racial mixture or impurity; cf. the Jamaican category "Jamaica white."

chino – a person of Asian appearance. Usually *trigueños*, but the crucial marker is the appearance of the eyes. Generally, these are the descendants of the roughly 100,000 Chinese immigrants brought to Cuba as indentured laborers in the nineteenth century; today, chinos are uncommon in Cuba, and their actual skin color varies as the result of intermarriage. Abstractly, however, *chino* continues to denote an Asian appearance and status within overall *raza blanca* (the white race).

jabao/a – light, but barely not white skin, and somewhat wavy or curly hair.[25]

capirro/a – a person with "bad" but blonde hair; "of doubtful parentage." Somewhat obscure term with contestable or variable associations. "Neither white nor black."

azafrán – with freckles, reddish-brown skin, and curly red hair.

sidio/a – originally a term used to describe Ethiopians or other East Africans as black but handsome, with "facciones finas" (fine features) and "decent" hair.

mulato/a – a person with medium dark skin, with either "bad" hair (in the case of a *mulato oscuro*) or "good hair" (in the case of a *mulato claro*).

yucateco/a – literally "from the Yucatan." Used for Cubans of indigenous/mixed or partly Mayan appearance.

mestizo/a – person with caramel colored skin with "good" hair. Much less common than *mulato/a*.

indio – dark skin, dark but straight hair.

moreno/a – literally "dark brown." Intermediate category between *indio* and *moro*.

moro/a – literally "Moor." Persons of dark, dark skin, and straight or curly dark hair.

prieto/a – literally "dark." May be used in place of *negro*, or to modify other categories.

negro/a – literally "black." Dark, dark skin, "bad" hair.

niche – akin to *negro*, but generally more depreciative.

azul or *negro azul* – literally "blue." Close to *negro*, *azul* denotes persons so black that their skin has a bluish quality.

fosforescente – similar to *azul*. Literally "phosphorescent."

Classification of Eyes

ojos azules/verdes/ojos claros – blue/green/light eyes.

ojos negros/oscuros – black/dark eyes.

Classification of Hair

lacio/a – straight.

rizado – curly.

pelo bueno – literally "good hair."

pelo malo – literally "bad hair."

tener / no tener pelo - literally "to have / not to have hair"; i.e., to have straight hair / to have woolly hair—which is also sometimes referred to derogatorily as having *pasas* (raisins). Also in such a sarcastic, racist mode, one might hear the phrase *la pasión* (literally "the passion") to indicate unkempt or wild *pasas*.

spendrum or *afro* – an "Afro."

Classification of Noses

tener / no tener nariz – "to have / not to have a nose." That is, to have a prominent, European-shaped nose, or not (presumably having an African-shaped nose instead).

ñato – literally "flat-nosed"; used to denote African noses. I once heard a woman referred to disparagingly as *"una ñata,"* intended to imply not only a racial status, but an inferior intellect as well.

Many ethnographers working in Cuba have compiled their own lists of Cuban racial terminology; the most detailed lexicon published to date is that of Nadine Fernandez (2010, 20–24), representing terms she has heard in Havana since 1992.[26] It must be reemphasized, however, that *no* set of terms will adequately represent actual popular discourse on race in Cuba, with its ever-proliferating signifying slang, obfuscation, allusion, and metaphor. At the same time, basic terms such as *blanco*, *mulato*, and *negro* are more common than *fosforescente*, *sidio*, and *capirro*; indeed, I will argue that the former are not only terms but are also three fundamental Cuban cultural categories. Given that in actual usage, listed attributes (skin color *plus* hair texture *plus* features) are likely to be variously combined and given the subtle losses inherent in translation,[27] it is likely that not even my list and other ethnographers' lists together come close to the ethnographic realities; as we have understood at least since Saussure, lexigraphic closure is impossible. The point of such compilation and comparison, thus, is *not* to determine the "real" terms of the Cuban vernacular, but rather to track the degree of slippage and incompleteness as well as overlaps that point to recurring categorical divisions recognized throughout the republic.

Beyond their necessary incompleteness, what hypotheses or conclusions do such lists support? One is immediately tempted to propose a seemingly uncontroversial and limited empirical claim: the sheer variety of Cuban racial or color terminology is unmatched in everyday North American discourse.[28] But the risks of such an approach are perhaps best exemplified by a quick review of a foundational fable—the supposed linguistic wealth of Boas's Eskimos. Like many undergraduate anthropology majors, I was taught that while conducting fieldwork in Greenland in the 1880s, Franz Boas discovered that Eskimos had no single word, "snow," but rather, some eighty terms for snow (and ice) of different types, grades, and uses—the implication being that the richness and depth of human language and linguistic precision varies wildly and directly reflects the given environmental conditions or central preoccupations of a culture. Even leaving aside the problematic grouping "Eskimo" (Inuit? Aleut? Yupik?), it turns out to be a myth nearly without a founder. Boas barely mentions the topic in his introduction to *The Handbook of American Indian Languages* (1963),[29] and Whorf (1956) reiterated the idea. From there, the story really snowballed, with the supposed number of terms rising at each textbook retelling, while Boas's own critical awareness of issues like the problematic definition of "a word" as a fundamental unit of meaning are overlooked (Martin 1986; Pullum 1991). This does not imply that there is no logic to Cuban racial categories; clearly the lesson is that we not ascribe meaning directly from an ethnographic vocabulary list. But given the fluidity of racial terms and their various permutations and overlaps, the patterns are not easy to sort out. Is there an underlying racial structure? What would it be: a two-tier (white:black) or a three-tier (white:mulatto:black) system? Or, as the Cuban state often argues, just one-tier, "Cuban"? Or should classification be judged strictly by context? This debate will be addressed below; for the moment, it is worth highlighting that in our just-cited lexicons, both Nadine Fernandez and I concluded that *blanco*, *mulato*, and *negro* are basic categories of Cuban popular discourse (Roland 2011, 23). Meanwhile, there is more remaining to illustrate the dynamics of popular racial categories in action.

On "Afro-Cuban"

Among the many common Cuban racial terms listed above, there is one notable absence. Although the category "Afro-Cuban" or "Afrocuban" is almost ubiquitous in English-language scholarly work on Cuba, no such term is used in a like manner in normal Cuban speech.[30] *Afrocubano* exists as a recognizable word and even has a certain scholarly space, corresponding to the *afrocubanismo* movement of the 1920s and 1930s and to studies and publications concerned with folkloric culture. However, I believe that, as a term to describe Cuban *people*, the imported expression presupposes that which must first be ethnographically demonstrated. Not only is it *not* in common use among the population, but it is often resisted by those it purports to describe. The following ethnographic vignette illustrates this dynamic.

The Entre Cubanos Conference

Shortly after I arrived in Cuba, I attended a conference held in honor of Cuban anthropologist and national hero Fernando Ortiz. Titled "Between Cubans," after his book,[31] the conference revisited his adaptation of Malinowski's "acculturation" to "transculturation" (Ortiz 1995) and considered African influences in Cuban culture, especially in syncretic *santería* religious practices. I soon discovered that I was the only non-Cuban present, the only person paying an entrance fee in dollars (for me, CUC$20.00; for Cubans, CUP$20.00) and the only person wearing a tie. I was warmly welcomed, however, as a student of a well-known Nigerian religious expert, Andrew Apter. The final paper of the session, delivered by

Jesús Guanche Pérez, a well-known, European-looking man, was titled "Santería cubana e identidad cultural" (Cuban *santería* and cultural identity). In attempting to describe regional variations of santería, however, Guanche Pérez was suddenly confronted by a number of the darker-complexioned listeners, who would not allow him to finish. They were upset, it turned out, because he had used the term "Afrocuban" to refer to a group of persons.

"There are no 'Afrocubans,'" said one young man heatedly. "There are only Cubans; we are all Cubans alike. As the saying goes, '*El que no tiene de Congo, tiene de Carabalí.*'"

"No, well, of course," said Guanche Pérez. "I was simply trying to describe a historically based population; no lack of respect was intended. Just as North Americans are all Americans, but have "African-Americans," or "Asian-Americans," I did not mean to suggest that we are not all Cubans alike."

This pleased no one; an older black woman in the audience stood and said: "How can you compare Cuba to North America? The struggles of people of color there are different; we must respect their struggles in that racist system, but here, we are all Cubans, lighter or darker, it makes no difference. We are all Cubans, period."

In this case, the darker-complexioned Cubans in attendance not only presented a case that might be endorsed by biologists or geneticists but one that is also virtually indistinguishable from the argument of the Cuban government, which, as we have seen, has generally not permitted public discussion of "race" as a valid social variable since the beginnings of the socialist system and which seems to have taken as its mantra on intra-island racial division the already-cited Martían phrase "The Cuban is more than white, more than mulatto, more than black."[32] Although in certain other contexts *of course* there were and are expressions of identity made by black Cubans, it is frequently the case that arguments for separate racial groupings come from lighter-skinned Cubans and are resisted by so-labelled "Afrocubans." It may be that black Cubans' resistance to the term in this case had much to do with a relation to a specific nationalist project—perhaps particularly within a nationalized system of allocation by citizenship—that is totally elided by the too-facile translation. Underlying this inversion of North American identity discourse, however, are many similar issues and frustrations, which the Cuban government—supported by many black Cubans—has addressed explicitly in Marxist terms as a function of eliminating economic prejudice and inequality. Interestingly, in this situation, the one identity that was hegemonic or beyond question to both whites and blacks as well as to José Martí was "Cuban." While Marc Perry's work points to a similar exchange as a generational contrast to the younger generation of *raperos* (rappers) certainly more interested in an "emerging black public sphere" (2004, 276; 2009), the sort of dynamics outlined here help fill in a distinctive context within which even a new generation does or does not challenge certain common-sense understandings.

In any case, this example is evidence for caution in presuming that the term "Afro-Cuban" adequately groups Cubans. Not surprisingly, those North American ethnographers who have expressed reservations about this concept have lived in Cuba for particularly long periods of time. Nadine Fernandez (2010) explains that she uses the term only reluctantly and in particular contexts; Marc Perry (2004, 17–18) and Rebecca Bodenheimer (2015, 15) are similarly cautious. Ivor Miller is even more adamant, arguing in part that

> by avoiding the term "Afro-Cuban," I am not denying contemporary uninstitutional racism in Cuba, but searching for better ways to articulate the centrality of African heritage in Cuba. . . . Words like "Afro-Cuban" are now obsolete signifiers used to negate African influence in the general social fabric. Many of the people I quote throughout this text use the term "Afro-Cuban," and I translate their voices as literally as I am able. In my own writing I search for terms that more accurately reflect Cuban reality. (1995, xx)

My judgment on the term "Afro-Cuban" is similar. Too often, I believe, it does more to confuse than to clarify Cuban classifications, and I avoid it to the extent possible. Instead, I prefer to draw on the (untranslated but now defined) "native" Cuban racial terms cited above, as appropriate to a specific context. I will revisit this idea below in relation to the debate over the most appropriate representation of the tiers of Cuban racial structure through history (Helg 1997). Meanwhile, several other ethnographic moments further exemplify certain popular racial dynamics in fin-de-siècle Cuba.

"Black by Definition," or, The Hat Thief

Walking down a hilly street in Centro Habana one afternoon, I was suddenly smacked on the back of the head as a teenager on bicycle grabbed my baseball hat. While making his escape with all the speed provided by his carefully chosen hill, the punk looked at me over his shoulder for a long moment, and I got a good look at him. Mad at myself (I knew better than to wear my good Red Sox hat in that area) and at Cuba and with ears still ringing, I continued on my way to the office of an academic center I visited often, although *not* my own department at the university, where I was better known. Greeting the secretary there, I recounted the mishap:

"Lourdes, you know what just happened? Some kid on a bicycle stole my baseball hat right off my head."

"*¡Ay, Dios Mío!* Where were you?"

"In Centro Habana. I knew better, it was my own fault."

"Those black kids, they're no good," she replied sympathetically.

For a moment, I was speechless. Despite her dyed-blonde hair, in North America Lourdes would be black. In Cuba, she was *una mulata*, but actually several terms darker than the hat thief, who was light-skinned and had straight hair (and therefore "white").

"Well," I manage, "no, I don't think he was black. He had my complexion, and straight hair."

"No, no. You were in Centro Habana, and he stole your hat. He was black," she said with finality.

I tried twice more, with increasing confidence and detail, to indicate that the hat thief was whiter than she or I, but her position would not change: a thief in Centro Habana is black by definition.

Lourdes here defines race neither by descent nor (as is most common in Cuba) by appearance, but rather by location and occupation.[33] Implicit here is her attempt to extend herself to me as sympathetic to my disaster. While my high status as a foreigner was not irrelevant to her sympathy, she fully expected me to respond as a Cuban. Thus, she did not interpret my reluctance to classify the thief as "black" as other than the terminological confusion of a foreigner, and, subsequently, my repeated attempts to describe the hat thief as *blanco* failed. I very much doubt that Lourdes would have questioned *my* racial category as "white," however, even should I have proven to be a thief. Perhaps to an extent, foreign status would have exempted me from the painstaking racial evaluation to which Cubans subject themselves and each other. Also, it would be worthwhile to consider the constitution of "crime" here (see treatment of the "parallel economy" in Chapter 1). This secretary would not automatically treat theft from the state as criminal, whereas the theft of my baseball hat was personal property, and therefore taking it was both immoral and criminal. Moreover—and this is crucial—although Lourdes describes herself (and would be described by others) as *una mulata*, like my neighbor Roberto, the *blanco cubano*, she does not here identify with a presumptive community of "Afro-Cubans." If anything, the implicit identification is with an imagined category of respectable, normal, moral persons, in contrast with a constructed association of *negros delincuentes* (Fuente 2001, 265; also see Queeley 2010b).

More on *Mestizaje*

If conclusively establishing the existence of the category *mulato* in the contemporary vernacular is difficult, finding a consensus about it on the street is impossible. One white schoolteacher proposed to me that *blancos*, *mulatos*, and *negros* were each endogamous groups. Others, like a white homemaker I interviewed, insisted that the only relevant distinction was between *la raza blanca* and *la raza negra*: "black or mulatto, it makes no difference, it's the same shit." As we have seen, however, many insist that "Cuban" is the only valid distinction. And many of intermediate color often describe themselves as of the middle, *mulato* or *mestizo*, "neither white nor black."[34] Such seeming contradictions cannot be resolved from a strictly synchronic perspective and thus demand further historicized consideration (see below). Meanwhile, I propose that "*mulato*" cannot be presumptively dismissed as a category in its own right simply because of the ambiguous manner in which it is used. In other words, perspectival challenges must not be mistaken for categorical confusions or for an absence of cultural coherence. A few ethnographic examples of a separate identity claimed, at certain moments, by contemporary self-identified *mulatos* illustrate this point.

"I am not attracted to black people," a young *jabao* once told me. Seeing my look of shock, he added: "Look at me! I have African ancestors, and it's not that I am a racist. But I simply am not attracted to them, physically." Here is another account, from a conversation with a *mulata* friend:

> After we left the others at the theater, Niurka was tremendously critical of Hermes in racialized terms. "Although I have the blood of Africa in my veins, a black like that I can't stand." What she was critical of, she added, was that he talked grandiloquently but without substance—*porquerías*, garbage. Neither of the *blancos cubanos* present commented one way or another. What about the other black man there, José, I protested: He was not talking trash. Didn't that complicate her stereotype? "Look at this nose! Even with the *ñata* that I have," she replied, "I am very racist." (Ryer, field notes)

While, as we have seen, the state media is generally silent on racial matters, a heartrending expression of *mulato* vs. *negro* discrimination is documented in the film *Si me comprendieras*, directed by a Cuban expatriate with independent Spanish financing (Díaz 1998). In a powerful, powerful interview with a Cuban *mulata*, Alina Jerez, and her family (including her black daughter and white son), her *mulato oscuro* father's anti-black racism is openly captured on film. While he listens, Alina talks about how angry her father was when she had a black boyfriend and daughter, and then she describes his own grandmother from Calabar as the source of the blackness in the family (Díaz 1998).

Examples like these proliferate in a range of contexts. One older woman, who described herself as a *mulata clara*, launched a (factually incorrect) tirade, which I had heard from many white Cubans, about how much better "*los negros*" were doing relative to the white population during the Special Period. "They are on top of all the things that pay well [in hard currency]: sports, music, *jineterismo*. Fidel Castro has liberated them," she concluded with some bitterness (Ryer, field notes).[35] Perhaps nowhere does the common sense of racial identity become more evident than in the incessant circulation of jokes, aesthetic commentaries, and adages throughout Cuban neighborhoods and households. Many of these commentaries correspond to patterns of race that I have already touched on in this chapter. I have already recounted one aphorism that I have heard many times in different forms, the "joke" about a young white woman marrying a black doctor with a car; Nadine Fernandez (1996, 157) and Kaifa Roland (2011, 35–36) each also describe this aphorism, which is, of course, virtually the same one Professor Trouillot knew from Haiti. Such accounts of the apparent interconvertibility of economic status and racial categorization have been widely reported throughout the Caribbean (see I. Miller 1995, 186; Raymond Smith 1988, especially chapters 6 and 7). Peter Wade (1993, 338–39) reported a similar phenomenon from Colombia but cautioned that the represented social mobility is itself structured and greatest for those toward the middle of the racial spectrum. Is this simply a postcolonial universal? After all, in Marx's view the underlying principles *are* universal:

> What I am and am capable of is by no means determined by my individuality. I am ugly, but I can buy for myself the most beautiful of women. Therefore I am not ugly, for the effect of ugliness—its deterrent power—is nullified by money. I, in my character as an individual, am lame, but money furnishes me with twenty-four feet. Therefore I am not lame. I am bad, dishonest, unscrupulous, stupid; but money is honored, and therefore so is its possessor. (Marx 1987, 138)

While certainly Marx's critique is relevant to analyzing these Cuban aphorisms on the whitening power of money, there are also distinctively Caribbean patterns at play here. Not only are economic and social status very complexly and ambiguously correlated today in Cuba, where medical doctors currently make less money per month than a taxi driver makes in a day yet maintain relatively high status. In general, however, the social mobility of money is disproportionately weighted toward the middle of the color spectrum—where many of the cited overlapping racial terms tend to concentrate (Stolcke [1974] 1989; N. Fernandez 2010, 22). Thus, in considering Cuban global self-positioning, mixture matters. Toward a deeper understanding of the nature of its fundamental divisions, there is no substitute for studying the changes in these categories over time.

The Tannenbaum Tradition and Cuban Categorical Historiography

Whether slavery in Latin America was, and racism is, significantly distinct from that of the Anglophone Americas has long been debated in the wake of

Frank Tannenbaum's proposition that Iberian slave colonies, including Cuba, were fundamentally less brutal than northern European ones. Inspired partly by Gilberto Freyre's ([1933] 1971) work on Brazilian slavery, Tannenbaum ([1940] 1992) proposed that differing legal structures derived from divergent European religious systems—Protestant and Catholic—accounted for the differing forms of plantation slavery in the New World. Dismissing the complications introduced by the "intermediate" French, Tannenbaum argued that religious ideology and law, from the pope downward, were crucial (65). Not only could slaves buy their own freedom, but, unlike the situation in the northerners' colonies, in the Catholic Iberian territories: "More important in the long run than the condemnation of the slave trade proved the church's insistence that slave and master were equal in the sight of God. . . . The slave had a right to become a Christian, to be baptized, and to be considered a member of the Christian community" (63). To Tannenbaum, such differences explained even the differing timetable and means of abolition of slavery. Since his book was published in 1940 and continuing through contemporary historiographic work, scholar after scholar (see Elkins 1959; H. Klein 1989; Mintz and Price 1992) has either explicitly reworked the Tannenbaum thesis or dismissed the role of ideological forces (Catholic:Protestant or Anglo:Iberian) for more material forces. Among the former, Hendrik Hoetink (1967) wrote a supportive elaboration entitled *The Two Variants in Caribbean Race Relations*, and in 1967, Herbert Klein (1989) compared the colonial systems of Virginia and Cuba. In 1970, however, Franklin Knight's *Slave Society in Cuba during the Nineteenth Century* challenged the two variant hypothesis, suggesting instead that

> what is abundantly clear from any study of Cuban slavery during the nineteenth century is not merely that it was significantly different from slavery in the United States. . . . Instead, what emerges, somewhat surprisingly, is that slavery on the sugar plantations of Cuba and slavery on the sugar plantations of the other West Indian islands bore a strong resemblance and were comparable. Plantation slavery—and particularly of the sugar plantation type—was a distinctive system. (1970, 83)

In short, a generation of Marxist scholars such as Franklin Knight and Verena Stolcke argued against the Tannenbaum school that comparison must be made in relation not to chronological time, but to the type of economic organization. In other words, the plantation mode of production—the Plantation, in Benítez-Rojo's (1992) Deleuzian formulation—arrived in Barbados centuries before arriving in Cuba but always brought with it characteristic types of organization and repression, irrespective of the legal or religious ideologies of the specific islands or of the century in which it arrived.

From its discovery, there was slavery in the colony: Columbus's scribe, the priest Bartolomé de las Casas, famously petitioned the Spanish crown to alleviate the conditions of the native inhabitants, but his remedy infamously involved importing greater numbers of African laborers. A full-blown plantation system like that of the English or French Caribbean colonies did not immediately develop, however. In the first centuries of colonization, Cuban slavery evolved out of medieval legal and Christian practice, resting in part on the distinction between "believer" and "infidel" (see H. Klein 1989; Stolcke [1974] 1989) and in conjunction with imperial policy that saw Cuba more as a military outpost or way station than as a sugar island (Moreno Fraginals 1995, 3). Even early in the slave era, intraslave distinctions were made between African-born *bozales* and Spanish-speaking *ladinos* or Cuban-born *criollos*, who were believed to be more civilized and tractable (Paquette 1988, 35–38). As exhaustively documented by Anderson (1983) and many others, the distinction of birth between Spanish-born *peninsulares* and white American-born *criollos* was a fundamental division in colonial Cuba as throughout the Spanish Empire. In the late eighteenth century, several events contributed to a massive change in Cuba's status and mode of production. In 1762, the island was briefly captured and occupied by the British, who restructured much of the sugar-producing economy before returning the colony to Spain ten months later. And, in 1791, the Haitian Revolution shattered the plantation system of nearby Saint Domingue, the dominant sugar colony of the time, dramatically raising the price of sugar and sending waves of experienced plantation owners fleeing to Cuba, where conditions were ideal for sugarcane.[36] Thus, at beginning of the nineteenth century, Cuba was poised for a transformation into the world's sugar bowl.

With the slave-dependent sugar boom and its massive importation of enslaved African labor came *increased* racially based repression throughout the nineteenth and into the twentieth centuries, including the infamous La Escalera repression of 1843–44, in which free blacks and mulattos—of the *pardo* and *moreno* elites—were suspected of conspiring to lead a rebellion against slavery, and many were tortured and executed (Paquette 1988). For my review of Cuban classificatory change, the most useful study of this era is that of Verena Stolcke ([1974] 1989). Based largely on her archival work with Cuban marriage records and especially marriages between persons of differing color classifications,[37] Stolcke interprets color in Cuba as a symbol of the division of labor. She argues that initially African origin implied slavery and a distinct socioeconomic position. As long as there were just blacks and whites, and each had a distinct place in the field of labor, the system was sustainable. But with miscegenation and the growth of middle groups—often prosperous mixed-race families—"the system contained its own seeds of destruction" (81).

Stolcke's treatment of the then-emerging *mulato* as an analytically important category is exceptionally helpful to the argument of this chapter. Recognizing that "the status of the mulattos was often a source of incoherence" to the colonial order (80), Stolcke does not then make the mistake of dismissing the category. Rather, the contradictions exposed and revaluations forced by the new group uniquely illuminate the overall order:

> With progressive miscegenation and the appearance of a free coloured group, colour as a distinguishing mark of a person's occupational status became increasingly equivocal and unreliable. Typical in the ambiguous nature of their status were the free negroes and the slave and free mulattos. As M. Douglas writes, "whenever the lines are precarious we find pollution ideas come to their support." In effect, in the Cuban case once the racial attributes became blurred recourse was taken to the more abstract notion of "purity of blood" that had already been applied in Spain throughout three centuries, or to its equivalent, legal colour. (80)

Thus, the idea of blood purity, which was also noted above, emerged from late medieval Spain, where it was religious and national unity at stake rather than a systemic division of labor as in Cuba. Just as the notion was being discredited in nineteenth-century Spain, it was revived and reworked in a new Cuban context. While the link between racism and slavery in Cuba is clear, it is precisely this kind of changing valuation of "purity" that, Stolcke points out, "should make one wary of an interpretation of racism in simply economic terms" (75). Similarly, the see-sawing priority given to legal color and physical appearance in the documentary record suggests that the underlying issue in the colony was the social origin of individuals rather than the color of their skin. And thus, not surprisingly, Stolcke found that the most likely tolerated intercategorical marriages were ultimately between poor *blancos* (white males) and relatively well-off *mulata* women.[38] Ugly as it certainly was, the system was thus developing new racial distinctions adapting and transforming older logics from Spain and beyond. This, then, is a deeper Cuban and Caribbean background to the doctor "joke" discussed earlier.

The other valuable notion developed by Professor Stolcke that I have already described and have adapted for this book is what she called the "classificatory embarrassment" of the order of things in nineteenth-century Cuba. With the decline of the slave trade—largely owing to British naval pressure—expanding sugar plantations faced a labor shortage in the mid-nineteenth century, a shortage partly resolved via the importation of indentured Chinese laboring men. However, these laborers confounded the system of that time: while their labor status was at the very bottom of the scale, their skin color was often lighter than that of the Spanish upper classes. So how should they be classified? Would they be able to marry whites? *Mulatos*? Blacks? In the end, the Chinese issue was resolved by exempting them from the normal requirement of having a marriage license; *they were given no legal color at all.* Thus, theoretically, they could marry individuals of any color. In practice, they faced much more prejudice from upper-class whites than from any other group and thus tended to marry *poor* whites, *pardas*, or *morenas*. Stolcke argues that "it is plainly the conflicting racial and occupational status that prevents a social classification of the Chinese along traditional lines" (76). Similarly, although less dramatically, the Cuban racial system struggled to classify a wave of Yucatecan Mayans "indentured" (enslaved) to Cuba for their role in the Caste War, circa 1850. Like the Chinese, the Mayans were of relatively fair skin for their *de facto* occupational status. Stolcke describes the classificatory challenges presented by these two groups at length:

> If the status of the mulattos was often a source of incoherence, more so was that of the American Indian and the Chinese. The mulatto was the product of the mixture of the two groups themselves, and by instituting the principle of hypodescent the problem involved in his classification was, at least in theory, solved. The Indians and the Chinese, however, were extraneous elements for which the system made no provisions. A special third category could have been created to take up Indians and Chinese. Yet such an additional category would have reduced the clarity

and workability of the system in terms of the interaction between the different categories, apart from the integrating rather than segregating effect of an intermediary category.

In the case of the American Indians official policy revealed a degree of incoherence, which, however, never reached the point of an admitted incapacity of the system to accommodate a category of people, as was the case when the Chinese were declared wanting of any legal colour. The Indians were always considered as legally white. Their skin colour, however, was probably closer to *pardo* and their social status as regarded income ranged from medium to desperate in the case of the Yucatecan indentured labourers.

The Chinese and the Indians (especially the Yucatecan labourers) were then in varying degrees a classificatory embarrassment. For while they were physically rather white—in comparison to Spaniards— occupationally they were as if of African origin. . . . The defenders of slavery would have wanted to enforce a neat dividing line between the racial-cum-occupational groups. Only coloured people should be slaves, and only free people white. But the system contained its own seeds of destruction. . . . The mulattos, the free coloured artisans, the Yucatecan Indians, the Chinese indentured labourers are all instances where the system of classification breaks down. (80–81)

There is, of course, much more to Stolcke's work than I will address here—particularly with regard to gender, marriage, and the role of the Catholic church. She also argues that in the nineteenth century Cuba was stratified at its base by economic division, an unequal division of means of production, and hereditarily preserved inequality that used the strict control of female sexuality (partially circumvented by strategies of elopement) to preserve a family's honor and social status. Ultimately, in Stolcke's view, "race relations are class relations," and the system contained inherent risk and instabilities (124). This view, of course, precisely mirrors the socialist Cuban government's view of race as an epiphenomena of class; today, decades later and long after the state seizure of all means of production, I am not sure the two could not be just as productively inverted for Cuba, making "class" the epiphenomena to a still profoundly racialized cultural order. Nevertheless, in putting the emergence and revaluation of Cuban categories in historical perspective, Stolcke's study once again provides valuable insight.

More recently, two well-known US-based historians, Aline Helg and Ada Ferrer, have proposed alternate interpretations of the history of Cuban racial categories. For Helg (1995; 1997), the fundamental Cuban division is between white and black, within which the *mulato* is subsumed. Thus, she argues that although it does not follow the "one-drop" rule of descent, Cuba's notion of race is much more akin that found in the United States than it is to those found elsewhere in Latin America. In partial support of Helg's thesis, it is certainly true that in the Cuban documents she analyzes, which I have also examined (see Ryer 2006), a variant of the binary term "la raza de color" is used, often in relation to abstract/general membership in the *Partido de Color*. However, *individuals* are also often referred to triadically, as *blancos*, *morenos*, or *pardos*, and even then different designations are contested or simply not observed. Ada Ferrer's approach, also focusing on the late nineteenth and early twentieth centuries, is different. As she put it, "sometimes historical protagonists drew multiple lines, sometimes one, and sometimes (more rarely) they drew none" (1999, 12; also see Sartorius 2013). There is also an exhortative element to the rhetoric here, which is more ideological than hegemonic: one has a sense that in the newly founded republic, the categorical value of "Cuban" is particularly in play.

One could continue to scour the historiographical literature of Cuba or primary documents of the time, but the central point is clear: ultimately, the reduction to a two-tier model does some fundamental violence to the complexities of identities and distinctions noted by historical actors themselves, which at times are three-tier, two-tier, one-tier, or some mixture of the above. Like other North American-based scholars writing about Cuba, however, rather than recognizing this factor and adding nuance and flexibility to her model, Helg dismisses substantial and varied evidence—apparent even within the conventional historiographical archives she cites—that complicates and at times refutes her two-tier structure. Why? How? Perhaps here it is helpful to revisit the *processes* examined by Michel-Rolph Trouillot, not only to consider silencings inherent in historical narratives, but also to consider the context of both the production and the consumption of a given historiographic narrative (Trouillot 1995, 146; Fuente 2001, 8–9). Rather than trying to fit Cuban categories awkwardly into North American ones (or worse, simply presuming they are universal), an approach such as Ferrer's seems both more humble and more powerful:

By using categories from both biracial and triracial systems of racial categorization, I do not answer the familiar question about the number of Latin American color lines; that is not my purpose. But I do hope that using language from both binary and ternary racial systems shifts the terrain of the debate somewhat—from structural questions about lines drawn a priori to questions about the way race, racial boundaries, and the ideologies of race are made and remade on the ground. And if the racial labels sound sometimes strange, it is my hope that this strangeness, rather than deterring readers, will function to remind them, first, of the non-universal nature of North American understandings and, second, of the unnatural character of all these categories. (Ferrer 1999, 11–12)

All the ambiguities and disputes encountered in this brief examination of Cuban categories of a century ago resonate in the contemporary ethnographic context described earlier in this chapter. As noted above, it is not difficult to find Cubans, particularly self-identified "whites," who posit a binary racial scheme today. Others propose a three-tier system or claim to not care. And what about those people of intermediate color—*mulatos*—who Helg buries in endnotes, but who, at times, seem to be claiming a third tier for themselves? Judging by contemporary complexities, there are strong arguments for a third (self-identified) category. At times enfolded into *negro*, *mulato* is, in other contexts, more autonomous or even expands to putatively include all Cubans (as when, for instance, the racial term *blanco cubano* specifically casts doubt on "white" Cubans' claim to whiteness or blacks are described as looking more African than Cuban). Just as since 1959, on an *official* level, racial categories have been relentlessly suppressed and compressed into one national term, "Cuban," think again of the popular saying *El que no tiene de Congo, tiene de Carabalí*. In challenging the "white" category, does the aphorism not expand the notion of Cuba as a single mestizo or mulato tier? It is in this sense that nationalist terms such as cubanidad (Cubanness), as well as "mixed" icons from the Virgin of Charity to Antonio Maceo or the state-championed Calibán, are arguably synonymous with *mestizaje* (Kutzinski 1993, 7).

Drawing largely on ethnographic encounters with race in Cuba over the past two decades, this chapter has explored some of the sometimes unexpected ways that race operates there—from the uneasy relationships of white Cubans to the presumed mixtures of *cubanía* and the sometimes visible differences with North America race rules (including official silences and national doxicities), to problematic terms such as "Afro-Cuban," the too-easily overlooked importance of the category *mulato*, and the nationally specific character of Cuban *mestizaje*. Given evidence such as the racial term *blanco cubano*, I have proposed that, together, national and racial boundaries ultimately outline entangled strands of a wider classifying discourse, which we might call "metaracial," perhaps. Such emerging linkages raise new questions. Where do racial or national categories come from, who has the power to define them, and what kinds of patterns are evident across a *longue durée*? Exactly *where* are putative racial purities (and impurities) located: in day-to-day consciousness? in "Spain" and "Africa"? Minimally, one could say "elsewhere." Not in Cuba. How, after millennia of their own *mestizajes*, could Spain or Africa come to represent racial purities in the Cuban imagination? And what, then, might the self-positioning, sense of belonging, and identities of Cuban-educated Africans, once they have left Cuba behind, suggest about the relative weight of these matters to those who have experienced them at length but who, as border-crossing diasporic selves, illustrate the processual nature of identity?

CHAPTER 4

BEYOND A BOUNDARY

What I want to suggest is that despite the dilemmas and vicissitudes of identity through which Caribbean people have passed and continue to pass, we have a tiny but important message for the world about how to negotiate identity. . . . Identity is not in the past to be found, but in the future to be constructed.

Stuart Hall, "Negotiating Caribbean Identities"

Because of what happened to us we feel more Latino than African, because we were taken there [when we were] young. So we feel more like Latin Americans than African.

Carol Berger, "From Cattle Camp to Slaughterhouse"

Caribbean migrations are routinely more complex than they at first seem. For instance, the story of Puerto Rican emigration to New York, Chicago, and elsewhere in the United States is widely known, but there are also simultaneous long-term *im*migrations to Puerto Rico from Cuba and the Dominican Republic (Duany 1999), to say nothing of what Juan Flores (2009) has called "re-asporicans" who have migrated from the diaspora back to the island.[1] While many in New York are familiar with emigration from the Dominican Republic to Washington Heights, there has also been the simultaneous immigration of hundreds of thousands of Haitians to that republic (Sutton and Chaney 1987; Martínez 2007; Derby 2009; J. González 2011). While there are over 160,000 Belizeans in the United States today (and only twice that number at home), since the convulsions of the 1980s Belize has also been on the receiving end of immigrations from neighboring Central American nations. While more than half of Grenada's citizens have emigrated to the United States, the United Kingdom, Canada, Trinidad, or Barbados, that nation has also faced immigration from Dominica and elsewhere; Jamaican diasporic patterns are similar (Chamberlain 1998). Kamala Kempadoo (1999) has detailed the excruciating migrations of sex workers throughout the region; even in Port-au-Prince there are immigrant communities of Dominican sex workers. Not an exhaustive list, these examples illustrate the general point—that whether a result of political upheaval, remittance economics, or what Mark Padilla (2007) has eloquently termed the "Caribbean Pleasure Industry," Antillean migrations today are never unidirectional. For all its political distinctiveness, revolutionary Cuba nevertheless follows this broad pattern.

Wrestling with this multidirectional, doubly diasporic quality of its contemporary migrations—layered on the scars of earlier voluntary and involuntary diasporas—scholars of the Caribbean have often emphasized that there are no essentialized, autochthonous bases from which to build Caribbean national identities. In his seminal examination of hyphenated Cubanness, Gustavo Pérez Firmat writes: "When pondering the shakiness of my foundations, the mobility of my cultural home, I take consolation and courage from the knowledge that insular Cuban culture rests on similarly shifting grounds. . . . The reasons for this are complex but the principal ones have to do . . . with the extermination of Cuba's aboriginal population [and] with the island's strategic location at the entrance to the Americas. This has meant that Cuban culture has always lacked a stable core or essence" (2012, 13–14). I take seriously the notion that diasporic identities are best traced processually, through lived experience rather than in relation to some authenticating originary essence. Other ethnographers and scholars of diaspora make similar points. As Kamari Maxine Clarke has recently argued, "because diasporic connections have been made and remade through time, scholars need to go beyond the mere charting of modern notions of territorial descent and instead demonstrate the ways race and diaspora are shown to be *processes in the making* rather than stable categories" (K. Clarke and Thomas 2006, 151; emphasis added). And yet, it is a struggle to let go of an imagined concreteness, the foundational islands of identity; our common sense is not so easily displaced. It is somehow easier to add a hyphen to the Antillean homeland (Cuban-American, for instance) than the reverse. Thus, because they are not Cuban citizens and are African- rather than Cuban-born, Cuban-educated students—who, I will argue, would otherwise fulfill the criteria of a hyphenated "1.5" generation—are never considered "really" Cuban and are thus invisible or irrelevant to even the best subsequent studies of contemporary Cuban migration and diaspora (e.g., O'Reilly Herrera 2001; D. Fernández 2005; Eckstein 2009; Stepick, Rey, and Mahler 2009; Berg 2012). In exploring the cases of Cuban-educated students who "don't quite fit" commonsense cartographies, this chapter seeks to push beyond the merely descriptive toward rethinking the borders of Cubanness more processually.

Originally developed by Cuban-American sociologist Rubén Rumbaut (1991, 1997) while working with refugee youth from Southeast Asia, the "1.5" or "one-and-a-half" generation concept has been repeatedly deployed in the scholarship of the Cuban exile experience (Pérez Firmat 1994; O'Reilly Herrera 2001; Rumbaut and Rumbaut 2005) and has since been adapted for many diaspora literatures. In Rumbaut's formulation, a member of the 1.5 generation is someone who is born and partly raised in one cultural and linguistic setting but displaced to another during adolescence, becoming entirely and distinctively bilingual and bicultural. It is not a description of those who spend a year or two studying abroad, but rather of those whose formative years and lives are fundamentally split in two. Because of the potentially decontextualized, personalized, and ahistorical orientation of the theory, anthropologist Mette Berg has articulated a valuable set of concerns about the 1.5-generation hypothesis in relation to her own work with diasporic Cubans in Spain. Berg argues that historical context mattered more than age at time of migration. Among Cubans in Spain, she describes three distinct generations: "Exiles," who arrived to Spain in the 1960s; "Children of the Revolution," who grew up in and were shaped by revolutionary Cuba before leaving the island; and "Migrants," who have immigrated in the wake of the post-Soviet economic crisis. These generations, or cohorts, Berg argues, shaped "different modes of remembering and relating to home and away" (2009b, 272). In the case of the Cuban-educated students I am considering in this chapter, it is certainly true that those who lived in Cuba in the 1970s and 1980s had a different experience than those studying there today; however, unlike Berg's material from Spain, we will see evidence of intergenerational post-Cuban studies solidarity among graduates, as well as their own reflections on the importance of the age at which they were sent abroad (see below). In any event, what is important here is not only the 1.5 model itself, but the critical stance its deployment opens up in order to rethink the taken-for-granted island originaries of Cuban diasporic studies. As we will see, more recent work (Ossman 2013) will add further nuance to understanding identities and describing lives lived across systems. Furthermore, as I have argued elsewhere (Ryer 2010), the 1.5-generation paradigm is apt for these Cuban-educated students but contains yet *another* unresolved issue: doesn't a hyphen necessarily imply the linking of separate or distinct cultural wholes? This is a now well-recognized dilemma of hybridity (Tsing 2005, 26; García Canclini 1995). The contents of this chapter challenge us to take seriously an experiential understanding of identity, to rethink the tools—for example, remittances as well as passports—by which we measure it, and, ultimately, to reimagine kinship, belonging, and identity writ large as indeed a future to be constructed rather than a past to be found.[2]

Cuban-African Educational Internationalism

I have already addressed the Cuban state's internationalist educational project in more detail in Chapter 2, but to reiterate: from the 1970s through the 1990s and beyond, in the context of its simultaneous involvement in wars in Angola and Ethiopia, the Cuban government brought tens of thousands of students from more than thirty African nations or political movements to be educated in Cuba, intending them to become the leading professionals and vanguards of their respective socialist nations. Divided by nationality, most arrived as middle school-aged students and were initially placed in work-study boarding schools on the Isle of Youth that combined study and agricultural labor. From there, those who did well and mastered Spanish were able to enroll in high schools with students of other nationalities and eventually move on to universities and professional schools on the main island, studying medicine, law, engineering, and many other fields, side by side with Cuban peers (Jané 1988; McManus 2000; Blum 2011). Drawing on my own ethnographic work as well as documentaries, online communities, and recent scholarly work (Berger 2001; Lehr 2008; Hickling-Hudson, Gonzalez, and Preston 2012; Bernstein 2013; Nibbe 2013), this chapter presents data from just three of the many Cuban-educated African groups. I look first at the case of the southern Sudanese and Ghanaian students and then in more detail at the "Cubarauis," using a set of recent documentaries to explore certain themes and patterns of these groups. In the process, I propose, we will have to rethink the borders of belonging and cubanidad as well as revisit the matter of remittances and *yuma* style.

Perhaps one of the best ways to unpack the complexities of belonging is to consider doubly hyphenated identities, groups that "don't fit" the standard "Cuban-American" model—a model of a single ethnicity living in exile.[3] Like these African-Cubans, the Jewish-Cuban community in Miami does just that. Ninety percent of Cuba's Jewish community of about ten thousand people, who mostly arrived in Cuba in the 1920s and 1930s, moved to the United States following the 1959 revolution. Although anthropologist Ruth Behar, one of the best-known members of this community, argues that the engagement with the Jewish diaspora is present in everyday Cuban life and sensibility outside Cuba, and even that the Cuban idea of *exilio* (exile) stems from Cubans living in close proximity to Jews in Miami Beach (1996, 145); nevertheless, the small community of Spanish-speaking Cuban Jewish exiles remains relatively unrecognized in Miami, with its much larger American Jewish and Catholic Cuban populations. Caroline Bettinger-López has concisely described the situation of this community: "The Jewish Cubans belonged nowhere in Miami. Among other Cuban exiles, they became 'Jews.' . . . Whereas in Cuba they had stood out as Jews, in Miami Beach [then a predominantly Jewish-American area] they stood out as Cubans. Those who had arrived on the shores of the United States as 'Jewish Cubans' thus became 'Cuban Jews' in Miami Beach" (2000, 34–35). By the late 1960s and early 1970s, after a formerly important distinction between Ashkenazi and Sephardic was silenced, the Miami category "Cuban Jews" was further transformed into "Jewban." Indeed, Bettinger-López (2000) argues, the Jewban identity is still transforming, is now the domain of what Pérez Firmat calls the 1.5 generation, for whom the United States is increasingly home, and Cuba—or "Juba"—is "an imagined homeland" (Behar 2009).

I suggest that the 1.5 paradigm can be productively stood on its head: rather than looking at a cohort that began as Cuban and acquired a hyphenated, second identity through the dislocation of exile and migration, what about looking at those who began elsewhere and acquired a Cuban identity? Again, I am not referring to recidivistic tourists, nor even to those who take up residence in Miami or Havana for a year or two, but rather to those whose lives, languages, experiences, and fundamental sense of identity are inexorably split, bifurcated, or hyphenated because of long-term dislocation during adolescence—born elsewhere, made in revolutionary Cuba. Identity, in other words, is a process of lived social relations as much as it is an accident of birth or geography. In fact, there are such groups that I argue fit the 1.5 paradigm, even though to date they have been entirely ignored by US-based Cuban studies, for reasons that should be considered. I am referring, of course, to Cuban-educated African students.

Cuban-Educated Sudanese Students

In 1985, a group of 619 young Dinka, Nuer, and Shilluk boys and girls were sent from southern Sudan to boarding school in Cuba. After thirteen years in the Cuban educational system, where they had limited contact with their families and were schooled to see themselves as "New Sudanese," these students often came to describe themselves as "Africans" in the context of internationalist and pan-African educational projects sponsored by the Cuban state. Following political changes in Africa and economic crisis in post-Soviet Cuba, in the late 1990s, approximately 250 of the remaining, stranded Sudanese students were granted refugee status by the Canadian government, transported to Alberta, and given work in a slaughterhouse near Edmonton. While most are still in Canada today, some have returned to newly independent South Sudan, where their professional skills are in demand. To other Sudanese, however, they have since come to be known as "the Cubans." They are noted for lacking knowledge of Nilotic tribal or clan divisions and age-sets; for different expectations of appropriate gender roles; for speaking Spanish as their first language; for having unexpected attitudes toward the handling of money and remittances; and for different food preferences, musical tastes, and favorite dances. Today, facing new forms of racialization in rural Canada or in their secondary migrations, the self-identification of these cosmopolitan migrants continues to change: recently, one Cuban-educated student described himself as doubly hyphenated to a reporter in Calgary: "I always call myself Sudanese-Canadian-Cuban" (Bill Kaufmann, *Calgary Sun*, March 26, 2006).

Although beyond the scope of this chapter, questions of identity involving the Nuers and Dinkas of southern Sudan may have particular resonance for many anthropologists, due to the famous segmentary theses of E. E. Evans-Pritchard (1940). Also present, however, are questions of recent history—of rebellion, refugee camps, the Cold War; of interactions between southern Sudanese Dinka, Shilluk, and Nuer, as well as with Ethiopians and northern Sudanese Arabs and Muslims. Of the 619 students sent to Cuba, 60 were girls; the youngest were six years old, the eldest twenty-two. All were then affiliated with the nominally Marxist SPLA resistance and most were especially well-connected to military officers or otherwise privileged to be selected from among the eighty thousand southern Sudanese in refugee camps in the mid-1980s, and for virtually all, the date and details of their initial trip to Cuba are still vividly recalled. In Cuba, the Sudanese faced a number of adjustments, both in terms of the specific pedagogical project envisioned for them and in relation to a near total isolation from their families and from news of home. In accord with Marxist ideology:

> In Cuba, the youth increasingly experienced a group identity consistent with the stated aim of the SPLM to create a single [New Sudanese] nationality—one which de-emphasized tribal or geographic affiliation.[4] As well, neither Christian nor traditional southern Sudanese religions were taught or practiced at the Sudanese school on the Isle of Youth. At the same time, however, events in northern and southern Sudan were creating conditions for a resurgence of ethnic and religious identification. (Berger 2001, 46)

The students also had to make adjustments to Cuban practices. To mention just two: Cuban teachers were opposed to corporal punishment within the schools and, as Berger has noted, pork, popular in Cuba, is not eaten by Nilotic people (2001, 44). On the Isle of Youth, rivalries with other African schools were encouraged for the sake of agricultural production, and these rivalries at times became violent. For those students who succeeded in school and were sent on to polyclinics or universities on the main island, however, a certain pan-African sentiment often emerged between students of different nationalities. As we have seen, all African students, in fact, shared a certain set of issues resulting from their foreign status. Because of their citizenship, they could not receive housing or food without student status; however, they could legally purchase scarce and prized goods from the *diplotiendas* reserved for non-Cubans, creating a niche for black marketeering, and many students survived by re-enrolling in schools and by illicit trading during the hungry years of the early 1990s following the collapse of the Soviet Bloc. By the mid-1990s, the students were finishing their educational programs but could not return to Sudan; some were sent back to refugee camps in Ethiopia, but the remainder waited in limbo until the Canadian government granted them refugee status and resettled them in Alberta.

Anthropologist Carol Berger, a former journalist posted to the Sudan, conducted extensive interviews, interaction, and observation with these Cuban-educated Sudanese over several years around the millennium. Her interviewees noted the immediately evident difference between those arriving from Cuba and other Sudanese immigrants:

> Those who came from Cuba are different from those who come from Ethiopia or Kenya [referring to absence of tribal division]. When we came from the airport, they start to separate us. . . . When I was in Windsor [Ontario, still in transit to Alberta] even some of my cousins came and said "Why are you living with those [Nuer] guys?" We are three Dinka and one Nuer [living together]. . . . Even they say, "Look, these communists.[5] See how they think." (2001, 78)
>
> We Cuban guys, we never fight. We've been living together—Dinka, Shilluk, Nuer—we all stay together. We think differently [from other Sudanese]. Even the other Sudanese here, they say we are "the Cubans." All these differences [between tribes], we don't agree with it. (80–81)

Even with the certain shock of being transported to the northern plains and suddenly employed in a slaughterhouse straight out of *Fast Food Nation* (Schlosser 2002), conflicts and differences with other directly arrived Sudanese compose the bulk of Berger's interview and observational data. Such differences include the "Cubans'" lack of observance of age-sets (2001, 15); near total ignorance of clans and subclans (88); and changed gender roles and expectations: "This is the other shock [for non-Cuban Sudanese]. Some of the girls coming from Cuba, they don't want husbands but they want boyfriends" (74). The informant continued: "The men from Cuba have also been chastised and corrected by other Sudanese" for things such as slouching, dressing with too much hip-hop style, and drinking in front of older people (74–75). The misunderstandings, extending even to serious fights between long-separated cousins, are mutual:

> The "Cubans" use the Spanish word *gaucho* to describe Sudanese coming to Canada directly from Africa. The word refers to what the youth from Cuba consider the unsophisticated ways of their relations. The Sudanese, for their part, sometimes use the Dinka word *ah cheebel,* meaning "fools," or "people who are lost" to describe those who were in Cuba.

Whether in the manner that they speak or their actions, the Cubans are considered uncouth and disrespectful. (Berger 2001, 87)

Another set of differences has to do with expectations of reciprocity and remittances (for more on Cuban norms of reciprocity, see Rosendahl 1997). "The contrast between [a direct Sudanese interviewee's] sense of community and that of the Cubans was marked. Cuban informants routinely remarked on the absence of solidarity among other Dinka; in particular, that they failed to offer assistance to those in need" (Berger 2001, 86). For their part, non-Cuban Sudanese felt that the Cubans remitted "too much" to kin in Africa (83–89, 112). Some of the slaughterhouse-earned money was earmarked for family to buy cattle, or for bridewealth, or simply to support scattered and long-separated kin. "Said informant 'J': 'If I need help I can go to my friends, even to a Nuer, as long as you come from Cuba you can always find help, financially, emotionally. But if I go to one of those other Dinka [coming from Egypt or Kenya] they will say no'" (82). Such differences, as well as different languages, food preferences, musical tastes, and favorite dances, I propose, mark the Cuban-educated as "one-and-a-halfers," although the relevant detail is their age of *arrival* in Cuba, not their *departure*. But like Pérez Firmat's Cuban-Americans, those sent at especially young ages tilt more heavily to the acquired culture—in this case, toward the Cuban side. Indeed, many describe themselves not only as Cubans, but as Latinos: "We speak not very good English, not very good Arabic, not very good Dinka. What we speak well is Spanish. We are Latino" (Cuban-Sudanese interviewee, quoted in Berger 2001, 71; also see Oleschuk 2011, 31).

Berger repeatedly chronicles the ex-students' nostalgia for Cuba, even as there is a consensus among them that in the last years of their stay the economic situation there was far from ideal. She describes one Cuban-educated Sudanese woman's apartment, with much carefully preserved Cuban memorabilia, and writes: "Because the informant was very young when she traveled to Cuba, no more than eight years old, she shows a particularly strong Latino or Cuban identity" (93). She then describes how hard this young woman works to support her mother and extended family in Africa. Another student comments: "I miss Cuba so bad. I want to go back. Sometimes, when I think of my memories they're all in Cuba. Spanish is really my first language now." When Berger asks her if she would like to see Sudan again, the student replies: "I want to see how Sudan looks like. . . . Like a tourist I could go. If you ask me now about Sudan I know nothing, only what I hear and see on the TV" (73).

Beyond the clear personal distress evident in this lament, one has to wonder in what ways, or to what extent, these Sudanese students' nostalgia for Cuba is sharpened by encounters with new groups and structures elsewhere (such as the racial order of rural western Canada, for instance). And how is African students' attachment to Cubanness (cubanidad) likely to change over years to come? Merin Oleschuk has more recently noted that both Cuban and Sudanese foods represent "home" for these former students (2011, 164), and indeed, as noted earlier, some of them have returned to now-independent South Sudan and congregate at the Havana Café in Juba, which one of them opened and named as a way of "giving back" to Cuba (Hannah McNeish, *Voice of America*, August 13, 2012).

ESBEC 22 and Beyond

Unlike other student groups, Ghanaians were not displaced to Cuba from armed conflict, nor from refugee camps. Like the others, however, they arrived in waves as early or preteenagers from 1983 on, and began their extended residency in Cuba isolated at ESBEC 22, a boarding school on the Isle of Youth, with most eventually scattering to a wide range of professional programs at universities and technical institutes throughout the republic.[6] With some 1,200 students thus far, today only a limited number are engaged in professional studies there. Like other Africans, they have since dispersed further; some are still in Cuba, many have returned to Ghana; others are in the United Kingdom, the United States, the Bahamas, or scattered around the globe. Many have been quite successful in careers that may or may not correspond to their chosen studies in Cuba. Sabine Lehr (2008), in particular, has examined the program and subsequent trajectories of Cuban-educated Ghanaians, particularly back in Ghana and in an enclave in the Bahamas (see also Hickling-Hudson, Gonzalez, and Preston 2012). Samuel Kaba Akoriyea, who has since returned to Ghana, with his Cuban wife, Dr. Yanet Pina, to work as a neurosurgeon, speaks in particular about the role of his high school on the Isle of Youth in developing an awareness of African realities beyond Ghana:

> The school consisted of students from Mozambique, Ethiopia, Cape Verde, Mongolia, Sudan, Namibia, Burkina Faso, South Africa, and

Ghana. Although we were all under the same roof, the students of each country formed their own academic groups, and we did not mix in the classroom for lectures.

This was a period to socialize, listen, and learn from other nationalities. It was a time to learn about the situation in Mozambique, Namibia, South Africa, the Darfur crisis, and to share experiences as to how we all got to Cuba. Contrary to the selective procedure that took place in Ghana, many students from the Sudan, Mozambique, and Angola explained how they had to flee their country as refugees. Whereas we received letters from our parents, they never saw their parents before leaving their home lands. (Kaba Akoriyea 2012, 227–28)

This account speaks clearly to both the general and particulars of the Esbecan experience in relation to other student groups. For the remainder of this section, let me focus on the patterns of self-identification evident among those graduates active online—at least among the several hundred registered at ESBEC.com or who participate in *EsbecRadio* (*www.blogtalkradio.com/ esbecradio*), which are two linked sites by and for the "Esbecan" community.

Hosted by college professor Samuel Darko, aka "Buggy," from the group sent to Cuba in 1983 and now residing in Columbia, South Carolina, *EsbecRadio* has broadcast some forty shows since May 2008. Shows are broadcast live and then posted via BlogTalkRadio to the web, where they are freely accessible. The format is simple: after a theme song, "Yo soy el punto cubano" by Celina González, Buggy announces a topic, perhaps has a few community announcements or a cohost for the day, and encourages listeners to call in. Up to five callers can be online at once, so it can become quite a conversation; at other times, there are few callers and more music. Musical selections focus on songs popular in Cuba and among Esbecans in the 1980s and 1990s, from Los Van Van to zouk to reggae (e.g., Bob Marley, "Africa Unite"). Callers often remark that the song list evokes good memories or nostalgia for Cuba. Frequently, callers are asked to play an on-air quiz, "Dime lo que tú sabes," focusing on remembered people, events, and miscellany from the boarding school, with questions like "What was the Ghanaian nickname of the tall black professor at ESBEC 22?"

The dominant language of the show is English, with frequent code switching to Spanish or Cuban expressions and slang and occasionally to Ghanaian languages as well. Much of the airtime is filled with queries and updates about Esbecans around the world. Often, however, Buggy takes up a particular topic—from the theme of reconciling with each other, to the status of Esbecanas (as with the Sudanese and POLISARIO students, there were fewer female than male students in the school), to the importance of maintaining ties with Cuban families and children left there. Those who have recently traveled to or know of couriers to Cuba occasionally report this as well, for the sake of facilitating communication and remittances. The kinds of self-identification deployed by the "serial migrants" (Ossman 2007) on the show remind us again that identity is always partial, processual, and contextual, and not to be essentialized or reified. At times, participants refer to themselves as cubanos and Ghanaians, but most commonly as Esbecan or esbecanos/as. At times, Buggy or his guests refer to Esbecans as "a people" and at other times as a family, as, for example, in this comment from the first episode: "We actually are basically family. . . . Most Esbecans feel most comfortable around other Esbecans" ("Our Very First Show," originally broadcast May 20, 2008, minute 56; also see "Mending Fences," originally broadcast June 21, 2008). Or, in planning the twenty-fifth anniversary of their arrival to Cuba: "What have we done as a people, to see the benefits of being an Esbecan? That would make us proud in celebrating our anniversary?" ("General Esbecan Topics," originally broadcast May 22, 2008, minute 8). Like the Cuban-educated Saharauis described in the next section, Cuban-educated Ghanaians have found their own experience so distinctive, so hyphenated, that a new term, Esbecan, has emerged among them, and they recall and commemorate the precise dates of their dislocation. And like the Sudanese, they can and do rely largely on each other for emotional and material support (e.g., "Show #3: Donde esta las Esbecanas?" originally broadcast May 24, 2008, minute 74). Interestingly, they have been fundraising and planning a new iteration of the Cuban ESBEC—a work-study school in Ghana, taught, run, and funded by themselves (e.g., "General Esbecan Topics," minute 27). Whether *conciencia cubana* or *nostalgia socialista*, the pattern is also similar to that of other Cuban-educated groups.

Cuban-Saharan Internationalism

The specific history of Cuba's involvement with Saharaui students from the Western Sahara goes back to a Cold War–era Cuban governmental fact-finding mission in 1977.[7] In the wake of the Moroccan/Mauritanian invasion of the former Spanish colony in 1975 following the vacuum created by the slow death of General Franco, many surviving Western Saharans fled to refugee camps near Tindouf, Algeria, where the young anticolonial POLISARIO reorganized to resist the US-allied Moroccan forces occupying their territory (see Chatty 2010; Zunes and Mundy 2010). In a gesture both humanitarian and political, Cuba offered to educate some of the children from these impoverished camps, and the first Saharaui students arrived in Cuba in March 1978, shortly after similar programs had been established for Angolan, Namibian, and other African students. Technically organized by the POLISARIO-dominated RASD government, the Saharaui-Cuban program has been one of the most successful and long-term international educational exchanges in revolutionary Cuba and, according to many interviewees, has endured well into the twenty-first century partly owing to Saharauis' head start in Spanish—their second language and one that they, as former Spanish colonial subjects, have already studied and heard before traveling to Cuba. In any case, since 1977, there have been well over 4,000 total Cuban-educated Saharauis out of an estimated 165,000 Saharauis in the refugee camps (Chatty 2010).

Although some young Saharauis have been educated in Libya, Algeria, and elsewhere in the region, Cuba's free education is sought after, and students are generally selected from families with POLISARIO or RASD ties; while in the 1970s and 1980s, boys and girls of middle-school age were sent, today the program is only for somewhat older boys. Under the terms of the agreement between the Cuban and RASD governments, Saharaui students are eligible for long-term Cuban residency papers, renewable upon ongoing satisfactory progress in their studies; however, they are not permitted to remain in Cuba following the completion of their degrees, even if they have married a Cuban citizen in the interim. There is an RASD embassy in Havana that coordinates the educational program, and thus in addition to the students, a very few Saharauis do live and work in Cuba. Some of the other specific conditions they have encountered in Cuba have changed over time. As discussed earlier, until the 1990s, international students had the right to purchase goods in the diplomatic stores off limits to Cuban citizens and thus often served as middlemen for quasi-legal transactions for Cubans looking for certain scarce appliances, clothing, and other items. Once Cubans were allowed into these stores in 1993, that opportunity vanished. By all accounts, during the early 1990s finding adequate food was particularly difficult for

Saharaui and Cuban students alike, as noted in documentaries and interviews (e.g., see Boicha 2009b; Fiddian-Qasmiyeh 2010).

Another change involves the work-study expectations of the international schools. As mentioned earlier, initially, Saharaui schools followed the work-study ideas of José Martí and the design for other international schools in Cuba: to pay for their education, room, and board, students were required to do a half day of study and half day of agricultural work, primarily in the local citrus industry. There are a range of ex post facto descriptions of the work-study nature of Cuban international education, with the great majority painting a nostalgic picture: "'Yes, we worked in the fields in the afternoons, but we didn't mind,' admits Aftaim, who studied for 12 years in Cuba and now works as a nurse in the clinic in the February 27th camp. 'They paid us to study and live for over a decade, so it wasn't too much to ask us help clear a one-square meter plot once a day'" (Blue_Woman 2009). However, at least one Cubaraui, Saldani Maalainine, has denounced the program as exploitative (see Fiddian-Qasmiyeh 2009). In any case, while Saharuis still begin their time in Cuba at a boarding school on the Isle of Youth, they are no longer expected to do agricultural labor there.

The remainder of this case study is divided into three sections. First, I explore Saharan students' encounters with Cuban society, the effects it had on them, and their struggles upon returning to the Sahara in order to better evaluate their fit with the 1.5-generation model. Second, I examine resulting complexities of Cubaraui kinship and belonging and challenge our common sense of distinction between "real" and "fictive" kin. And third, I propose that attending to *actual* patterns of remittances and reciprocity allows a rethinking of belonging and "home" and provides evidence of a distinctively Cuban-Saharan (and Cuban-African) *conciencia*, which I leave untranslated in order to retain the sense of both "consciousness" and "conscience."[8] One note about methodology: as with other transnational, multisited research, this chapter necessarily looks beyond the traditional ethnographic single site, seeking rather to follow people in motion (Tsing 2000, 346). While my first encounter with Cubarauis was part of my ethnographic fieldwork in Havana in the 1990s as noted, here I draw on a range of scope-extending sources, including blogs, social media, and documentary films. As we will see, three films, in particular, provide a distinctively mobile but highly curated lens into Cubaraui lives, and I reference them frequently but not uncritically.[9] Just as Trouillot exposed the *inevitability* of silencing within any historical narrative, similar processes are at play in the production and editing of these films, all of which were directed by Spaniards for a Spanish audience, with secondary circulation in global film circuits, primarily in the Spanish-speaking world. The first documentary, *Las Cubarauis* (Márquez 2005), focuses on the experiences of Cubaraui women in Cuba. The second, *Caribeños del Sáhara* (I. Pérez 2007), goes back and forth, interviewing Cubarauis in Cuba and in the Saharan refugee camps. The third and most powerful film, *El Maestro Saharaui* (Muñoz 2011), follows the interlocking, transnational lives of Cubarauis and their kin in Algeria, Spain, and Cuba.

The clearest example of the importance of attending to the dynamics of silencing within the editing processes is the preeminence of Cubaraui women throughout the documentaries despite the reality that girls' participation in the program has declined drastically. Why is this so? In an inspired analysis of *Las Cubarauis* (Márquez 2005), Elena Fiddian-Qasmiyeh notes the careful staging of that documentary, which "highlights certain characteristics and images [of both the Saharan students and of Cuba] in order to elicit a specific response from the audience" (2009, 341). The intended audience of the film, in fact, is the Spanish public and Spanish NGOs, which provide much of the camps' often-meager assistance. Thus, as she notes, the POLISARIO leadership is happy to situate Cuban-educated women "at the center of their international public relations campaign directed to European audiences," even as, *internally*, following several pregnancies resulting from liaisons with Cuban men in early years of the program, "these women have been perceived to be potential threats" to both moral standards and the political status quo of the camps, and their participation in the program has therefore virtually ceased (341). Again, this is an important reminder to look critically at any of the representational modes considered here as well as to foreground the always-lurking reality of silencing—namely, that any narrative comes at the expense of others. Here, then, rather than discarding these sources, my strategy is akin to Trouillot's repositioning of evidence (1995, 27).

Cubarauis: Caribeños del Sáhara

Cubarawi. (coo-ba-ra-wee) n. A person of Saharawi birth who has spent at least five years studying in Cuba, and thus currently displays a mix of the two lifestyles and is fluent in both Spanish and Hassaniya. You won't find this definition in Webster's Dictionary, World Book Encyclopedia, or even Wikipedia. It is not a recognized word in any language, but it is an expression

with considerable meaning for hundreds of Saharawi refugees here in the
camps outside of Tindouf, Algeria. A Cubarawi, by definition, has spent
anywhere from four to sixteen years—oftentimes uninterrupted—studying
in a Cuban secondary school and/or university. Usually, he or she left the
Saharawi refugee camps or the Occupied Territories (the part of the Western
Sahara currently under the control of the Kingdom of Morocco) at a young
age, because there are many more educational opportunities in the cities of
Cuba than in the sands of the Saharan Desert. Cubarawis eventually leave
the Republic of Cuba and return to the refugee camps with degrees in general
medicine, nursing, mechanical engineering, law, literature, English language,
and a plethora of other areas of study.

Blue_Woman, "Profile of a Cubarawi"

More than any words could, the contrast visible in each of the documentaries about Cuban-educated Saharans—switching between life in the refugee
camps in inland Algeria with naught but sand and dust in sight and the
verdant blue and green rural and urban life of tropical Cuba—sets the stage
for thinking about the stark dislocations of this migration. Like many 1.5
cohorts (e.g., Pérez Firmat 1995), they vividly describe the details of their
date of arrival—boat or plane, the Caribbean sea, the strangeness of smells
and sounds: "To see the sea . . . see a green and infinite earth . . . because
I was born [during the flight to the camps] I had never seen free Sahara,"
(Muelimnin Said, quoted in I. Pérez 2007). Or as blogger Ebnu puts it:

> I recall those first days with a sad, bitter sensation. With the perplexity
> and the curiosity of a new experience that was just starting, a different
> world full of expectations and surprises. Mango, guayaba, mamey . . .
> delicious! The "ball," the baseball. How can they play such a game? Do
> they even know football? The contrast with sweet and salted. The sweets
> were too sweet, the salty food was too salty. How can someone eat rice
> every day, day and night? When I do not like rice. (quoted in "Western
> Sahara: Cubarawis," *Global Voices*, December 17, 2008)

But among the many difficult adjustments—language, food, dress,
sports, gender expectations, and religious context—the greatest shock they
most commonly cited was isolation from their Saharan families, which
was exacerbated by poverty and limited telecommunication infrastructure

on both sides. In the beautifully produced *El Maestro Saharaui*, Azman, in Cuba since 2004, discusses how he has never met his elementary-age brother: "Some have been [gone] seventeen years and we've never been able to talk on the phone or send money." Slaka Ahmed recalls, "I thought I'd be gone five years, but it was five years until my first *phone call* home" (Muñoz 2011). With stays in Cuba averaging ten to fifteen years (Fiddian-Qasmiyeh 2009, 332), many students who arrive in Cuba as young as nine to twelve years old, have spent more than half their lives in the Caribbean by the end of their studies. As mentioned earlier, the challenges faced by Saharan students have varied over time, of course, and conditions during the Special Period were especially difficult for international students, as they were for Cuban citizens (see Berg 2009b). However, to my surprise, one of my Saharan informants insisted, *in 1996*, that once one learned how, one could live well enough in Cuba even as an international student from a refugee camp (Ryer, field notes, 1996).

Like other international students, Saharauis in Cuba routinely faced Cuban ignorance of and stereotypes about their homeland. For instance, several times Cubaraui informants in Havana complained to me about a Cuban stereotype about them—namely, that as Arabs they must have no water, but that each must have his/her own oil well or wealth. Elena Fiddian-Qasmiyeh reports from the refugee camps in Algeria that:

> many of the interviewees commented on the way that Cubans approach, evaluate, and criticize Islam. According to the students, gender-based notions play a pivotal role in Cuban understandings of Islam: most students claimed that when Cubans first learnt that they are Muslims, they immediately said "Muslims beat their wives," "you force your women to wear the veil" and "you keep them indoors." [Ironically], as doctors and medical students working in the Accident and Emergency departments of various hospitals [in Cuba] they regularly witnessed the physical results of "disrespect, violence and abuse" towards Cuban women. (2010, 147–48)

El Maestro Saharaui records several initial interactions with Cubans encountering a Saharan student for the first time. One exchange, between Brahim Breih and a Havana *taxista*, is particularly interesting in this regard, as the taxi driver immediately asks whether it is true that Muslims can have four wives. Clearly having faced the question before, Brahim has a quick answer, that it is the same as Cuban men having multiple girlfriends, only legal. Notably, both Saharans and Cubans commonly make a clear distinction between "Arab" and "African" students (e.g., see Embarka Luchaa's interview in Muñoz 2011); indeed, Arab, or *árabe*, is often used in the Cuban vernacular color terminology described in the previous chapter.

Cuba confronted both male and female Saharan students with additional adjustments in terms of gender relations and expectations. In the words of Mohamed Salem Cori, "It's a little freer here. I can have . . . the girlfriend I want, but in the Sahara it's different. . . . Until I get married, I can't have a girlfriend" (in Muñoz 2011). As I saw firsthand in Cuba, and as one can see in the Cubaraui documentaries, romantic relationships between Middle Eastern or African students—the majority of whom were and are male—and their Cuban peers were and are common. As we will see, these relationships have sometimes led to marriages and/or to children. But the cultural switch also set up new gender horizons in other ways: for example, in *Caribeños del Sáhara*, Muelimnin Said, a doctor, speaks about changed gender role expectations among Cuban-educated professional women like herself—of learning to want more than to stay at home and care for children (I. Pérez 2007).

Most Cuban-educated students, however, describe the greater shock as that of leaving Cuba and returning "home."[10] It is the date of *departure* from Cuba that is most vivid in student narratives: "It was one of the saddest days in my life, when I got on the plane and saw the island disappear behind me, everything turning into blue, heading for the mid-Atlantic, that day was, if not the saddest, then one of the saddest days of my life" (Abdi Ami Omar, in Muñoz 2011). Indeed, one of the central narratives of *El Maestro Saharaui* concerns the graduation of Ayub Ali Mohamed, his separation from his Cuban girlfriend and young daughter, and return to the Algerian camps to take up a position as the new *maestro saharaui* (Muñoz 2011). While the wrenching shock of dislocation is shown rather than told in Ayub's case, it would be hard to overstate the centrality of this moment in most graduates' narratives. "In Cuba I left [my] fiancée . . . when I went to the airport, she came with me and cried much" (Nanah Bidi in I. Pérez 2007).

It would also be difficult to overstate the challenges of reintegration described by student after student. Many described being particularly teased about their lack of mastery of the traditional tea ceremony and Hassaniya language, which, in many cases, was no longer their primary tongue and in which they struggled to communicate appropriately. Mahafud Mohamed went to Cuba at age twelve and earned a pharmaceutical degree there before returning to the desert: "I arrived here at night . . . I said: 'my God, where am I?' [I saw] my aunt and I said to her: 'Hello mother' and she says to me: 'I am not your mother, I am your aunt'" (I. Pérez 2007). He then goes on to describe speaking to his mother in Spanish, having forgotten the appropriate Hassaniya words, even though she does not speak Spanish. As evident in written texts and interviews, and as visible in the documentaries, returned Cubarauis describe, often with accents and gestures more Cuban than Saharan, struggles with the language and the difficulty of reintegrating with their families.

> "It was definitely difficult to come back," confesses Saleh, a Cubarawi after twelve years in the Republic of Cuba. "There are still some words in Hassaniya that I don't know, and people look at me funny when I can't think of them. . . . But you know what I really miss?" he continues, with a playful grin. "Walking around my apartment in my underwear. There's no privacy here. I just can't do it." Having left the camps at an early age, the Cubarawis picked up not only some Cuban customs, but also the Caribbean mind-set. Because of this interesting mix of cultures, they understandably connect best with each other. (Blue_Woman 2009)

Arguably, these difficulties have had as much of an effect as memory and affective nostalgia for Cuba in forming a strong Cubaraui cohort consciousness:

> One of the ways in which students cope with the initial ridicule and marginalization on their return is by maintaining the peer networks that they had established while studying abroad and tapping into them for emotional support. A former Saharaui student from Cuba describes it as follows: "I have many friends, especially from Cuba. We have the same mentality and stick together. We gather for coffee from time to time and try to help and understand each other. We have something like a club and we meet girls and boys and give them advice." (Chatty, Fiddian-Qasmiyeh, and Crivello 2010, 71)

This intensified post-return cohort formation is strikingly akin to the case of the "re-asporicans" noted earlier (Flores 2009), as well as to

Cuban-educated Sudanese, Ghanaians, and others (Berger 2001; Lehr 2008; Hickling-Hudson, Gonzalez, and Preston 2012). Indeed, Luis Pérez has described similar dynamics of feeling like a stranger in one's homeland among those Cubans who returned to the republic after extended studies in the United States a century or more ago (1999, 419; also see López 2013). Both the "Cubaraui" neologism and its attendant cohort support network, I submit, are the outcome of the combination of the extended cultural gap and the proportionately large scale of return—again, roughly 4,000 Cubarauis in camps of some 165,000 Saharaui kin. After returning to Algeria, Ayub, the *maestro saharaui*, goes to see his brother, Saleh Ali Mohamed, himself an older Cubaraui:

> **Saleh**: What are your plans?
> **Ayub**: Practice my profession.
> **Saleh**: That way you can adapt better, because it's a difficult process. You must also seek support from the lads you studied with, because they can help you more than the people here. This society has changed a lot, [lit. *demasiado*], it's not the way you left it in '96. . . . I didn't have anyone to give me refuge . . . [At this point Ayub's brother fans a fire to light it.]
> **Nearby woman**: May God bless us, and may we be free . . .
> **Saleh**: You've got to struggle, that's the way life is.
> **Woman**: And ask for God's help.
> **Saleh [with clear impatience]**: You don't just ask for God's help.

Clearly, the filmmakers intend us to infer that at least these Cubarauis are more secular, more cosmopolitan than their Saharan kin. Recall, however, the previous comments of Cubarauis confronting Cuban ignorance regarding Arabs and Islam, documented by both Fiddian-Qasmiyeh and myself; here again, we must treat the documentary film critically, as one particular, partial, interested viewpoint with its own political, economic, and ideological agenda.

Nevertheless, these particular Cubaraui narratives do have value for rethinking the a priori of Cuban diasporic studies as well as for opening a window to the parallel processes confronting Cubarauis upon their return to the Sahara. Like 1.5 Cuban-Americans, they are liminal yet distinctively and advantageously positioned. Once again, Gustavo Pérez Firmat artfully frames the dilemma: "Life on the hyphen can be anyone's prerogative, but it is the one-and-a-halfer's destiny. I diverge from Rumbaut, though, in stressing the beneficial consequences of this situation. Although it is true enough that the 1.5 generation is 'marginal' to both its native and its adopted cultures, the inverse may be equally accurate: only the 1.5 generation is marginal to *neither* culture" (2012, 3; emphasis in original). On the one hand, interview after interview and source after source makes clear that it is a shock and a struggle for Cubarauis to return to a place in which their training and skills are often of little use. "In Cuba we got an education, learnt a way of life, that is of no use here. Here, what we learnt in Cuba is multiplied by zero" (Muñoz 2011). POLISARIO officials put it slightly differently: in a context in which the only industry is war, "you do a university degree and arrive in circumstances in which you cannot use it" (Muñoz 2011). But at the same time, many *do* ultimately use their degrees and their in-between status in some productive way. Many interviews with Cuban-trained doctors and medical professionals are filmed at their rather bare-bones workplaces, for instance. And as fluent Spanish speakers, Cubarauis have privileged access to international visitors, serving as guides, translators, and the like (see Chatty, Fiddian-Qasmiyeh, and Crivello 2010, 70). As a concluding question, Fiddian-Qasmiyeh asked a number of Cubaraui men and women whether they would send their own children to Cuba, given the chance. The consensus reply seems to reinforce a vernacular 1.5 logic: Yes, they would send their own children, but as older adolescents so they would maintain a greater degree of Saharaui identity (Fiddian-Qasmiyeh 2010, 151; also see Berg 2009a).

To summarize, we see that Cuban-educated Saharans, or Cubarauis, are betwixt and between families, languages, cultures; they certainly have not simply become indistinguishably Cuban (see Fiddian-Qasmiyeh 2010, 148). Like other 1.5 cohorts, their lives are definitively fractured in adolescence, leaving them both marginalized and empowered, misfits in the broadest sense. By speech, style, gestures, attitudes toward gender, sexuality, religion, and—as we will see—money, politics, and social *conciencia* (both in the sense of consciousness and conscience), Cubarauis stand out; they are neither 100 percent Cuban nor 100 percent Saharaui. Just as they stand out in Algeria as Cuban, in Cuba, they stand out as Saharan. If their *gestos* haven't, their accents will mark them; in taxi rides from the airport, or in clinics, they are marked as different in both places.[11] Like Desi Arnaz, they might well come to have an accent in two languages (Pérez Firmat 2012). And "the period of time which students may have spent abroad . . . together with the age at which they left their families . . . are key issues which influence youth experiences of returning home" (Chatty, Fiddian-Qasmiyeh, and Crivello 2010, 64–65). In all these key ways, Cubarauis do indeed form a 1.5 cohort.

And yet, beyond the issue of directionality, there is one clear difference, at least from Cuban-born one-and-halfers, of course: Cubarauis can and do eventually return to their birthplace. One of the distinctions of contemporary Cuban emigration, and possibly the reason it has always fit awkwardly with standard transnational migrant circuit models that describe communities of people communicating and continually circulating between sites in two nations (Rouse 1991; see also Kearney 1995; Schiller and Faist 2010; Schiller and Simsek-Caglar 2011), has, at least until very recently, been the political constraints on returnees resettling at "home" as we see many Cubarauis (and Cuban-educated Africans) doing. Perhaps this is why, within Cuban diasporic studies, hyphenation rather than transnational circuits has been a dominant paradigm. In any case, I submit that what we have considered thus far *does* mark them as one-and-a-halfers, as much so in Tindouf as in Havana.

There is an additional element to consider, however: many of the Cuban-educated have migrated again, to a third country.

> When I left Cuba, twenty-two years old, grown-up and with a degree in hand . . . I didn't know exactly where I was going, but wanted to go, to see my family for the first time in thirteen years was the most urgent. [But] one day I separated from them directly, and, in fact, we were also separated by our manners and attitudes, and I did not remember their faces nor their words. My re-encounter with them was lamentably cold, but intense—I did not shed a tear, and even my mother hardly shed a few drops. I had a strange feeling in those moments, a sensation that later would be transformed into confusion, misunderstanding, incoherence, strange thoughts, obligations. . . . So, almost exhausted, I did everything possible so that, a year and a half after my return to Tindouf, I landed in Gran Canary island, in March 1997. (Yazid 2009; my translation)

Many have gone on to Spain—often specifically to the Canary Islands—as frequently noted in both the written and cinematic resources cited here.

Indeed, Brahim Breih, one of the central figures in *El Maestro Saharaui*, is at one point filmed leaving his family and home in Spain to travel to both Cuba and to the Sahara. Here is another example, by Cubaraui Poet Limam Boicha (2009a), in a poem titled "Polygamy:" "I have three . . . / Three lovers: / Sahara, Cuba, and Canaries; / And of the three / I love them equally" (my translation).

How then are we to characterize such secondary permanent moves to yet another nation-state, and what do they suggest about the 1.5 paradigm and belonging in general? Aihwa Ong's (1999) notion of "flexible citizenship" is relevant, although we are not really talking here about powerful tycoons with a fistful of passports. More immediately productive, I think, is Susan Ossman's recent work on "serial migrants." Focusing on "how ways of moving produce forms of life" rather than giving "primacy to ethnicity or culture a priori," she argues that serial migration—making a second migration to a third national, cultural, linguistic space—can be a liberation from the duality of immigration. In the process, borders become signposts in one's life story, and place is subordinated to time (2013, 1–2). Not all Cubarauis have become serial migrants, but for those who have, Ossman's conceptual work is helpful. At the same time, the specific Cubaraui context of traditional Saharaui mobility *and* contemporary Cuban remittance migration shape the immediate motives and goals of a second migration:

> The POLISARIO/SADR'S highly successful campaign to educate its people has resulted in a new generation of Sahrawi youth who are comfortable with cyclical patterns of movement away from the extended family and kin group. It is a movement reminiscent of traditional migration patterns. . . . Many members of this new generation . . . are now looking to continue their migrations in order to contribute to the well-being of their kin back at home. . . . However, on their return to the camps after protracted periods abroad and with established social networks transcending national borders, many are now flexing their ability to take charge of their lives and to contribute actively to their families, kin groups and the state. For many highly educated youth, this means considering emigrating in another cycle of movement in order to set up a chain of remittances to support their society, from afar. (Chatty, Fiddian-Qasmiyeh, and Crivello 2010, 77)

This is a great description of the logic of a remittance economy, which ought to look familiar to students of contemporary Cuban out migration (e.g., Berg 2009a; 2012), but it also takes for granted something I am questioning—that Cubarauis have *one* society, and *one* set of kin, based in the desert camps around Tindouf. In the next section, I go back to the available evidence in order to assess and challenge this presumption—which, after all, is remarkably similar to the unidirectional assumptions of Cuban diasporic studies (as emigration only) with which I began this chapter.

Complexities of Kinship

Without exhaustively reviewing this classic anthropological topic, my specific point of departure for thinking about Cuban-African kinship, primarily using Cubaraui data, is to take seriously the perspective articulated here by Kath Weston: "My inclination while yet in the field was to treat it as an instance of what anthropologists in the past have termed 'fictive kin.' The concept of fictive kin lost credibility with the advent of symbolic anthropology and the realization that *all* kinship is in some sense fictional—that is, meaningfully constituted, rather than 'out there' in a positivist sense" (1997, 105). That "all kinship is in some sense fictional," or rather, meaningfully constituted, may start to explain how we might come to see a step-sibling as more closely related than a faraway cousin. More recently, Marshall Sahlins has extended and inverted such a Schneiderian perspective to argue that all kinship ultimately involves culturally meaningful "mutuality of being" rather than biology *per se*: "kinfolk are persons who participate intrinsically in each other's existence" (2012, ix; see also Härkönen 2014b). Surely, when Cubarauis speak of Cubans as family, as they often do—for example, when Ayub's Cuban host mother in Santa Clara tells him, at his farewell dinner, "You must keep in touch with us, because you're a son to me that'll now be far away" (Muñoz 2011; also see I. Pérez 2007)—such claims are familiar to those who have lived with or returned to Cuban families. It is a two-way assertion of relatedness within a genre I have seen and heard in relation to many Cuban-educated students as well as other resident foreigners. Such statements often seem genuine yet metaphorical, rhetorical, and often threaded with the underlying realities of an increasingly embedded remittance economy. When Brahim Breih returns to Havana partway through *El Maestro Saharaui*, we are shown something we had not seen in previous documentaries: the return of a Cubaraui *to Cuba* and to Cubans.[12] Right away, we see him head to his old dormitory in Havana to greet the staff, who greet him with "Brahim!!!" and "This is my nephew, my son!" with big embraces and queries back and forth about other students and staff. While clearly affectively meaningful, this greeting may be challenging to accept from the outside as more than a rhetorical assertion of kinship—that is, as "fictional" rather than "real" (blood) kinship. But if all kinship in the final analysis is fictive—or rather, determined by mutuality of being rather than biology—then the instances above are more than mere metaphor and should be treated as seriously as any genetic linkage. If this is a leap too far into the symbolic constitution of meaning for some, fortunately there are two more "concrete" examples available that illustrate my overall interest in examining the relatedness of Cubaruis and Cubans. Both are central storylines in *El Maestro Saharaui.*

In the first thread, the film crew follows Ayub as he goes about his daily life in Santa Clara, finishing his thesis and preparing to return to the camps. We see him at the beach, playing, in an almost pitch-perfect rendition of a Cuban father, with his toddler-age daughter, Miriam, and her young Cuban mother and grandmother. Later, we watch his almost unbearable farewell, and then the film follows him back to Havana, to the airport, onto a plane, and arriving back to the Sahara; his sense of loss and dislocation is not verbalized, but it is palpable in his dazed movements. This, then, is an excruciatingly emotional separation of "real" kin, familiar to anyone who has spent time in the Miami terminal of José Martí International Airport.[13]

The second storyline starts with an interview with Slaka Ahmed, an older Cubaraui now residing in a tent in one of the Algerian camps. Slaka relates how, as a student in Cienfuegos some two decades earlier, he had met a Cuban woman, fallen in love, married her, and had a son, Basiri, but (like Ayub) had to leave upon the completion of his studies, when Basiri was six months old. This was not a unique case, of course; in *El Maestro Saharaui,* former Cuban official Regla Fernández recalls that there were a number of Cubans who made attempts to move with their partners to the Sahara, and who had to be dissuaded in light of the refugee camp context (unlike, say, Cuban-Soviet marriages [see Loss 2013; G. Pérez 2006]).[14] In any event, Brahim Breih becomes the key connector here, first meeting with Basiri in Cuba, talking about the pain of this sort of separation and promising to help deliver a letter and photographs: "I'll look for him in the camps." Later, we see Brahim deliver the letter to Slaka, who says: "I swear to God I've never stopped trying to go see him." These are emotional yet everyday scenes, of course, in Cuba and its diaspora as well as in a world full of migrants and familial separations, and, although certainly filtered through the edited film, they speak to the affective reality of transnational kinship. The storyline wraps up, finally, with Slaka actually returning to Cuba and meeting eighteen-year-old Basiri for the first time, and the emotion is filmed but not staged: "Basiri! [hugs, tears] How are you, son? Are you alright? [between tears] I'm so glad. . . . I'll be able to sleep tonight. I had this thing inside me, remorse that gave me no rest. . . . I came to see you so that you know you have a father [more kisses, tears from both, especially Slaka]. . . . That's enough, men don't cry. We're Arabs, and men. Sahrawi don't cry, alright?" (Muñoz 2011). The scene concludes with Slaka laying out a plan to spend the next twenty days with Basiri, day and night. Slaka, of course, is in the minority of Cuban-educated, in that he has been able to return to Cuba. And Basiri, of course, is Cuban rather than Arab, technically. But does it matter? What strikes one over and over in this context, from the epigraph above to this family reunion, as well as in interviews and online commentaries, is how little birthplace or formal citizenship weighs in the affective *cubanía* of Cubarauis, and how enduring that rupture.[15]

While these two cases, like others involving the Cuban children of Cuban-educated students, may seemingly legitimate the students' ties to Cuba and any claims to Cubanness, I am reluctant to play into that common-sense reading of "fictive" vs. "real" kinship between Cubarauis and Cuban kids, finding the understanding of kinship as "mutuality of being" to be more powerful. What is at stake here, as throughout the new Cuban diaspora, are lives lived, identities as process rather than as the automatic outcome of birth (K. Clarke and Thomas 2006). Is it not more productive to focus on the visible realities of with whom Cubarauis identify, feel a sense of kinship, build lives, and, in the broadest sense, support? Perhaps we already have a marker for studying some of this in thinking about the patterns of Cubaraui remittances writ large.

Rethinking Belonging: Remittances, Reciprocity, and Conciencia

Generally, the concept of "remittances" refers to money and commodities sent home by migrants in support of their kin or in preparation for a more successful future upon return, with both positive and negative changes resulting from the establishment of local remittance economies (e.g., Robert Smith 2006; Vertovec 2009). Since people transmit new practices, values, moral codes, ideologies, and interests as well as money, we have more recently been challenged to rethink the category, toward what Peggy Levitt (2001) called "social remittances" and are now often glossed as "cultural remittances" (see also Brettell 2003). Cultural remittances, for Juan Flores, are "the ensemble of ideas, values, and expressive forms introduced into societies of origin by remigrants and their families as they return 'home,' sometimes for the first time, for temporary visits or permanent re-settlement" (2009, 4). But in the Cubaraui case, as we have seen, "home" and "kin" are more complex than our common sense might suggest. Whether they migrate again or not, as Cuban-educated students re-establish themselves (often, but not always, as relatively successful professionals), we can and must take seriously their own choices in terms of where they find mutuality of being, where they look for and send support. In other words, if we examine Cubaraui identity processually and in relation to wider contemporary Cuban diasporas, we should attend to *actual* Cubaraui cultural and material remittance practices. In written texts and in the documentaries, we see evidence of remittances—of clothes, letters, money, videos (e.g., I. Pérez 2007; also see Knauer 2008)—traveling back and forth between families in the camps and Saharan students in Cuba. But thus far, we have not seen much of Cubarauis' actual postgraduate practices comparable to the Esbecan or Cuban-Sudanese cases. Here *El Maestro Saharaui* again shows us something new to consider, and again Brahim Breih is the central connector.

In the documentary, we see a series of scenes in which Brahim first recruits Cubarauis and Spaniards in Spain to help fund a *Cuban* school.[16] Brahim outlines the project, while others listen and interject approvingly:

> "As I was saying, the main project is the Cuban children's school. This week we're contacting the guys so they can pitch in. On this project the ex-students, the 'Cubarahwi,' are working as a gesture of gratitude to the Cuban Revolution."
>
> "To give something back."
>
> "Yes."
>
> "The idea is that everyone in the Cubarahwi group buys each of the one hundred Cuban students a notebook and a toy. We've given the embassy a printer and three sets of football gear with the Sahrawi logo."

In a later scene, he travels to an elementary school in Cuba named for the founder of POLISARIO where he is the central guest of a performance by the school's Cuban *pioneros*, who sing about the hero Luali Mustafa Sayed and are then addressed by Brahim. He presents them with a Saharaui flag, and says: "I'm going to explain something. This . . . is a small donation from we students who came to study in Cuba. When I returned to my country with a group of Sahrawi students, we got the idea of a project to help Cuban children. With this year's aid, we've tried to ensure that every student has a notebook, a pencil, an eraser, a ruler, a pencil sharpener, colored pencils, and a compass" (Muñoz 2011).

I have already described how Brahim reconnects with his own associates and locates Slaka's son Basiri in Santa Clara. But he also makes a trip to visit the still-functioning Saharaui ESBEC on the Isle of Youth, bringing packages from the Sahara, checking that conditions are good and that the students have items for tea and are generally well. In showing Brahim reconnecting with "fictive" Cuban kin *and* working to strengthen ties between Saharan families and Cubarauis in Cuba as well as between Cubarauis and their Cuban children—couriering letters, plane tickets, and information; chatting with students; checking up on the condition of their schools; and organizing the school sponsorship—this case illustrates not only elements of Cubaraui one-and-a-halfness, but also the multiplied kin, remittance, and reciprocity ties binding Cubarauis to each other and to their Saharan *and* Cuban kin. The focus on schools and education as sites of remittance and "giving back" illustrated here actually extends further. Another Cubaraui, Maima, has founded a successful school for women in the camps (Follina 2007); as we have seen, other Cuban-educated students are funding and building ESBEC-style schools elsewhere.

The directionality of remittances is thought-provoking; tracing Cubaraui remittances to families in camps *and* to Cuban schools and Cubans provides one way to rethink belonging and "home." But the underlying impulse "to give back" is also interesting. There are signs that the often-noted intensity of Cuban patterns of reciprocity (e.g., Rosendahl 1997) have been adopted by many Cuban-educated students. Recall Carol Berger's reported tensions between Cuban-educated Sudanese and their non-Cuban, directly diasporic kin, who felt the "Cubans" remitted *too much* back home. Cubarauis evince some of these revolutionary attitudes as well: compared to Cubans, says Mafoot, "sometimes Arab people are too concerned with money and planning for the future" (Blue_Woman 2009). And, as one of my Cubaraui informants in Havana reminded me earnestly, "there is more to life than money!"

So Brahim's drive to connect and to give back, to a Cuban school, to other former students, and to their scattered kin is not unique, but rather it echoes the *conciencia* of many Cuban-educated international students. Dare we call this "conciencia revolucionaria"? Or even "conciencia socialista"? Although it varies according to the speaker as well as, perhaps, the era, Cuban-educated students do sometimes articulate revolutionary values—often more strongly than their Cuban peers might. Take, for example, the first two sentences of *El Maestro Saharaui*, spoken by Cubaraui El Kaid Yadi: "I always carry something to remind me of Cuba, which is the Commandante [shows photo of Fidel Castro] whom we see as a father: Fidel Castro. He is a hero, an example, and truly a father" (Muñoz 2011). In any case, regardless of their individual political stance, Cubarauis, like other Cuban-educated graduates, have a revolutionary *hombre nuevo*–inflected discourse as part of their distinctive repertoire. Speaking of distinctive repertoires, I now turn back to the post-Cuban Sudanese in their process of adjusting to rural Canada. Here, the work done in Chapter 1 helps to make sense of the Cuban meanings of global styles returns, but with a twist.

A Rodeo in Alberta

Not surprisingly, following their relocation to rural Alberta, Cuban-educated Sudanese have been in an intense ongoing process of adaptation to new Canadian cultural dynamics, including rigid, monolithic racial separation and the existence of a provincial Canadian working class. In this situation, "black" and "cosmopolitan" are increasingly terms of self-identification for the Cubans (Berger, personal communication). As Berger notes, "living in a white, racist society contributes to the creation of a 'black' as opposed to Sudanese or African identity. This follows their previous, Cuban experience, in which being southern Sudanese, Dinka, Nuer or Shilluk, was overtaken by the group identity of 'Sudanese'" (2001, 206). Self-description these days can be a challenge: recall the Cuban-educated student in Alberta who described himself as doubly hyphenated (Bill Kaufmann, *Calgary Sun*, March 26, 2006).

Perhaps more surprisingly, they are also in an uneven process of renegotiating their cultural identity vis-à-vis other Sudanese, torn between impatience with pressure to conform to tribal rather than national (Sudanese) identity and "a stated desire to be 'Dinka' or relearn Dinka culture. Cassettes of recorded Dinka stories and songs were sent to the new arrivals to Canada by relatives in refugee camps in Kenya" (Berger 2001, 88). Dinka brides have arrived in Alberta—an "experiment" for the disproportionately male Cubans (Berger 2001, 114–16). Although social separations remain, the Cuban-Sudanese have come under pressure from the wider Sudanese community (in Canada and Africa both) to re-establish tribal identities, to break off close contact with fellow former students, and to literally once again become Nuers and Dinkas (Berger 2001, 79).

Berger's thick description of the Cuban-Sudanese youth ends, appropriately enough, with a "Latin Explosion" party held at Rodeo Hall on September 2, 2001. For those familiar with post-Soviet Cuban fashions, a short excerpt should suffice:

> "F" was wearing a flowing, West African-styled robe . . . heavy embroidery on the chest of the garment has been sewn into the shape of the African continent. . . . At eleven p.m., a group of women who were raised in Cuba arrived. All were wearing long, tight dresses. They greeted the young men they grew up with in Cuba with kisses on the cheek and brief embraces. . . . The music was salsa from Cuba and Brazil and all from Cuba were expert dancers. [One of the Cuban-educated women] wore a cut-off top with the logo "Tommy" across the front, a small glittery gem placed in her navel. (2001, 117–18)

While for the Canadian ethnographer the passage above really was simply thick description, a reading of this scene informed by the material of Chapter 1 suggests that the "Tommy" (Hilfiger) top is far more than just a shirt for the young woman wearing it. Recall that at the time the Sudanese were departing from Cuba at the turn of the millennium, Hilfiger wear had just surpassed Nike as the most desirable brand in the country and, I argue, was a status symbol marking the wearer's privileged position in a transnational remittance circuit.[17] Again, as Naomi Klein outlined, Hilfiger first became popular by presenting a yacht club image to poor urban youth, whose adoption of the style was then emulated by more numerous, whiter, wealthier suburbanites: "Once Tommy was firmly established as a ghetto thing, the real selling could begin—not just to the comparatively small market of poor inner-city youth but to the much larger market of middle-class white and Asian kids who mimic black style in everything from lingo to sports to music. . . . [Thus Hilfiger] feeds off the alienation at the heart of America's race relations: selling white youth on their fetishization of black style, and black youth on their fetishization of white wealth" (2000, 76). In this process, the brand reached 1990s Miami and, from there, was literally carried to Cuba alongside Nike and star-spangled stuff. But if in Havana it marked a certain remittance-privileged status, what might it mean in Alberta?

I submit that as it moves into diaspora with young Cubans and Cuban-educated Africans alike, this Tommy T-shirt has become an emotionally and symbolically saturated statement of belonging—of being *Cuban*—and of nostalgia for a recently past Cubanness as well as a sign of Cuban high fashion circa 2000. Surely it is not signifying pro-American politics here. This is, of course, my over-their-shoulder reading of a reading so local that, in Alberta, at least, it would only make sense to a few hundred people. But if you reread the sections on *yuma* fashion (Chapter 1) and on pan-African style (Chapter 2), it does make perfect sense. And one wonders, in this rodeo hall, might not one of the participants have shown up wearing US flag–patterned apparel? What would *that* mean? I am speculating now, of course, but I do not think it would be surprising to see, with now-transformed sentiments of nostalgia rather than remittance status, just as an American car from the 1950s in Miami actually marks nostalgia for Cuba (João Felipe Gonçalves, personal communication, 2011). Imagine a star-spangled bodysuit among former Cuban-educated students, now transformed into a sign of *Cubanness*. Truly, the semiotic transformation is complete: meaning *is* like a grace that descends upon the object, as Barthes put it so well.

To really consider the semiotics of style among migrants or in diaspora, one would first have to be familiar with the terrain they have moved through, in the appropriate timeframe since, as we have seen, imported brands may cross (or create) boundaries in ways unanticipated in a global or etic perspective. Doing so might in turn suggest some adjustments to ethnographic methods, but it also promises, I think, a better way of assessing belonging as affect rather than as something given by formal citizenship papers. In the end, belonging is about the meaningful *transformations* of relationships and ethnographic entanglements, not essences. Looking at branded goods in motion, this chapter proposed that even with its ethical entanglements, ethnographic work can make an important contribution here in making sense of local meanings, transnational semiotic transformations, and instabilities of identity in the world today.

* * *

What, then, does all this African-Cuban data indicate? Does the notion of a 1.5 generation fit these students? Indeed it does, although in reverse: the date and their age at time of arrival *to* Cuba, rather than their age at time of departure *from* Cuba, together with the overall length and depth of their social experience there, are the crucial factors. The younger they were when they arrived and the more centrally immersed they were in Cuban dorms and residencies, the more their hyphen tends toward the Cuban side. But in so many ways, Cuban-educated Africans uncannily reproduce the lived characteristics of the 1.5 generation. Like those in Miami and elsewhere in the Cuban diaspora, they were dislocated as adolescents, often from contexts of violence and refugee camps to a calmer and more peaceful social context; like Cuban-Americans, the date and details of their voyages to/from Cuba are emotional, often keenly recalled moments. Like other hyphenated Cubans, they are cultural translation artists, now frequently successful professionals. Like other one-and-a-halfers, they self-identify as cultural hybrids who have necessarily sought out new terms of reference for themselves. ("Cuban-American," after all, is no less a neologism than "Cubaraui" or "Esbecan.") Their cultural preferences in food, dance, dress, sports, etc. are distinctive. Like those "made in the USA," they have confronted new patterns of racialization, reciprocity, gender, and sexuality and, like the Cuban-born Pedro Pan (Conde 1999), have done all this while largely cut off from their birth-family networks.

Of course, there are differences as well: Cuban-educated Africans went to Cuba, to a revolutionary socialist system: if Cuban-American one-and-a-halfers were "born in Cuba, made in the USA," these one-and-a-halfers were "born in Africa, made in Cuba *socialista*." And most now have a secondary hyphenation many years later (e.g., Cuban-Canadian-Sudanese; Ghanaian-Esbecan-American), becoming truly world citizens and serial migrants. But none of these differences undermine the central elements of the 1.5 paradigm. That they have not been embraced as hyphenated Cubans within the diaspora is no doubt partly due to their small number and global dispersal, but (despite the explicitly anti-essentialist position of both

Rumbaut and Pérez Firmat) it may also still rest on an underlying linkage of "real" identity to one's place of birth rather than to a process of lived social relations. Or perhaps it may speak to a *longue dureé* of elite ambivalence about the "Africanization" of Cuban culture (Helg 1995; Ferrer 1999).

In any case, in this chapter, I have explored the dizzying migration of three small groups of Cuban-educated students from Africa to Cuba and back, or onward, not only to push Pérez Firmat's notion of life on the hyphen into new terrain, but also to rethink the seemingly clear boundedness of cultural Cubanness as lived and remitted and not simply given by paper status. The grounds for considering only *emigration* from Cuba, only hyphens attaching to an original islandness, are exposed as essentializing. By their multinational ties of kinship and mutuality of being, as by their subsequent choices in terms of where and how to "give back," to whom to reciprocate, we see that Cuban-educated students are entangled in *both* African and Cuban kinship and remittance networks for the long haul. The issue here is *not* whether they are "really" Cuban—a claim they do not themselves make—for they are also "really" Saharan, Ghanaian, Sudanese, and more. Not one of them is simply "Cuban." Nor is the issue which side of their hyphen is which or assigning some magic proportion of Cuban to Saharanness/Ghanaianess/Sudaneseness, etc. It is, rather, that they really have been deeply shaped by the lived experience of many years spent in revolutionary Cuba as well as by their birth societies in Ghana, South Sudan, the refugee camps of Tindouf, or any of the thirty-plus African nations that sent students to Cuba, for that matter. It is in attending to that actual experience—not in essences, genetics, heritage, or history—that we see that identity is more *process* than birthright and that these extraordinary Cuban-educated people are complexly working out kinship, home, and belonging betwixt and between, reflecting a consciousness of peoplehood with respect to, not an imagined nation, but a lived experience of stark rupture, startling contrasts, and uncommon movement. Born in Africa, made in Cuba, perhaps now residing in Alberta, South Carolina, or Madrid, these young men and women thoroughly embarrass any category they are put in. And that is the point: it is not ultimately about cultural authenticity or asserting an island-bound "culture," but about showing both the artifice and the enduring power of such boundaries in geographies of imagination and geographies of management. The question is not, then, just whether these are "real" African-Cubans, but whether there really is such a thing as "Cuban."

Do Nuer-Dinka-New-Sudanese-Cuban-Canadians, for instance, have the right to call themselves Cuban? Certainly, as much as anyone. There have been many media stories about these young professionals returning to South Sudan, as we have seen. But perhaps a more interesting question is: will they ever return *to Cuba*, and how will they be welcomed back—as Africans, as *yumas*, or as Cubans—by those left behind, and who they are remembering with such longing as they bring salsa dancing to Alberta?

CONCLUSION
GEOGRAPHIES OF IMAGINATION

This book has sought to advance the scholarly understanding of contemporary Cuban society—in *both* its distinctiveness as the sole state socialist system in the hemisphere *and* its simultaneous *longue durée* postplantation, postcolonial Caribbeanness. Cuban society, I have argued, becomes distinctively visible in its people's everyday mappings of a rapidly encroaching world and their changing place in it. Thus, for example, despite its changing but persistent political standoff with the United States and despite distinctive state controls, over the past twenty years, Cuba has fundamentally shifted from an agricultural mode of production (of sugarcane) to today's tourism and transnational remittance-based economy—a change that precisely mirrors transformations in the Caribbean at large (Black 2001). And thus, readers familiar with *both* the postcolonial Caribbean and socialist or formerly state-socialist societies might well recognize here kinships with Cuba. I also hope that Cuban readers might see themselves here, not unsympathetically, but through the eyes of someone who has long worked to understand their society accurately and to represent it as honestly as possible.

Beginning with the uncanny way in which a ubiquitously commonsense Cuban tale is also Haitian and a vignette contrasting my early disorientation in Cuba with that experienced by a long-term resident taken out of the republic, one can also read the text as an argument for the value of long-term, close-contact ethnographic fieldwork. The book ultimately proposes that through both state action and everyday aspiration—in the relation between a geography of management and a geography of desire (Trouillot 2003)—the ostensibly national category "Cuban" has, in effect, itself become a racialized term, as mapped against putative purities imagined to be elsewhere. In this sense, both Trouillot and I are following the oft-cited insight of Arjun Appadurai: "The imagination has now acquired a singular new power in social life," and the task of ethnography has indeed become "the unraveling of a conundrum: what is the nature of locality as a lived experience in a globalized . . . world?" (1996, 52, 53). In this book, I have fundamentally focused on the two imagined elsewheres that, although not exhaustive (the Soviet Union and Spain, here woven into the text, come to mind), have been the most ethnographically accessible in the post-Soviet era. The first of these, glossed as La Yuma, is, as we have seen, a particularly socialist popular idealization with a distinctively New World racialization. This dehybridized space in the Cuban geographic imagination, La Yuma—both a popular term for the United States and an idealized capitalist world—is accessed primarily by examining the appropriation and idealization of symbols and goods from the USA and places contemporary transformations of aesthetic value in relation to Cuba's post-Soviet crisis. Brands such as Nike and Hilfiger, symbols such as the US flag, and spectacles such as the Oscars all carry associations with La Yuma to the extent that local industries and imitative branding have emerged, flourished, and eventually declined as La Yuma has been both domesticated and critiqued. The desires, appropriations, and local resignifications are complex, as we have seen. Indeed, the too-facile equation of the deployment of the US flag and Hilfiger brands with simple opposition to the Cuban state or self-identification with blackness is belied by a more thickly ethnographic reading. In fact, Cuban deployments of these global symbols are often only intelligible with local knowledge—the swoosh on the sock, the unexpected meanings that a flag may carry in an emergent remittance economy. Although it would be equally mistaken to fetishize the "local" to the exclusion of properly acknowledging imported "global" values, here too, one may certainly read this text as an argument for the value of close, careful observation in curtailing misleading generalities and poor theorizations. To put it another way, presuming that fashionable star-spangled Obama t-shirts visible in Cuba today signify an uncomplicated, obvious pro-Americanism is akin to US analysts' disastrous assessments of Cuban popular sentiment in 1961 as "anti-Castro" (see Ryer 2014).

If La Yuma represents the personal embrace of capitalist style, the second imagined elsewhere, África, is its antipolitics, carrying connotations of socialist ideology, poverty, and even erasure, and, thus, I investigated this other "originary" stock, taking África to represent Cuban ideologies about Africa. Certainly Mbembe's reading that "narrative about Africa is always a pretext for a comment about something else" (2001, 2–3) is a good starting point. But how might Cuba's own Marxist, postcolonial position and unusually close contemporary contact with Africa and Africans—four hundred thousand Cubans having served internationalist missions in Africa and tens of thousands of African students having been long-term residents of the revolutionary republic—alter his argument?

As we have seen in painful detail, many, many Cubans described their emotionally laden experience in Africa as an encounter with a primitive, barbaric, and underdeveloped world. Looking at "development" discourse as part of a wider evolutionist ideology harkening back through Marx and Morgan to the old European scale of savagery, barbarism, and civilization, despite common coexisting affirmations of Cuban-African solidarity and kinship such as Castro's "We are a Latin *African* nation," Mbembe's point is well-taken. África as such cannot possibly be real. Rather, it only makes sense as an imagined and dehybridized geography against which Cubans can and do define themselves and their Cubanness. That since the end of the war in Angola and the end of the Soviet era África has receded as an explicit object of discourse does not mean that it lacks a place in the Cuban imagination; it is still present if even as a symbol of poverty, blackness, and socialism that many would prefer to leave silent or to resignify, particularly in a tourist economy. In the end, these disparate elsewheres support an understanding of national categories as racialized, wherein "Cubanness" is not presumptively black or white, but brown, in contrast to the presumedly nonhybrid spaces of La Yuma and África.

Keeping in mind that this project is a study of Cubanness rather than an ethnography of African students (although international students provide a key lens through which the former emerges in a distinctive light), the book then examined Cuban-educated students as comprising a "1.5 generation," but one with an inverted hyphen and an acquired, rarely recognized Cubanness. In other words, just as Cuban emigrants become Cuban-Americans, African immigrants become Sudanese-Cubans, Ghanaian-Cubans, Saharan-Cubans, or similar hyphenations, even after they leave Cuba and return "home" or serially migrate again. In pushing the boundaries of what it means to be Cuban, Cuban-educated Africans illustrate the complexities of kinship and belonging even as they now send remittances to those they recognize as kin in Cuba and to their birth families and as they further adapt the meanings of the fashions and brands they once wore in Cuba.

This panorama of contemporary Cuban emplacements in a racialized global geography and the mixed-up racial and national patterns of daily life in Cuba and its diasporas has perhaps led to more questions than it has answered. As Clifford Geertz famously commented,

> Cultural analysis is intrinsically incomplete. And, worse than that, the more deeply it goes the less complete it is. It is a strange science whose most telling assertions are its most tremulously based, in which to get somewhere with the matter at hand is to intensify the suspicion, both your own and that of others, that you are not quite getting it right. But that, along with plaguing subtle people with obtuse questions, is what being an ethnographer is like. (1973, 22)

Clearly, trying to *prove* a thesis through ethnographic elaboration is an aporetic endeavor. Thick description can *illustrate* a theoretical point, perhaps, but, in the end, the best rationale for ethnography and all its years of effort, cost, and dislocation, may be that, with its real-world examples, its strength is the capacity to challenge poorly founded theories and superficial presumptions like those displayed in the parade of recent media images of star-spangle-clad Cubans.

Ultimately, the material of this book suggests that, as in other Caribbean and New World societies (Whitten and Torres 1998), in Cuba, the national category Cuban is imagined as mestizo, mulato, mixed, or brown compared to imagined elsewheres such as La Yuma and África. In this light, José Martí's previously cited quote, "the Cuban is more than white, more than mulatto, more than black," and Ortiz's variation, "there are Cubans so dark they seem black, and there are Cubans so light they seem white" (quoted in Pérez Sarduy and Stubbs 1993, 233), resonate strongly. But they beg the question: if the local *here* is hybrid, it is only so by making *elsewhere* pure, and that is why an interrogation of the dehybridized, imagined spaces of África and La Yuma is so important. In his last major work, Trouillot proposed a re-examination of the relation of the geography of management and the geography of imagination that jointly underpinned the rise of global capitalism and the legitimacy of the West as the universal unmarked (2003, 45). A cursory answer to the question of how Cuba is racialized would likely describe a geography of management: state policies, economic structures and scarcities, the reproduction of historical silences. These have surely all contributed to the racialization of the nation. But there is also at play here a geography of imagination: the painful and contested categories and divisions of daily life, imaginary far-off purities, motivating silences and desires. Together, the two geographies have shaped a nation and defined its color, not by the colors of its flag, but as the midpoint of a global racial scale. Perhaps someday Marx will be proved right, and within some future mode of production, race will disappear. But before that day, the very notion of nation must also necessarily disappear, for that distinction, too, is one of race, writ large.

NOTES

INTRODUCTION

1. Unless otherwise noted, or in the case of public events or figures (such as Professor Trouillot), names and identifying details have been rearranged to protect the identity of the speaker.

2. Such paradoxes are well summarized by a Cuban parable which has circulated for decades:

   > [The President of the United States] sent a spy team to Cuba to gather facts for his anti-Cuba campaign. The team returned several months later with much data but no conclusions. The President, furious at the waste of time and money, asked why.
   >
   > "It's like this Mr. President," explained the team leader. "In Cuba there's no unemployment but nobody works. Nobody works but they always overfulfill their production goals. All the goals are overfulfilled but there's nothing to buy. There's nothing to buy but everybody has all they need. Everybody has everything but everybody's always complaining. Everybody complains but everybody goes to the square to pledge their lives for Cuba and Fidel, and then they go home and complain some more. So you see Mr. President, we have lots of data but no conclusions." (Benjamin, Collins, and Scott 1984, 81)

3. In this work, Benítez-Rojo is directly applying the insights of *A Thousand Plateaus* (Deleuze and Guattari 1988).

4. Throughout this book I will italicize all Spanish words or short phrases, followed by my translation as appropriate. In general, these italicized words should then be understood to reference *Cuban* categories. For longer translations from print-media sources, I will put English in the main text with the Spanish original reproduced in footnote form. Unless otherwise noted, translations are my own. Conversational exchanges reproduced in English may reflect modifications made to protect the individual identities of speakers as well as to condense and clarify the exchange.

5. To be clear, these geographies are not the *only* ones one could productively study! As we will see, places like Spain and the Soviet Union have their own particular places in the Cuban everyday as well.

6. Anthropologists have long considered the relationship between space and place and for the most part concur that "*space* is constituted by individuals' practices within particular places" rather than the reverse (Certeau 1984, quoted in Allen 2011, 21).

7. This was in 1979, during the second Duvalier dictatorship, Hurricanes David and Frederick, and the height of the exodus of the so-called "Haitian boat people."

8. Much influenced by works along the lines of Noam Chomsky's *Managua Lectures* (Chomsky 1987), I was not entirely indifferent to concurrent *Soviet* imperialism in eastern Europe or central Asia. Nevertheless, it was difficult to escape the binarism of the era, and I generally interpreted the Caribbean through a World Systems worldview (Frank 1970; Wallerstein 1976). But even at this early stage, one generally overlooked difference between Cuban and eastern European socialism seemed important: T-72s do not float. That is, any military threat to Cuba was and had long been from the empire next door, the United States, rather than from the much more distant Soviet Union. This distinctive relationship between socialist ideology and the culture of Cuban national identity may well resolve a reality inexplicable to mainstream academic theories and theorists—the survival of the socialist state in Cuba more than two decades after the fall of the Berlin Wall.

9. During the summer of 1994, an estimated thirty thousand Cuban *balseros* (rafters) set out for the United States on homemade rafts, leading to mass detentions in the Guantánamo Bay Naval Base, and new migration accords between the two governments.

10. Travel to Cuba was restricted under the Trading with the Enemy Act. This act effectively controls travel through the Office of Foreign Assets Control (OFAC), a branch of the US Department of the Treasury, on the grounds that the expenditure of US currency in Cuba would prop up an enemy regime and thus pose a risk to national security.

11. This was related to the notorious closing of the Cuban Center for American Studies (CEA), which has been exhaustively described in the problematic book *El caso CEA: Intelectuales e inquisidores en Cuba ¿Perestroika en la Isla?* by Maurizio Giuliano (1998). Dismantled for its critical work and too-close contacts with American academics, CEA is an area studies center equivalent (and physically adjacent) to CEAMO, where I had intended to affiliate. Each of these centers reports directly to the Communist Party of Cuba (the PCC, or simply, the "Party"). In light of this event, I was widely advised to avoid close contact with CEAMO in order to spare them further scrutiny, and, in the end, it was fortunate for us all that I had not already obtained an affiliation there.

12. This *carné* also permitted access to the subsidized transportation and ticket prices of the peso economy, which was not significant economically as much as it was transformative in contacts with everyday Cubans—particularly the many who were reluctant to be seen as hustling tourists—and it allowed me to interact in myriad ways otherwise off-limits to tourists and short-term visitors.

13. While anthropologists, like social scientists from other disciplines, do conduct interviews, we take to heart James Brown's insight that *sayin' it* and *doin' it* are often two different things, and we generally are wary of using interview data in a decontextualized manner. Thus, the excerpted interviews and ethnographic vignettes in this book are generally followed by substantial analysis of the broader cultural context.

14. In dealing with this issue in a very different field context, Ira Bashkow writes: "How [westerners] appear to Orokaiva differs markedly from how we appear to ourselves, since the version of us they see is constructed from *their* cultural standpoint and rendered meaningful in their cultural terms" (2006, 255; emphasis in original).

15. For more on the difference between Anglo-American and Cuban "white," see Chapter 3.

16. If my accent did not clarify the matter, once introduced or conversing with someone I would of course explain my nationality and, importantly, my residency status. The latter was often helpful in that being a student resident generally held a positive value and permitted more confidence than if I had either been in Cuba as a tourist or on a research visa. The striking lack of hostility toward US citizens on the part of the Cuban people has been the subject of much comment by travel writers and visitors to the island (e.g., T. Miller 1996, 20). Indeed, at least before the 2014 rapprochement led to greatly increased US travel, finding an American was often an opportunity for an animated discussion about a brother in Miami, an uncle in LA, the latest Hollywood movies, or Cuban players in the Major Leagues.

17. To clarify, discussion of specific events of *conspiración* as such, as conspiracies, has long been Cuban; to consider such discussion as representative of a genre or modality, as conspiracy theory, is my own device. In Cuba, such narratives would be called *teorías de conspiración* only in a very academic setting. In everyday use, they would be roughly grouped as a subset of *intriga*. In popular contexts analogous to those in the United States in which "conspiracy theory" is dismissive, in Havana one would hear phrases—the very number and variety of which speak to the prevalence of the modality in vernacular discourse— such as the following: "¡Oye, como te gusta la intriga!"; "¡Chico/a, pero mira que tú inventas!"; "¡Qué cuento es ese [fulano/a]!"; "¡Ay niño/a pero déjate de cuentos!"; "¡Óyeme este/a niño/a, pero qué imaginación tú tienes!"; "¡Oye

como te gusta el enredo!"; "¡Déjate de intriga, anda!"; "Oye, para mi que tú eres chivato, chico, porque tú siempre tienes una explicación pa' todo"; "¡Ay hijo/a, no compliques más las cosas!"; "¡Oye, tú eres la intriga misma!"; or "¡Coñó mi hijito/a, qué teje'maneje!" (Iván Noel Pérez, personal communication, 2014).

18. For a fascinating study in how conspiratorial explanation becomes "self-sealing," see Bavelas in Watzlawick (1977, 48–50); for an excellent analysis of recent Cuban conspiracist theorizing, see Humphreys (2012).

19. Former Secretary of Defense Robert MacNamara has publicly acknowledged such conspiracies (Rather 1996), in this case vindicating long-standing theories regarding anti-Cuban CIA operations. On the same program, Grayston Lynch, CIA Brigade 2506 Commander, describes some 2,104 missions of sabotage and warfare conducted against Cuba under the infamous Operation Mongoose following the debacle of the Bay of Pigs. Operations such as the Bay of Pigs and Mongoose provide the general backdrop for the Cuban state's use of the conspiracy modality. Paranoia within reason, indeed.

20. Although common among Cuba researchers (e.g., Carter 2000, 20), this strategy was doomed in the sense that any real spy would doubtless operate in the same manner. For the record, I am not an agent of any state, nor have I been paid by any state, nor have I collected any information for any organization or with the goal of damaging either the Cuban people or their government. My aspiration, rather, has been for "a ruthless criticism of everything existing" (Karl Marx, quoted in Tucker 1978). This is not to deny that, given the politicized context that surrounds this work, there are not some careful silences here, as Cubans and colleagues alike will realize. When asked about censorship in the Cuban cinema, the renowned director Tomás Gutiérrez Alea once insightfully commented that there is censorship of some kind everywhere—if not by the state, then by the market ("Cuban cinema pokes fun at tough reality," *Reuters*, November 1, 1999); analogously, there are surely public or scholarly silences in US discourse as glaring as any in Cuba.

21. Researchers have come to an array of conclusions about this, ranging from Mona Rosendahl's assertion that "As in all political systems, the person who lives a quiet life within the limits of the system has nothing to fear. Conformity guarantees freedom, which is the essence of effective social control" (1997, 159), to Sean Brotherton (2012, 138–44) and Katherine Hagedorn's nuanced reflections on the topic (2001, 21–39) and much more tense if not paranoid readings of surveillance and resistance expressed in particular encounters (e.g., Hirschfeld 2007, 84; Weinreb 2009, 49–51). One of the complicating factors in these encounters is that the state has so thoroughly penetrated "dissident" circles, which are largely unknown to and atypical of average citizens, that to

be approached by someone like Amelia Rosenberg Weinreb's Elena (2009, chapter 2) is quite possibly a state security test of one's own attitude toward dissidence in general. In any event, while I did have such encounters, I found them convoluted, atypical of everyday conversation, and most productive to avoid (Hofstadter 1965).

22. See *etnocuba.ucr.edu/?p=1288*.

23. I once had a conversation with a US diplomat in Havana, whose express goal was to identify and highlight the "repression" of the Cuban system, which he freely admitted that he had never found, and no one ever would find, Cubans missing fingernails or similarly tortured, but that control in Cuba was "more subtle" (Charles Blaha, personal communication). Yes, state power could be frustratingly capricious in the experience of Cubans I knew, but compare this to the sometimes spectacular violence of US-supported regimes elsewhere in Latin America and the Caribbean. In other words, relative to neighboring regimes, undue terror of state power never seemed particularly distinctive to Cuban daily life: I once watched a driver passionately argue a speeding ticket with a policeman for well over an hour; eventually I was somewhat concerned for the safety of the cop, who was unarmed.

24. Put another way, each international researcher most likely has two files, one in Havana and the other in Washington (Garton Ash 1997). Katherine Verdery's recent examination of her own file from the Romanian secret police archives provides a thought-provoking comparative case (2014).

25. Notable travel accounts include Columbus (1989), Alexander von Humboldt (Humboldt et al. 1998), Richard Henry Dana (1859), Joseph J. Dimrock (L. Pérez 1998a), Maturin Ballou (1897), Langston Hughes (1993), Jean-Paul Sartre (1961), José Yglesias (1968), Lee Chadwick (1975), Carlo Gébler (1988), Tom Miller (1996), and Isadora Tattlin (2002), among many others (also see Luis Pérez [1992], *Slaves, Sugar, and Colonial Society: Travel Accounts of Cuba, 1801–1899*, and Luis Martínez-Fernández [1998], *Fighting Slavery in the Caribbean: The Life and Times of a British Family in Nineteenth-Century Havana*).

26. The title "Third Discoverer" was coined by Juan Marinello, as cited in the prologue to *Etnia y sociedad* (Ortiz and Barreal 1993, x). In many ways, Ortiz's position in Cuba parallels that of his contemporary and colleague Jean Price-Mars, the foundational figure of Haitian ethnology. Note, however, that the Anthropological Society of Cuba had already been founded by Luis Montané y Dardé, among others, in 1877 (Guanche Pérez 1983, chapter 8).

27. Ortiz's sister-in-law Lydia Cabrera (1899–1991) is undoubtedly the second most frequently cited Cuban ethnographer. Educated in Paris from 1927 to 1938, Cabrera returned to the island with a newfound dedication to Cuban religious

practices (e.g., Cabrera 1975). A third contemporary, New York–educated folk-lorist Rómulo Lachatañeré (1909–1952), is best known for his collection of West African-derived myths and parables (Lachatañeré 1992a, 1992b).

28. For an overview of revolutionary Cuban archeology, see Curet, Dawdy, and La Rosa Corso (2005), *Dialogues in Cuban Archaeology*. Physical anthropology endured in part owing to the efforts of Manuel Rivero de la Calle (1926–2001), who persevered for many years within the School of Biology at the University of Havana (e.g., Rivero de la Calle 1984).

29. *www.revista-batey.com/index.php/batey.*

30. For further detail, see Ryer 2000a.

31. "I use the words 'inspiration' and 'inspired' when writing about the African-inspired societies of Palo and Ocha/Santo . . . instead of 'African-derived,' which is common among researchers but implies people and the materials they engage to an originary and inescapable African essence to which it is beholden" (Ochoa 2010, 6).

32. Also see Duany 1999; Burke 2001; Behar 2002; Carter 2007; Perry 2008; Hansing 2009; Ryer 2010; Daniel 2011.

33. There are many additional worthwhile volumes on the arts in Cuba that are based on other research methods (e.g., Chávez and Chakarova 2005).

CHAPTER 1

1. In Trouillot's formulation, the North Atlantic geography of imagination is an ideological byproduct of the internal narrative of modernity for which chronological primacy is a central tenet (2003, 43). In this sense, Cuban notions of development and underdevelopment which frame La Yuma and África are exemplary—deriving, as we will see, from European ideas about the move from savagery to civilization over time, wherein a local Cuba is projected against that background. By "geography of management," Trouillot means to highlight modernization and those material and organizational features of world capitalism in specific locales, which create places for explicitly political or economic purposes (2003, 37). Presuming that the Cuban state would fit this model—Cuba has certainly been increasingly re-inscribed within global capitalism since the Soviet era—one might equally point to the state's deployment of race-silencing strategies or deployment of *internacionalistas* to Africa as elements of a specific socialist geography of management.

2. For the sake of clarity, I will capitalize La Yuma as a spatial term, but not *el/un/una/la/las* or *los yumas* when these refer to people or are used as adjectives.

3. L. Kaifa Roland notes that while *yumas* are to be envied, they are also seen as somewhat stupid, at least in the way they navigate Cuban realities.

Interestingly, she also describes Cubans identifying her as a *yuma* by smell (2011, 78).

4. The intriguing exception to this state of exclusion would be the US naval base at Guantánamo Bay, which, in addition to functioning as a camp for Al Qaeda detainees à la Agamben (1998), also includes Cuba's only McDonald's.

5. As we will see, Jacqueline Loss explores more recent Cuban nostalgia for the Soviet Union (Loss 2011, 2013; Loss and Prieto González 2012); also see "Nostalgia de Misha," a special issue of *La Gaceta de Cuba* (Anonymous 2010); G. Pérez (2006); Peter Orsi "Restaurante brinda homenaje a la ex unión soviética en La Habana," *El Nuevo Herald*, August 24, 2014; Nora Gámez Torres, "Cubanos de Miami tienen nostalgia por productos rusos," *El Nuevo Herald*, November 14, 2014).

6. In the same vernacular register as *yuma*, Miami Cubans (but not other diasporic Cubans) are often specifically referenced as *comunitarios* or *de la comunidad*. Both of these terms derived from a change in official discourse in the partial rapprochement of the late 1970s, when the state began to refer to the Cuban exile as "la comunidad cubana en exterior," rather than as "gusanos." Interestingly, Cuban emigrants often jokingly replace or rhyme "La Yuma" with or to "La Llama" (used here in the sense of a burning fire) to index the shock of discovering just how hard they have to work and how difficult life in capitalism turns out to be. "¡Asere, esto no es La Yuma, esto es La Llama!" The expression is known but not common on the island.

7. The eastern German term *Möchtegerns*, literally "would-bes," is used to describe recently successful upwardly mobile locals (Veenis 1999, 81). Kaifa Roland notes that even Cuban-born foreign residents can ultimately become *yumas* (2004, 239, 89–91), and Marc Perry discusses one rare case in which a bilingual black Cuban was able to pass for one (2004, 180).

8. Although Adidas and Reebok (also desirable *yuma* goods) were by then legally available for purchase in dollar shops, Nike shoes, shirts, or hats were distinctly more popular: if all *cosas más yuma* are good, some are clearly more good than others! This is, I argue, related to the "remittance circuit" I describe later in this chapter.

9. Such imitative branding has become so distinctive since the mid-1990s that post-millennium the term *michi-michi* emerged to describe brand-imitating goods such as fake Nike shoes, the belts in the artisans' market, and the like. Partly taking the semantic space of the earlier socialist-era term *chapucería* described earlier, *michi-michi* refers to something that is fake, unoriginal, inferior, or even trashy. It can also be used to describe someone who tries too hard to dress slickly. Etymologically, the term is often believed to come from the English-language term "Mickey Mouse" and certainly has similar connotations

(also see Pertierra 2011, 29). Interestingly, there is an inverse Miami-based industry making US or Dominican-based knockoffs of Cuban-branded products—for example, Cubita coffee, Cohiba cigars, and Hatuey malta, among others (Ryer 2011).

10. For a more thorough historicization of the allure and consumption of North American goods, services, brands, and movies before the 1959 Revolution see "Fichu Menocal," in Geldof (1991); Hermer and May (1941, chapter 2); Rosalie Schwartz's *Pleasure Island: Tourism and Temptation in Cuba* (1997); Levi and Heller's *Cuba Style* (2002); and especially Luis Pérez's *On Becoming Cuban* (1999, 279–353). For a comprehensive recent ethnographic study of Cuban consumption, see Pertierra (2011); also see Weinreb (2009).

11. "The first time Gary Buxton went to Havana, Cuba, to play softball two years ago, he brought New York Yankees hats. This time, he's bringing Old Glory" (Murphy and Murphy, *Metro West Daily News*, October 31, 2011). Occasionally, one might also see the patterns of the Union Jack or the Stars and Bars of the Confederacy, but the Stars and Stripes is by far the dominant motif of this style (although see fig. 1.4).

12. Note that this was a local discussion, *not* an official Party-wide policy.

13. Thus this is *not* a struggle for the ordinary, as D. Miller and Woodward argue is the case for the enduring popularity of blue jeans in the United Kingdom (2011).

14. The Grammy, and more recently Latin Grammy, awards generate nearly as much interest. Chucho Valdés and Los Van Van have been Cuban winners; Cuban musicians in diaspora (e.g., Celia Cruz, Gloria Estefan, Arturo Sandoval) are often noted as well. Indeed, both the Grammy and Oscar awards are at the pinnacle of the aforementioned emphasis on US movies and music (e.g., see *Cuban Grammy Winners* 2001; Pertierra 2009).

15. Ironically, Hilfiger's popularity in Havana follows from a clever US marketing campaign tying "yacht club" and "ghetto" styles. "Once Tommy was firmly established as a ghetto thing, the real selling could begin—not just to the comparatively small market of poor inner-city youth, but to the much larger market of middle-class white and Asian kids who mimic black style in everything from lingo to sports to music. . . . [Thus Hilfiger] feeds off the alienation at the heart of America's race relations: selling white youth on their fetishization of black style, and black youth on their fetishization of white wealth" (N. Klein 2000, 76).

16. With the opening of shopping centers and sporting goods stores selling hard-currency goods principally imported through Panama, a limited selection of North American brands like Nike and Hilfiger became available in "*la chopin*"

(hard-currency state shops) often in both "real" and *michi-michi* versions. Indeed, North American goods have proliferated:

> Pop-Tarts, Marlboro Lights, Sprite, Green Giant green beans, Jell-O pudding mix, Chiclets, Tabasco sauce, Bayer aspirin, Jack Daniel's Whiskey, Fruit of the Loom T-shirts, Tampax tampons, Revlon Flex shampoos and conditioners, Brut cologne for men, Kit-Kat, Reese's Pieces, Pringles potato chips, Gerber baby food, Dole canned pineapples, Pepto-Bismol, Dial bath soap, Dum-Dum lollipops. . . .
>
> These are just some of the U.S. products manufactured either by U.S. foreign subsidiaries or in the United States, then shipped through a third country . . . to Cuba. It isn't as if you could enter any store and stroll through isle upon isle [sic] packed with American brands. But each store carries a few items. (Corbett 2002, 130; also see Tattlin 2002, 78–79)

Such goods, sold only to those with convertible Cuban pesos (CUC), are largely alimentary, inconsistently available, and do not have the ubiquity or brand recognition of Nike or Hilfiger wear.

17. Also see Perry (2009). More recently, of course, reggetón has become more prevalent than rap.

18. This would have been the 9th US Volunteer Regiment's band (Rebecca Scott, personal communication; also see Sublette 2004, 324).

19. This is an excellent demonstration of Daniel Miller's observation that "societies have an extraordinary capacity either to consider objects as having attributes which may not appear as evident to outsiders, or else altogether to ignore attributes which would have appeared to those same outsiders as being inextricably part of that object" (1987, 109; see also Foster 2008, 29). Very few *yumas* would associate a can of Coke with Cuban entrepreneurship in the way that a Cuban might. Similarly for Nike, much of what "Nike" connotes internationally (its celebrity spokespeople and inspirational television commercials, as well as anti-globalization protests against the appalling labor conditions in its factories) is absent from the Cuban vernacular space "Nike" occupies.

20. "I liked the spirit of Cuba, but now it's like Miami. Very commercial. They don't even dress like before. They dress like they're in Miami Beach" (Italian fashion photographer Fabio Fasolini, quoted in Lydia Martin, *Havana Journal*, June 12, 2003).

21. Indeed, the 1990s idealization of La Yuma and its goods uncannily mirrors the idealizations of Cuban socialism in an earlier North American scholarship as well as more recent but equally reductive popular North American nostalgizations of Cuban reality such as those evident in the turn-of-the-millennium cigar craze and the film *Buena Vista Social Club* (Wenders 1999; also see Hernández-Reguant 2009, 13; Pertierra 2011, 246).

22. Many ethnographers have noted extensive social networks (referred to as *quanxi, blat, sociolismo,* etc.), distinctive patterns of reciprocity, and the circulation of certain prestige goods as characteristic of the state socialist societies in which they have worked from China to Estonia, East Germany to Cuba (e.g., Yang 1994; Verdery 1996, 22; Rosendahl 1997). Daphne Berdahl noted that, ironically, "some of the very products that sustain elaborate networks of friends and contacts under socialism are seen to be 'driving us apart' in the new market economy" (1999, 136). In *Dreaming in Russian: The Cuban Soviet Imaginary,* Loss opens with a story of recent Cuban nostalgia for simple Soviet-era underwear, which surely illustrates the semiotic processes by which *yuma* goods have lost their luster; in Peircian terms, the qualisigns are being transformed (Fehérváry 2012).

23. To reiterate, the context of *yuma* ideologies in Cuba was first one of scarce and shoddy socialist goods, culminating in the desperate crisis of the early 1990s; as the economic situation improved through the later 1990s, Western goods flowed in along with guarded optimism (Tattlin 2002, 196; Hernández-Reguant 2004). Unfortunately, if perhaps predictably, the recovery has been uneven, with variable access to hard currency and remittances. The resulting disillusionment and bitterness are now only accelerated by new distributional inequalities and limited opportunities that exist despite gradually improving conditions, including enhanced ties with Venezuela and China and rebuilt ones with Russia and Russian tourists. I am arguing, then, that this background correlates closely with the 1990s rise and 2010s decline of La Yuma as a vernacular cartography.

24. One might also analyze the extent to which contemporary Cuba is comparable to or different from a wider Caribbean context by briefly considering the hurricane as a social process. In this context, the very quantifiability of a cyclone makes clear the broad point that distinctive elements of a centralized command economy remain in place in Cuba today and are socially significant. Millions of Cubans are regularly mobilized and forcibly evacuated upon the approach of a hurricane, and "since 2001, sixteen hurricanes and tropical storms have hit Cuba, causing a total of only 35 deaths. Compare this to the 1,836 deaths in the U.S. as a result of Hurricane Katrina" alone ("Cuba Offers Valuable Lessons in Hurricane Preparedness," *Uprising Radio,* August 28, 2012; also see "Abandona Cuba el huracán Charley y avanza hacia la Florida," *Granma digital,* August 2004; Orfilio Pelaez and Haydee Leon, "Cuba Demonstrates Its High Degree of Preparation for Confronting Nature's Adversities," *Granma International,* October 24, 2005). The contrast is even more striking between Cuba and other nations in the region, where hurricanes from David to Frederic

to Georges to Mitch to Jeanne have killed hundreds or thousands. I would argue that *both* the high level of civil preparedness *and* the relative vulnerability of Havana's architecture reflect socialist planning priorities and the socialist structure of scarcity in Cuba.

25. Until the 1990s, the official peso-to-dollar exchange rate was strictly controlled at 1:1. In the early 1990s, the actual black market rate shot up to 120:1. Since the mid-1990s, one US dollar or convertible Cuban peso (CUC) has traded for between twenty and thirty Cuban pesos (CUP, or *moneda nacional*; CUP$ or MN$). Cuban salaries average between four hundred and eight hundred pesos per month.

26. While this varies, it is approximately six pounds of rice, forty ounces of beans, six pounds of sugar, four ounces of coffee, six eggs, one or two servings of chicken or fish, per person, per month. Several times per year, there are special offerings such as a half-liter of cooking oil. Some Cuban-produced foods (mainly oranges, cabbage, and potatoes) are available seasonally at subsidized prices (for more see Garth 2012, 2013). As economist Ana Julia Jatar-Hausmann has argued, such subsidies must be taken into account when calculating the value of Cuban salaries. Her formula, "real salary = 160 + 9W-160/UE," where 160 is the average value of subsidized goods available to a family of four, W is the monthly salary, and UE is the unofficial exchange rate, is a significant if imperfect step toward depoliticizing these statistics (1999, 113–15). For a comparison with Soviet-era food distribution, see Rosendahl (in Benjamin, Collins, and Scott 1984; Rosendahl 1997), and for a more recent update, see Padrón Hernández 2012.

27. Here is another variation of the parable of Cuban paradoxes cited at the beginning of the Introduction, as published in the *Atlantic Monthly*:

> Making sense of Cuba's economy is not easy. There's a joke I heard when I was in Havana recently: The CIA sends an agent down to live in Cuba and report back on the state of the economy. He returns six months later, babbling, and is carted off to an asylum. "I don't get it," he mutters over and over. "There's no gasoline, but the cars are still running. There's no food in the stores, but everyone cooks dinner every night. They have no money, they have nothing at all—but they drink rum and go dancing." (Gordon 1997, 18)

28. *Socio*, literally, associate, workmate, friend, or business partner; also see the Martinique's *débrouillard* (Browne and Salter 2004) and the Dominican Republic's *tigueraje* (Padilla 2007). Despite a slightly disreputable connotation, the term implies a reliable relationship or contact. The revolutionary slogan "*socialismo o muerte*" (socialism or death) is often wryly rephrased "*sociolismo o muerte*" (have a friend or die).

29. *Particular*: someone working independently, and in many industries, illegally.

30. One North American resident of Cuba has an in-depth description of this pattern in relation to finding veterinary care for her family pets: "the Cubans we talk to, even though it's only about cats, are adamant about our never going to an actual *clinic*. We are supposed to go to a veterinarian who *works* in a clinic but then works after-hours in his home: these veterinarians are the ones who have access to medicines" (Tattlin 2002, 92–93; emphasis in original).

31. Matthew Hill describes one complex method of doubling a steak by flattening it (2004, 161–62).

32. These would be parallel-market chickens, gathered from a variety of small producers in the Cuban countryside. Compare this scheme to a more straightforward case of the direct diversion of frozen chickens in Pérez-López 1995, 148.

33. Clearly, in Cuba today there is an issue of differential access to the means of crime: who gets the managerial positions, and in what ways is their selection racially inflected? Additionally, however, there is the issue of the *meaning* of "crime." As Mayfair Yang put it in the Chinese context some years ago: "the art of *guanxi* cannot be reduced to a modern western notion of corruption because the personalistic qualities of obligation, indebtedness, and reciprocity are just as important as transactions in material benefit" (1994, 108; also see Verdery 1996, 22).

34. For transportation, as with many industries, the state maintains one price, but two currencies; tourists are supposed to pay in CUC (approximately equal to the US dollar) and Cubans pay in Cuba pesos (CUP), as if the dollar and the peso were of equal worth. Thus, a train ticket would cost a foreigner CUC$23.00 and Cubans or resident students such as myself CUP$23.00 (remember, CUC$1.00 actually trades at about CUP$25.00). While the system is not unfair considering that Cubans' salaries are also in pesos, it certainly reinforces national:foreign distinctions.

35. *La mecánica*: literally "the mechanism," but connoting a recognized extra-official, often illegal or disreputable (but effective) manner of accomplishing some practical goal.

36. Another, more powerful *mecánica* was in operation here. A little more than one of my five dollars went to buy the ticket in Cuban pesos (CUP$23.00); the rest was split between the ticket agent and her *socio* with the "waiting list." Everyone except the government profited: I didn't have to spend twenty-three US dollars to buy a ticket; with my student ID she could legally record a ticket sale in pesos, the books balanced, and she did not have to risk taking an outright bribe; he made more from the transaction than from a full day's labor in any officially salaried occupation.

37. Probably his wife or girlfriend.

38. An estimated 60 percent of Cubans have some family in the United States, though only a few actually receive remittances. As over 90 percent of Cuban Americans identify themselves as white; lighter-skinned Cubans such as Niurka are more likely to have close contacts in the United States than are black Cubans.

39. Cheese, produced by state farms with state-owned cows and equipment, is one of many strictly controlled food products. Like coffee, it is produced mainly in eastern and central regions, where it is relatively cheap on the black market. The only times I have been stopped by police have been while traveling with Cubans, or on busses with Cubans, who have been variously searched for meat, milk, cheese, coffee, tobacco, and seafood. Depending on the type and supply, a pound of cheese might sell for about one US dollar in the provinces and twice that in Havana.

40. There is a fictionalized description of similar train-based lobster smuggling in the contemporary Cuban novel *Dirty Havana Trilogy* (Gutiérrez 2001, 230–37). While smuggling items such as these is one element of an economy wherein the means of production are in state hands, it is not entirely estranged from prerevolutionary Cuban or Caribbean history. As early as the seventeenth century, Cuban settlers systematically went to great lengths to outwit royal tobacco excise taxes, and smuggling everything from human beings to alcohol to household appliances to narcotics has long percolated through the region. For a longue dureé perspective, see *Pedro Blanco, El Negrero,* (Novás Calvo 1973) and *Contrabando* (Serpa 1982).

41. After finishing their free higher education, university students must do two years of state service in their field, receiving the minimum wage—at that time, about eight US dollars a month.

42. As so often in Cuba, the moral here seems to be "always have friends" (see N. Fernandez 1996, 2; also see Chávez and Chakarova 2005).

43. In a similar manner, the majority of the many hitchhikers in Havana are young women, as most drivers are men and less likely to stop for other men. Understanding the disquieting gendered implications of the pattern, many women nevertheless prefer to hitchhike rather than to wait interminably for a bus.

44. For the sake of simplicity, I am bracketing out legitimate spoilage of produce; I am referring here to the practice of taking home good food that has been deliberately labeled "rotten."

45. It is partly from this perspective that I am unconvinced by Weinreb's "citizen-consumer" model (2009) as well as Pertierra's argument that markets shape Cuban consumption (2011, 107; cf. 119), at least unless "market" is substantially

redefined. In any case, these approaches risk overlooking the distinctive and still state socialist distribution patterns I have described here.

CHAPTER 2

1. "At times, history evolves before our very eyes, yet we fail to understand it in all its meaning. We Cubans can understand it best by comparing it with our own experiences. What was Cuba in the last century, but a Spanish colony? What has Angola been until very recently, but a Portuguese colony? Two nations belonging to the same peninsula, and two equally exploiting and cruel colonial systems" (Castro Ruz 1989, 76).

2. To clarify, not all socialist international exchange was with Africa! Many Cubans traveled to and studied in the Soviet Union and the rest of the socialist world. In addition, there was historical precedent for military internationalism in the large contingent of Cubans who fought in the Spanish Civil War (Castillo Falcato 1981; Deutschmann 1989, 13). This is all-important context, and pre–Special Period internationalism with Africa is certainly popularly understood to be (and critiqued as) a socialist-associated project (Mueller 2010). But, as the next chapter will demonstrate, África carries a longer-term charge in the Cuban vernacular than the Soviet Union. Put another way, travel to the Soviet Union and Warsaw Pact countries was not put in precisely the same register as *internacionalismo con* África. It is something like the difference between studying abroad and joining the Peace Corps. Unless otherwise elaborated, it is *Africa*, rather than the rest of the Soviet Bloc, that was associated with *internacionalismo* or *cumpliendo una misión internacionalista* (doing an internationalist mission). Similarly, albeit for reasons of scale, the default association with resident foreign *becados* (scholarship students)—especially from the mid-1970s through the mid-1990s—was with African students.

3. Frances Robles, *Miami Herald*, August 13, 2003.

4. For the most important of those studies, which do temporally and politically frame the international event, see Benemelis 1988, 1990; Erisman and Kirk 1991; LeoGrande 1980, 1989; Mesa-Lago and Belkin 1982; as well as C. Moore 1988; Gleijeses 2002; and Gleijeses, Risquet, and Remírez 2007.

5. The word Julia used, *educados*, is literally "educated" but in this context could just as well be translated as "civil," "polite," or "well-mannered."

6. Res ipsa loquitor. Again, also see Mbembe 2001.

7. This is what Almer neatly calls "internationalism with interés" (2011, chapter 5).

8. *Algo más que soñar* (Moya 1984) was a Cuban-produced television miniseries about a group of young men who join the army and eventually go to Angola to fight and about their families and friends left in Cuba. While one of the men

is killed, the sentiment vis-à-vis the combat is relatively heroic, and the Cubans are shown defending unarmed Africans from racist and brutal white South African soldiers. The series also, however, illustrated some of the privileges of the so-called revolutionary bourgeoisie, and it is best remembered for sparking much discussion of social privilege in an ostensibly classless society. Also see *Caravana* (Oliver 1990); *After the Battle* (Bravo 1990).

9. Also see Almer, "The Backward Savage" (2011, chapter 3). In terms of Cuban evolutionist frameworks within which África is embedded, her interviews demonstrate tremendous continuities with ones I conducted in the 1990s and 2000s.

10. Ultimately, of course, these Western ideologies go much deeper than Marx or the nineteenth century. V. Y. Mudimbe traces ideologies of Africa as a "geography of monstrosity" to Pliny, for instance (1988, 78–80). In the specific case of Cuba, the seminal early work of Fernando Ortiz has already been mentioned (see the Introduction).

11. Gabriel García Márquez, of course, was Colombian. This quote, however, is extracted from his state-authorized report on internationalism in Africa, written in his capacity as a journalist of and for the Cuban Revolution.

12. Again, Marisabel Almer's recent dissertation elaborates on this and other dynamics I discuss in this chapter in much more, often painful, detail (e.g., "Sexuality and the Scent of French Perfume," in Almer 2011, chapter 5).

13. Others articulated the point more generally. For example: "We [Cubans] never compare ourselves to the third world. One always wants to better oneself, and if we have the health and education of the first world, we also want our style of life and our economy to also be powerful, also of the first world, and we never accept [that it is not]. Especially because we recognize the political and economic errors that have occurred and we know we could be much better. Thus [comparing Cuba to Africa] does not console us, even if that pattern of comparison at least gives us a little calm. Of course, I am very much in favor of interchanges, which are as enriching with the third world as with the first" (Félix Pérez, interview).

14. This is not to imply that nationalism in Cuba began with socialist Cuba's international interventions, of course. To reiterate, the Cuban Revolution was largely a nationalist, anti-imperialist event in the first place. José Martí was a nationalist in the 1890s; even earlier, Cubans replaced bullfights with baseball games in a surge of anti-Spanish sentiment (L. Pérez 1994). Rather, the internationalist experience has become part of the ground against which Cuban nationalism has been renewed and reconfigured.

15. Compare this to travel writer Tom Miller's report that in Cuba circa 1989, the two most incessant topics of conversation were Africa and baseball ([1992]

1996). Not surprisingly, a certain nostalgia for the Soviet era has recently become more evident (Almer 2011; Loss and Prieto González 2012).

16. There is clear evidence that this varies from western to eastern Cuba. Oriente, or eastern Cuba, after all, has been the principal site of successive waves of migration out of Haiti since the Haitian Revolution (Berenguer Cala 1979; McLeod 2000; Charlton 2005; Casey 2012; Viddal 2012).

17. The Isle of Youth or "La Isla," formerly called the Isle of Pines, is primarily known for its citrus agriculture and fishing, the major occupations of its fifty thousand Cuban inhabitants. The island was also once the site of a Benthamite penal colony which held Fidel after the failed 1953 Moncada attack. That prison image foreshadows the issue of how to view the international educational project of *la Isla*. Was it an ideally secluded space for learning (Rojas 1987), or a quarantine for difference (C. Moore 1988, 254)? (Also see Núñez Jiménez 1976; McManus 2000; Calderón 2007.)

18. The students were principally Yemenese, Ethiopian, Namibian, and Angolan youths, and formerly a few Nicaraguan and other socialist and nonsocialist students from Latin America and the Caribbean (e.g., N. García 2011). Approximately three-quarters of all foreign students in Cuba have been from sub-Saharan Africa, about 10 percent from North Africa and the Middle East, a sprinkling from the Pacific, and nearly all the rest from Latin America and the Caribbean (see *www.cyborg.ne.jp/~embcubaj/outlinee.html*). Certainly it is important to recognize and learn from the non-African element to Cuban internationalist education, and I have included some comparative consideration of West Indian and North African students for that reason. However, vernacular Cuban discursive frames for this phenomenon in a context of socialist rhetoric were, of course, of "those African students." Until the growth of the Latin American School of Medicine in the 2000s, discourse about other nationalized or regionalized student groups was simply overshadowed by that about "the Africans."

19. The educational project on the Isle of Youth declined rapidly following the end of Soviet support to the Cuban state. During the crisis of the mid-1990s, many of the roughly six thousand international students still studying there were unable to pay their way home and moved on to advanced degree programs in universities in Havana or other cities (see "The Fruits of Communism," *Economist*, February 12, 1994) or, as in the case of the Sudanese, were unwelcome at home and sought political refugee status in Canada (see Chapter 4).

20. Also see Oscar Corral, "Saharan Refugees Discuss Perils," *Miami Herald*, September 19, 2005.

21. Over the course of my fieldwork, it became much easier for me to pick African students out of a crowd of Cubans. Sometimes their attire was distinctive, with

African cloth, continental emblems, and then hard-to-find hip-hop styles; in other cases, they were taller or blacker than most Cubans. However, it was generally *in movement* that they most stood out. Ways of walking, standing, and gesturing would usually give them away. As a Cuban *internacionalista* I interviewed pointed out, the distinctiveness of *gestos* (gestures) went both ways: he had been in Angola and said that no one there confused black Cubans with Angolans for their manner of walking and their gestures—Cubans generally being much more gesticulative. Differing ways of moving, then, are a key element of the perceptible differences underlying a border commonly drawn between Cubanness and Africanity.

22. *Fulano/a* is an informal, generic designation for any unnamed person.

23. Acquired for me from a sailor by my Cuban host brother, the bicycle was a used Japanese ten-speed. Costing sixty-five dollars, it was seen as much more desirable than the heavy Chinese bicycles commonly assigned to working Cubans through their work centers, although perhaps not quite as stylish as an imported mountain bike. Nevertheless, it was certainly a *cosa más yuma*—the sort of desirable item I described in the preceding chapter.

24. Literally "taking" or "drinking." In this context, the implication was ambiguous—referring either to drunkenness or to being on stronger drugs.

25. For more on the foundations of Cuban work-study schools, see Martí 1959; Editorial Pueblo y Educación 1990; Buenavilla Recio 1995; Turner Martí et al. 1996; H. González 1997. Also see Paulson in Mesa-Lago 1971; W. Richmond 1973; Martí 1975; Figueroa Araujo 1976; Simpson 1984; Rojas 1987; Marx 1990; M. Richmond 1991; Coe 2005.

26. For a recent ethnographically detailed overview of the Cuban educational system and a variety of personal responses to it, see Blum 2011.

27. There are a series of important if politically tricky questions about law, marriage, and citizenship here, in the same manner that Domínguez (1989) pursued in examining the defining of Jewishness in Israel. Who decides who stays and who goes, and how are such decisions made? The short answer is that these decisions are controlled by a branch of the state bureaucracy and its socialist legal code and prioritize the wishes of the *Cuban* parent (Evenson 1994; Zatz 1994).

28. José Antonio Echeverría City University (CUJAE or *Ciudad Universitaria José Antonio Echeverría*) has six thousand full-time students, including about three hundred foreigners, mostly living in the *becas* (there are separate buildings for foreigners and Cubans, as in Santiago). Of the foreign students about 60 percent are African and 40 percent Latin American. Most are in Cuba by *convenio* (agreement) between governments, but now some are also there by *comercio* (commerce), in which they pay their own way. Most of the latter are from Latin America, but there are still some African students in this category as well.

29. In Chapter 4, I explore such cases in more detail, not only to add an interesting counterpoint to this study, but also to rethink the described boundaries as they are doubly transformed in crossing—both in the literal movement into diaspora and in the more complex consequences in identity among now-hyphenated African-Cuban serial migrants (Ossman 2013).

30. The "Five Heroes" were five Cuban spies incarcerated in US federal prison. Following the successful campaign to return Elián González to Cuba, the Cuban government expended a tremendous amount of effort toward their release, which was finalized in December 2014.

31. Literally meaning "jockey," or a rider of foreigners, in this context a *jinetera* would roughly translate as "sex worker."

CHAPTER 3

1. This aphorism implying that all Cubans, even putatively white ones, have some African ancestry is of course only one national variant of a popular Spanish-language phrase with a trans-Latin American circulation. As Whitten and Torres report, "A popular saying of white-*mestizo* intellects in categorizing the masses of their nations in Ecuador and Peru is this: 'Quien no tiene de inga, tiene de man-dinga (whoever is not of [the] Inca is of [the] Mandinga).' . . . in the Hispanic Caribbean the word *dinga* (for Dinka) is substituted for the Andean *inga*" (1998, 7). In any case, rather than diminishing the interest of the described aphorism (or its accompanying narratives), regional correlates underscore the importance, variability, and specificity of *mestizaje* to nationalist ideologies across Latin America. Interestingly, in each instance of *mestizaje* denoted by this aphorism, it is *sangre*, or blood, which is the medium of purity or of contamination. Other scholars have noted historically rooted linkages of blood, purity, and social division throughout the region. Thus, Virginia Domínguez argued that "the problem [of social division] . . . stems from the existence of widespread assumptions about the properties of blood—that identity is determined by blood; that blood ties, lineally and collaterally, carry social and economic rights and obligations; and that both racial identity and class membership are determined by blood" (1994, 89). While I agree that there is clear evidence that assumptions about "blood" are symptomatic of a certain complex of racial ideologies, it seems to me *sangre* is the reagent rather than the font of this racial labeling, and we must look beyond it to see exactly where the purities and impurities are imagined to originate.

2. Incidentally, this is an excellent example of a methodological principle: when one hears a story often enough to finish it oneself—as, indeed, Professor Trouillot was able to do in the opening vignette of the Introduction—that itself suggests a wider ethnographic pattern worthy of substantive consideration.

3. Again, while precise Cuban racial statistics are scarce, approximately half of Cuba's twelve million people would identify themselves as white. Among Miami Cubans, the proportion is much higher, roughly 90 percent white, which potentially adds a racialized twist to island:diasporic relations. In any case, while clearly each Caribbean (and Latin American) nationality's particular *mestizaje* is different according to the particular historical context in which it was shaped (Mintz 1971; Benítez-Rojo 1992; Hall 1995), just as clearly, one of Cuba's little-emphasized particularities vis-à-vis the region is the proportion and sheer number of self-identified whites.

4. For more on white Cubans' genealogies, see Santa Cruz y Mallen (1940). As for Anglo-Americans, the aspirational apical ancestor for establishing one's ethnicity is commonly that one who crossed the ocean. However, I am arguing that in these Cuban narratives, there is an additional racialized quality of establishing whiteness—that which is presumed in white North Americans' mythologies. Even Fidel Castro, whose father was from Galicia, has been sometimes recognized as a *gallego*, particularly during the course of his state visits to Spain. This is an interesting counterpoint to his widely cited descriptions of Cuba as a "Latin *African*" nation (Casal 1989, 484; Peters 2012).

5. This is comparable to the well-known Puerto Rican aphorism, "¿Y tu abuela, dónde está? (And your [black] grandmother, where is she [hidden in your family history]?" (see Whitten and Torres 1998, 20). Famously cited by Luis Carbonell and echoing the poetry of Nicolás Guillén, many Cubans have come to think of this as a Cuban cultural expression.

6. At the time, private rental of homes was a grey area, legally speaking. It has since been regulated and heavily taxed in an attempt to drive business back into hotels, which, of course, are state-owned. In turn, private renters are claiming foreigners as distant kin or close friends rather than as paying guests. This fits a classic pattern in which socialist legality struggles to catch up to and control or harness popular practices.

7. Although no neighborhood in revolutionary Cuba is completely white or completely black, Centro Habana is predominantly black, poor, and has a widespread reputation for petty street crime. Long-time residents of the capital often also associate the neighborhood with recently arrived *orientales*, or Cubans from the eastern part of the island. This, then, is another of the local racializations of geography that percolate throughout this chapter.

8. This Cuban pattern of dual households (also described by Schweid 2004, 192) closely resembles (or perhaps exemplifies) the Caribbean "dual marriage system" analyzed by Raymond Smith. Working primarily in the Anglophone West Indies, Smith demonstrates that such widespread systems have historical trajectories related to the steep social and class hierarchies of the region (1996, chapter 5).

9.   In both state and popular discourse in Cuba, "racism" is often used in the way North Americans use "segregation." Thus, when I referred to racism in Cuba, another white neighbor commented, "there's no racism here, because they (black Cubans) can go wherever they want." In such cases, translation issues have greatly impeded cross-cultural racial comprehension. While at times "racism" is understood in virtually synonymous terms as in North America, in other contexts, white or black Cubans sincerely propose that there is no racism in Cuba today without intending to imply there is no racial discrimination, but rather meaning that there is a lack of racial *segregation*. As have many anthropologists in various contexts, Susan Gal makes a relevant point in her work on the discourse of abortion in Hungary: the discourse *seems* transparent (it uses the same words), but in fact rests on specific embeddednesses, local history, politics, and concerns (1994, 259–60). The issue thus returns to the cultural constitution and historicity of categories. After describing a similar exchange with a racist/antiracist white veteran of Angola, political refugee Assata Shakur concluded: "The whole race question in Cuba was even more confusing to me because all the categories of race were different" (1987, 271).

10. This is commonly described as having (or not having) *nivel* (level), as in "*Un muchacho que tiene nivel*" or "*de nivel*" (A young man of good cultural or educational level). The term often is used either as emphasis or as a counterweight in conversations about blackness, and its evolutionistic tone is unmistakable. While conventional Marxist understandings of social class do not work well in contemporary Cuba—both because of the state's elimination of most all private ownership of the means of production and because of the upended economic situation described in Chapter 1—*nivel* has also assumed some of the semantic load we would assign to "class" (N. Fernandez 2010; Roland 2011).

11. I am deliberately trying to avoid the language of public and private spheres, particularly inasmuch as popular racial discourse is often quite "public," and the socialist state has largely dismantled the sites and institutions that compose the Habermasian public sphere (Habermas 1991; also see Verdery 1996, 45–46). By "state" or "public" discourse, I mean to indicate anything reproduced, distributed, disseminated, broadcast, or published by the Cuban mass media—all means of production controlled solely by the socialist government and/or the Communist Party of Cuba and their principal spokesmen. By "private," "popular," or "vernacular" discourse, I am indicating face-to-face, commonsense commentary heard in the homes of ordinary Cuban citizens as well as in neighborhoods and in the street; these terms should *not* be taken to imply "hidden" or "counterhegemonic" resistance to state power, as they are often unabashedly vocal and in many contexts simply mirror state ideologies.

NOTES TO PAGES 97–103   183

12. It would be reasonable to find fault with my grouping of more than forty years of state discourse as "contemporary." Notes Fidel Castro: "As the Greek philosopher said, one never steps into the same river twice." However, since 1959 the same cast of characters, with relatively fixed ideas about the reality of national boundaries, has held office, promulgating those ideas rather than others.

13. Because *patria*, literally "fatherland," is a feminine noun, it could conceivably be translated as "motherland." As either translation would lose a significant aspect of the original category, I will here leave it untranslated and italicized.

14. In Cuba, as elsewhere, biologists are routinely pressed into service by the mass media to explain that "race" is a social rather than biological (or scientific) concept.

15. Critical responses to Carlos Moore include Casal 1989; Pérez Sarduy 1990; and Brock and Cunningham 1991.

16. *Compañero*, literally "companion," is a term closely identified with the Cuban revolutionary project.

17. The state-issued ID, the *carné*, is derived from *carnet* and should not be confused with *carne* (meat). Shawn Alfonso-Wells, an anthropologist at the University of Pittsburgh, has studied the categories of the *carné* in detail (2004).

18. *Órgano Oficial del Comité Central del Partido Comunista de Cuba.*

19. The McDuffie riot has been carefully examined in the context of Miami, especially in relation to a recurring pattern of African-American riots and their aftermath (B. Porter and Dunn 1984; Dunn 1997; Harris 1999), and in relation to *la comunidad* (Cuban Miami). Alejandro Portes and Alex Stepick analyze this event at length as one of the major elements, along with the Mariel boatlift, of "the year to remember," which led to a "reactive ethnicity" among Miami Cubans (1993). Their concept of reactive ethnicity in Cuban Miami both foreshadows the further enclavization brought on by the Elián affair and, because no such reactivity occurred on the island itself, illustrates the frequently divergent meanings ascribed to such events (McDuffie in 1980 and Elián in 2000) on either side of the Straits of Florida. For a more up-to-date look at Cuban Miami, see Grenier and Moebius 2015.

20. Thus, while Cuba's state news service, Prensa Latina, provided much of the reporting on the McDuffie riot, the photographs reproduced are only attributed "radiofoto." This raises the question of the source of the Cuban data on US racism—attribution of which, like the source of satellite images used during hurricanes, is often left unspecified.

21. From Angela Davis and Stokeley Carmichael to Assata Shakur, many prominent African-American radicals have been public figures and refugees in

revolutionary Cuba (Williams, King, and Nelson 1962; Clytus 1970; Shakur 1987; C. Moore 1988; Brent 1996; Marable 1999, 93–100; Fuente 2001; Perry 2004; Sawyer 2006).

22. By paradoxical, I do not mean to imply inconsistency. The Cuban state's position here is indeed consistent with Marxist theory on race as a marker of class and class as a function of differentiated relation to the means of production. The paradox, however, is from the spectator's perspective of a "now you see it, now you don't" treatment of race.

23. A term, of course, is not the same as a cultural category. As the overlaps between terms such as *blanco* and *rubio* or *mulato* and *moreno* illustrate, there are likely to be fewer fundamental categories than terms in a given context, whether considered in synchronic or historical perspective. Some terms may be rarely used (e.g., *sidio*), newly fashionable (e.g., *fosforescente*), or not fully recognized throughout the community, whereas the overarching categories are universally recognized and shape the nuances of less common terms.

24. Note too that there is a geographic element to Cuban racial classification, most commonly noted as an *oriental:occidental* (east:west) division. By all accounts, the racial taxonomy of Havana and the western part of the island retains similar terms and structure in eastern Cuba but tends to shift toward the darker end of the spectrum moving east. Thus, for example, someone denoted as *mulato* in Havana might well be considered *blanco cubano* in the eastern provinces, or an *oriental* who considers herself *mulata* might be labeled *prieta* in the *occidente*.

25. Taxonomically, the labels preceding *jabao* are sometimes described as pertaining to *la raza blanca*, and those following, to *la raza negra*. Note, however, that the classification of a *jabao* (*jabado*) depends on the appearance of his/her hair; *jabaos* are sometimes classified as part of *la raza blanca* and sometimes as part of *la raza negra*. Here, then, is one crucially important, if indistinct, boundary for evaluating underlying Cuban racial boundaries.

26. Also note R. Moore 1997, 13–15; Hansing 2006, 64–66; Perry 2004, 18; Schmidt 2008; Roland 2011, 33–35.

27. Note that there are a number of Cuban dictionaries and lexical references that roughly trace these terms through time, and scholars such as Fernando Ortiz (1985, 1990) have relied on such sources in their own work. It is not possible, however, to derive sufficient meaning or pattern from such a method alone.

28. Similar patterns of proliferating racial terminology have, however, been extensively documented throughout the circum-Caribbean:

> Like Louisiana, the islands of the Caribbean have a history of extensive plantations and African slave labor. And like Louisiana, they have a history of extensive miscegenation, especially in the Spanish-speaking countries. Over the years, color terms other than white and black proliferated. The pattern holds throughout the

> Caribbean and those parts of South America with a history of African slavery. In a national sample of 100 Brazilians, Harris (1970) collected 492 terms he called racial or color terms. Sanjek (1971) discovered 116 terms in a similar study of a Brazilian village; Taylor (1959) elicited 40 terms in Runaway Bay, Jamaica, to denote 24 adult members of the community; Alexander (1977) elicited 12 terms from 9 informants in a study of middle-class Jamaicans; and Domínguez (1973) elicited 58 terms from a sample of 50 Cubans, 56 terms from a sample of 43 Puerto Ricans, and 25 terms from a sample of 11 Dominicans. . . . Every study of racial or color terms in the Caribbean documents widespread overlap in the use of these terms." (Domínguez 1994, 273–75)

    Among many other sources, also see Wade 1993, 2010; Whitten and Torres 1998; Twine 1998; Rahier 1999; Rahier, Hintzen, and Smith 2010.

29. For Boas's original text, see Boas 1963, 20.

30. The term "Afro-Cuban" is virtually hegemonic among scholars writing in English, to the degree that it is used without comment in many book and article titles (e.g., Brown 1993; Helg 1995; Bettelheim and Ortiz 2001; Palmié 2002). In some cases, the term is also adopted by Cuban academics in exile (e.g., Pérez Sarduy and Stubbs 2000; Fuente 2001), perhaps precisely owing to its incontestability here. Nevertheless, it is instructive to compare scholarship published abroad with much more specific, limited, and folkloric on-island usages such as those of Menéndez (1990) and León (1991).

31. Ortiz 1987.

32. As it happened, there were relatively few Cubans of intermediate color categories at this particular talk, and none of them participated in the represented exchange.

33. Interestingly, while provincial origin or municipal *barrio* and educational *nivel* are readily deducible by syntax, inflection, or accent, Cubans acknowledge they cannot distinguish each other's race or color over the telephone.

34. Writing as a long-time North American resident of Cuba, Assata Shakur recalls her initial reaction to Cuban color categories:

> I was shocked to learn that a lot of Cubans who looked Black to me didn't consider themselves Black. They called themselves mulattoes, colorados, jabaos, and a whole bunch of other names. It seemed to me that anyone who wasn't jet black was considered a mulatto. The first time someone called me a "mulatta," I was so insulted that if I had been able to express myself in Spanish, we would have had a heated argument right there on the spot. (1987, 271)

35. This narrative always started an argument, for, in fact, in an economy where the largest source of income is family remittances from the diaspora, where diaspora is disproportionately white, where the best jobs in tourism disproportionately go to white Cubans, and where black Cubans are often stopped by police while whites are not, the evidence that in the contemporary era "the blacks are on top" is weak at best (see Fuente 2001, chapter 8).

36. Undoubtedly the seminal revolution of the post-Columbian Caribbean, the Haitian Revolution also initiated a recurring pattern of white Cuban fear and repression directed against Haitians and black and mulatto Cubans. Even into the 1930s, there were episodes of violence against Haitian and Jamaican cane cutters in Oriente province. White fear of "another Haiti," and its "Africanization" of Cuba—as if "Africa" were forty-five miles from Cuban shores—has repeatedly resulted in severe violence against persons of color (see Helg 1995, 174, 197; Ferrer 1999, 112).

37. For more on marriages in colonial Cuba, see Fuente 1990.

38. Note the apparent inversion between this nineteenth-century pattern and the contemporary one described previously in the aphorism of the car-driving black doctor, whereby educated, affluent black men become acceptable partners for lower status white women. In both cases, however, the underlying logic demands a recognition of the interconvertibility of socioeconomic status and color.

CHAPTER 4

1. Juan Flores, writing about the ambivalence and divided loyalties of young adults from migrant families that have returned to Puerto Rico after growing up in New York: "The way that they hung out together and shared a sense of group belonging in an often unaccepting environment made them seem like a diaspora, or actually a kind of reverse or return diaspora with the homeland society itself. We joked, and made up the term 'Re-asporican'" (2009, 3).

2. Or more precisely, perhaps the past too was processual, as historian Luis Pérez argued in his magisterial work on becoming Cuban (1999, 8).

3. Even that standard Cuban-American model does not seem to me to fit well within the term "transnational," at least in Roger Rouse's original formulation of a "transnational migrant circuit," where a given community is "plurilocal"— existing simultaneously across multiple spaces (1991; also see Kearney 1995). Cuban exile over the past five decades has been too linear, too much of a one-way ticket, and it has not been necessarily a wage-labor migration, as are many more-studied "transnational circuits." Once one leaves Cuba, it is nearly impossible to return for more than a brief visit, and the "trans" is more accurately a transit, in the nautical sense.

4. This nationality came complete with its own flag, flown at the school in Cuba long before South Sudan's independence.

5. Berger describes Sudanese in Canada's "intense interest" in a documentary about Fidel and Ché in May 2000 in terms strikingly similar to those I described for other African students in Chapter 2, although in the now-altered political

context of Canada. "When the scene cut to Fidel Castro giving a speech, they roared with approval" (2001, 71–72). She continues: "After more than twelve years in Cuba, the young southern Sudanese strongly identify with the heroes of the communist state. None profess to be communist, having experienced the hard times which followed the collapse of the Soviet Bloc in the early 1990s. But there is a regard for the history of the region where they grew up, Cuba, and the socialist countries with which it was allied" (72).

6. *Escuela Secundaria Básica en el Campo*. See Figueroa Araujo 1976; M. Richmond 1991; Blum 2011.

7. The term Saharaui refers to the pre-1975 population of the Western Sahara as well as their descendants now residing in refugee camps near Tindouf, Algeria. Sometimes spelled Saharawi or Sahrawi, I use the former spelling except in cases of direct quotation. As we will see, the neologism Cubaraui or Cubarawi, discussed below, follows this pattern. The acronym POLISARIO, or POLISARIO Front, is from the Spanish Frente Popular de Liberación de Saguía el Hamra y Río de Oro, the Popular Front for the Liberation of Saguia el-Hamra and Gold River, and RASD stands for República Árabe Saharaui Democrática, or the Sahrawi Arab Democratic Republic.

8. Cf. *consciencia*.

9. Of these Cubaraui documentaries, *Las Cubarauis* (Márquez 2005) is the most difficult to obtain; a portion of the film is available at *www.youtube.com/watch?v=oadqsTU7xJA*. To view *Caribeños del Sáhara* (I. Pérez 2007, with subtitles by Alicia Osés Ilundain and Adriana Ahumada Naveros), go to *vimeo.com/11813252*. There is also a different version, *Caribeños del Desierto* (I. Pérez and Galdeano 2008) which focuses on interviews with the caribeños, available at *video.google.es/videoplay?docid=794963053040710622&hl=es*. Spanish and English subtitled streaming versions of *El Maestro Saharaui* (Muñoz 2011) are available for a small fee at *www.toma24.net/productions/el-maestro-saharaui*.

10. Or in some cases, such as the already described group of several hundred Cuban-Sudanese sent to Canada, the shock of going on to a third country.

11. Again, like the Jewish-Cubans, or "Jewbans," who, like the Cubarauis, stood out in both places—in Cuba as Jews, and in Miami Beach as Cubans (Bettinger-López 2000).

12. The question of why Brahim is so driven to return to Cuba is glossed in the text simply in terms of "giving back," as we will see below. Susan Ossman, however, traces a larger pattern: "certain territories thicken in their meaning for the life as a whole. . . . To return can be an uncanny reiteration of immigration" (2013, 100). This framework fits not only someone like Breih, but other Cuban-educated students who return, sometimes repeatedly, to Cuban friends,

families, and children (e.g., see "Tell Me a Story," *EsbecRadio*, October 18, 2008, *www.blogtalkradio.com/esbecradio/2008/10/18/tell-me-a-story*).

13. Flights originating from Miami are routed through a different terminal (Terminal Two) in Havana than flights originating elsewhere, and since the great majority of Cuban-Americans live in Miami (unlike most tourists), that particular space is something of a ground zero for Cuban family reunions and separations.

14. Speaking more broadly, another Cuban administrator comments:

> Sometimes it was not easy to gather some of the students to go home, because they got used to Cuba, liked it here, and wanted to stay. They spoke fluent Spanish and moved freely through the country. Sometimes we had to go looking for them and enlist the help of the embassies to send them home after their study program had come to an end. . . . Last but not least, all these students maintained links with the communities on the Isle of Youth. They went to parties, had boyfriends and girlfriends, and sometimes this caused problems. They left some seeds in Cuba, and today there are quite a number of Cuban citizens with one African parent. (Elejalde Villalón 2012)

15. For instance, in the blog post, "Profile of a Cubarawi," Blue_Woman (2009) states that "of the 11 Cubarawis interviewed before the writing of this article, every [one] of them looked back with fondness on their lives in Cuba, and above all, the Cuban people." If the earlier examples have not been sufficiently compelling, there is a fantastic collection of first-person accounts of life in Cuba and, especially, the trauma of return to the Sahara by a number of Cubarauis available at *generaciondelaamistad.blogspot.com/search/label/Cuba*.

16. For more on this project, see *elporvenirdelsahara.blogspot.com/2010/06/justificacion-de-las-cuentas-2010.html*.

17. Remember, these styles change quickly. In mid-1990s Cuba, it was all Nike; by 1997, Tommy Hilfiger apparel was hot and hard to come by in the republic. A couple of years later, Nike and Hilfiger were ubiquitous among young Cubans, who were clamoring for FUBU and for New York Yankees insignia. And so on. Among other things, then, the style is a clear temporal marker of an era or, in this case, the moment of departure from Cuba.

References

Agamben, Giorgio. 1998. *Homo Sacer: Sovereign Power and Bare Life*. Stanford: Stanford University Press.

Alafia, Joshua B., dir. 2004. *Cuban Hip Hop All Stars*. London: Papaya Records/ Raptivism. DVD.

Alcántara, Leyton. 2013. "ESBEC #53 Carlos Fonseca Amador." YouTube video, 16:50, posted August 16. *www.youtube.com/watch?v=pfzcW8HNwRk*.

Alfonso-Wells, Shawn. 2004. "Cuban Color Classification and Identity Negotiation: Old Terms in a New World." PhD diss., University of Pittsburgh.

Allard, Jean-Guy. 2012. "Falleció investigador de EE.UU. que vinculó a Posada Carriles con el asesinato de Kennedy." *Granma Internaciónal*, September 4.

Allen, Jafari S. 2007. "Means of Desire's Production: Male Sex Labor in Cuba." *Identities: Global Studies in Culture and Power* 14: 183–202.

———. 2009. "Looking Black at Revolutionary Cuba." *Latin American Perspectives* 36 (1): 53–62.

———. 2011. *¡Venceremos?: The Erotics of Black Self-Making in Cuba*. Durham, NC: Duke University Press.

———. 2012. "One Way or Another: Erotic Subjectivity in Cuba." *American Ethnologist* 39 (2): 325–38.

Almer, Marisabel. 2011. "Remembering Angola: Cuban Internationalism, Transnational Spaces, and the Politics of Memories." PhD diss., University of Michigan.

Álvarez Ramírez, Sandra. 2013. "El 'color de la piel' en los censos en Cuba." In *Situación de los Afrodescendientes en América Latina: La desigualdad reflefada en los censos*, 75–94. San José, Costa Rica: Instituto Afrodescendiente de Estudio y Investigación y Desarrollo.

Andaya, Elise L. 2009. "The Gift of Health: Socialist Medical Practice and Shifting Material and Moral Economies in Post-Soviet Cuba." *Medical Anthropology Quarterly* 23 (4): 357–74.

———. 2014. *Conceiving Cuba: Reproduction, Women, and the State in Post-Soviet Cuba*. New Brunswick, NJ: Rutgers University Press.

Anderson, Benedict. 1983. *Imagined Communities: Reflections on the Origin and Spread of Nationalism.* New York: Verso.

Anonymous. 1995. "América Nuestra: Una revista por la identidad." *América Nuestra: Una revista por la identidad* 1 (1): 24.

———. 2010. "Nostalgia de Misha." In *La gaceta de Cuba*, edited by N. Codina, 1. Havana: Unión de Escritores y Artistas de Cuba.

———. 2012. "Negros con clases, racismo y publicidad comercial, racialización, racialismo y racismo." Special issue, *Universidad de La Habana*, no. 273.

Appadurai, Arjun. 1996. *Modernity at Large: Cultural Dimensions of Globalization.* Minneapolis: University of Minnesota Press.

Báez, Carmen R. 2000. "Tribuna abierta de la juventud y los estudiantes en Mesa Redonda Internacional, el 2 de mayo del 2000, 'año del 40 aniversario de la decisión de patria o muerte.'" *www.cuba.cu/gobierno/documentos/2000/esp/m020500e.html*.

Ballou, Maturin M. 1897. *Due South; or, Cuba Past and Present.* Boston: Houghton Mifflin and Company.

Barnet, Miguel, and Esteban Montejo. 1968. *The Autobiography of a Runaway Slave.* New York: Pantheon Books.

Barreal Fernández, Isaac. 1998. *Fiestas populares tradicionales cubanas.* Havana: Centro de Investigación y Desarrollo de la Cultura Cubana Juan Marinello: Editorial de Ciencias Sociales.

Barthes, Roland. 1983. *The Fashion System.* New York: Hill and Wang.

Bashkow, Ira. 2006. *The Meaning of Whitemen: Race and Modernity in the Orokaiva Cultural World.* Chicago: University of Chicago Press.

Bataille, Georges. 1988. *The Accursed Share: An Essay on General Economy.* New York: Zone Books.

Bataille, Georges, and Allan Stoekl. 1985. *Visions of Excess: Selected Writings, 1927–1939.* Minneapolis: University of Minnesota Press.

Baudrillard, Jean. 1989. *America.* London: Verso.

Behar, Ruth. 1996. *The Vulnerable Observer: Anthropology That Breaks Your Heart.* Boston: Beacon Press.

———, dir. 2002. *Adio Kerida.* Distributed by Women Make Movies, New York. DVD.

———. 2009. *An Island Called Home: Returning to Jewish Cuba.* New Brunswick, NJ: Rutgers University Press.

———. 2013. *Traveling Heavy: A Memoir in Between Journeys.* Durham, NC: Duke University Press.

Bejel, Emilio. 2001. *Gay Cuban Nation.* Chicago: University of Chicago Press.

Beliso-De Jesús, Aisha. 2014. "Santería Copresence and the Making of African Diaspora Bodies." *Cultural Anthropology* 29 (3): 502–26.

Benemelis, Juan F. 1988. *Castro, Subversion y terrorismo en Africa*. Madrid: Editorial San Martin.

———. 1990. "Cuba's African Policy." In *Cuba: The International Dimension*, edited by G. Fauriol and E. Loser, 121–51. New Brunswick, NJ: Transaction Publishers.

Benítez-Rojo, Antonio. 1992. *The Repeating Island: The Caribbean and the Postmodern Perspective*. Durham, NC: Duke University Press.

Benjamin, Medea, Joseph Collins, and Michael Scott. 1984. *No Free Lunch: Food and Revolution in Cuba Today*. San Francisco: Food First.

Berdahl, Daphne. 1999. *Where the World Ended: Re-unification and Identity in the German Borderland*. Berkeley: University of California Press.

Berenguer Cala, Jorge. 1979. *La emigración francesa en la jurisdicción de Cuba*. Santiago de Cuba: Editorial Oriente.

Berg, Mette L. 2009a. "Between Cosmopolitanism and the National Slot: Cuba's Diasporic Children of the Revolution." *Identities: Global Studies in Culture and Power* 16: 129–56.

———. 2009b. "Homeland and Belonging among Cubans in Spain." *Journal of Latin American and Caribbean Anthropology* 14 (2): 265–90.

———. 2012. *Diasporic Generations: Memory, Politics, and Nation among Cubans in Spain*. New York: Berghahn Books.

Berger, Carol A. 2001. "From Cattle Camp to Slaughterhouse: The Politics of Identity Among Cuban-Educated Dinka Refugees in Canada." Master's thesis, University of Alberta.

Bernstein, Alissa. 2013. "Transforming Medical Education and the Making of New Clinical Subjectivities through Cuban-Bolivian Medical Diplomacy." In *Health Travels: Cuban Health(care) On and Off the Island*, edited by N. Burke, 154–77. San Francisco, UC Medical Humanities Consortium.

Bettelheim, Judith, and Fernando Ortiz. 2001. *Cuban Festivals: A Century of Afro-Cuban Culture*. Princeton, NJ: Markus Wiener Publishers.

Bettinger-López, Caroline. 2000. *Cuban-Jewish Journeys: Searching for Identity, Home, and History in Miami*. Knoxville: University of Tennessee Press.

Black, Stephanie, dir. 2001. *Life and Debt*. New York: New Yorker Films. DVD.

Blue_Woman. 2009. "Profile of a Cubarawi" El Por Venir Del Sahara (blog), May 8. *elporvenirdelsahara.blogspot.com/2009/05/profile-of-cubarawi.html*.

Blum, Denise F. 2008. "Socialist Consciousness Raising and Cuba's School to the Countryside Program." *Anthropology and Education Quarterly* 39 (2): 141–60.

———. 2011. *Cuban Youth and Revolutionary Values: Educating the New Socialist Citizen*. Austin: University of Texas Press.

Boas, Franz. 1963. *The Handbook of American Indian Languages*. Washington, DC: Georgetown University Press Institute of Languages and Linguistics.

Bodenheimer, Rebecca M. 2015. *Geographies of Cubanidad: Place, Race, and Musical Performance in Contemporary Cuba*. Jackson: University Press of Mississippi.

Boicha, Limam. 2009a. "Poligamia." Caribbean of the Sahara, accessed May 18, 2009. *www.caribbeanofthesahara.com/poemas.htm*.

———. 2009b. "El Repetidor." Caribbean of the Sahara, accessed May 18, 2009. *www.caribbeanofthesahara.com/poemas.htm*.

Bolívar Aróstegui, Natalia. 1994. *Los orishas en Cuba*. Havana: PM.

Brana-Shute, Gary. 1989. *On the Corner: Male Social Life in a Paramaribo Creole Neighborhood*. Prospect Heights, IL: Waveland Press.

Bravo, Estela, dir. 1990. *After the Battle*. Distributed by Cinema Guild, New York. DVD.

Brent, William L. 1996. *Long Time Gone*. New York: Times Books.

Brettell, Caroline. 2003. *Anthropology and Migration: Essays on Transnationalism, Ethnicity, and Identity*. Walnut Creek, CA: Altamira Press.

Brock, Lisa, and Otis Cunningham. 1991. "Race and the Cuban Revolution: A Critique of Carlos Moore's 'Castro, the Blacks, and Africa.'" *Cuban Studies* 21: 171–85. *www.jstor.org/stable/24485707*.

Brotherton, Pierre Sean. 2012. *Revolutionary Medicine: Health and the Body in Post-Soviet Cuba*. Durham, NC: Duke University Press.

Brown, David H. 1993. "Thrones of the Orichas: Afro-Cuban Altars in New Jersey, New York, and Havana." *African Arts* 26 (4): 44–59.

———. 2003. *Santeria Enthroned: Art, Ritual, and Innovation in an Afro-Cuban Religion*. Chicago: The University of Chicago Press.

Browne, Katherine E., and Rod Salter. 2004. *Creole Economics: Caribbean Cunning under the French Flag*. Austin: University of Texas Press.

Buenavilla Recio, Rolando. 1995. *Historia de la pedagogía en Cuba*. Havana: Editorial Pueblo y Educación.

Burke, Nancy J. 2001. "Creating Islands in the Desert: Place, Space, and Ritual among Santería Practitioners in Albuquerque, New Mexico." PhD diss., University of New Mexico.

———, ed. 2013. *Health Travels: Cuban Health(care) On and Off the Island*. San Francisco: UC Medical Humanities Press.

Butterworth, Douglas. 1980. *The People of Buena Ventura: Relocation of Slum Dwellers in Postrevolutionary Cuba*. Chicago: University of Illinois Press.

Cabezas, Amalia. 1999. "Women's Work Is Never Done: Sex Tourism in Sosúa, the Dominican Republic." In *Sun, Sex, and Gold: Tourism and Sex Work in the Caribbean*, edited by K. Kempadoo, 93–123. New York: Rowman and Littlefield.

———. 2009. *Economies of Desire: Sex and Tourism in Cuba and the Dominican Republic*. Philadelphia: Temple University Press.

Cabrera, Lydia. 1975. *El monte: Igbo, finda, ewe orisha, vititi nfinda: Notas sobre las religiones, la magia, las supersticiones y el folklore de los negros criollos y el pueblo de Cuba.* Miami, FL: Ediciones Universal.

Calderón, Ana L., dir. 2007. *La Isla de la Juventud: El sitio ideal para hacer realidad cualquier sueño.* Mexico: Zafra Video, DVD.

Calvo, Sara, and Alejandro Armengol. 1978. *El Racismo en el Cine.* Havana: Serie Literatura y Arte.

Carbonell, Walterio. 1961. *Crítica: Como surgió la cultural nacional.* Havana: Min. de Educación.

Carter, Thomas F. 2000. "Playing Hardball: Constructions of Cuban Identity." PhD diss., University of New Mexico.

———. 2002. "Baseball Arguments: *Aficionismo* and Masculinity at the Core of *Cubanidad.*" In *Sport in Latin American Society: Past and Present*, edited by J. A. Mangan and L. P. d. Costa, 117–38. London: Frank Cass.

———. 2007. "Family Networks, State Interventions and the Experience of Cuban Transnational Sport Migration." *International Review for the Sociology of Sport* 42 (4): 371–89.

———. 2008a. "Of Spectacular Phantasmal Desire: Tourism and the Cuban State's Complicity in the Commodification of its Citizens." *Leisure Studies* 27 (3): 241–57.

———. 2008b. *The Quality of Home Runs: The Passion, Politics, and Language of Cuban Baseball.* Durham, NC: Duke University Press.

———. 2011. *In Foreign Fields: The Politics and Experiences of Transnational Sport Migration.* New York: Pluto Press.

Casal, Lourdes. 1989. "Race Relations in Contemporary Cuba." In *The Cuba Reader: The Making of a Revolutionary Society*, edited by Philip Brenner, William M. LeoGrande, Donna Rich, and Daniel Siegel, 471–86. New York: Grove Press.

Casey, Matthew. 2012. "From Haiti to Cuba and Back: Haitians' Experiences of Migration, Labor, and Return, 1900–1940." PhD diss., University of Pittsburgh.

Castañeda, Tiburicio P. 1925. *La explosión del Maine y la guerra de los Estados Unidos con España.* Havana: La Moderna Poesía.

Castellanos, Jorge. 2003. *Pioneros de la etnografía afrocubana: Fernando Ortiz, Rómulo Lachatañeré, Lydia Cabrera.* Miami, FL: Ediciones Universal.

Castillo Falcato, Norma., ed. 1981. *Cuba y la defensa de la Republica Española (1936–1939).* Havana: Editorial Politica.

Castro Ruz, Fidel. 1981. *Fidel Castro Speeches: Cuba's Internationalist Foreign Policy, 1975–80.* New York: Pathfinder Press.

———. 1989. "We Are United by Blood." In *Changing the History of Africa: Angola and Namibia*, edited by David Deutschmann, 76–83. Melbourne: Ocean Press.

Centeno, Miguel A., and Mauricio Font, eds. 1997. *Toward a New Cuba? Legacies of a Revolution*. Boulder, CO: Lynne Rienner Publishers.

Certeau, Michel d'. 1984. *The Practice of Everyday Life*. Berkeley: University of California Press.

Chadwick, Lee. 1975. *A Cuban Journey*. London: Dennis Dobson.

Chamberlain, Mary. 1998. *Caribbean Migration: Globalised Identities*. London: Routledge.

Charlton, Audrey K. 2005. "'Cat Born in Oven is Not Bread': Jamaican and Barbadian Immigrants in Cuba between 1900 and 1959." PhD diss., Columbia University.

Chatty, Dawn. 2010. *Deterritorialized Youth: Sahrawi and Afghan Refugees at the Margins of the Middle East*. New York: Berghahn Books.

Chatty, Dawn, Elena Fiddian-Qasmiyeh, and Gina Crivello. 2010. "Identity With/out Territory: Sahrawi Refugee Youth in Transnational Space." In *Deterritorialized Youth: Sahrawi and Afghan Refugees at the Margins of the Middle East*, edited by D. Chatty, 37–84. New York: Berghan Books.

Chávez, Lydia, and Mimi Chakarova. 2005. *Capitalism, God, and a Good Cigar: Cuba Enters the Twenty-First Century*. Durham, NC: Duke University Press.

Chomsky, Noam. 1987. *On Power and Ideology: The Managua Lectures*. Boston: South End Press.

Clarke, Austin. 1980. *Growing Up Stupid under the Union Jack*. Havana: Casa de Las Americas.

Clarke, Kamari Maxine, and Deborah A. Thomas, eds. 2006. *Globalization and Race: Transformations in the Cultural Production of Blackness*. Durham, NC: Duke University Press.

Clytus, John. 1970. *Black Man in Red Cuba*. Coral Gables, FL: University of Miami Press.

Coe, Cati. 2005. *Dilemmas of Culture in African Schools: Youth, Nationalism, and the Transformation of Knowledge*. Chicago: The University of Chicago Press.

Cole, Johnetta B. 1980a. "Women in Cuba: The Revolution Within the Revolution." In *Comparative Perspectives of Third World Women: The Impact of Race, Sex, and Class*, edited by B. Lindsay, 162–78. New York: Praeger.

———. 1980b. "Race toward Equality: The Impact of the Cuban Revolution on Racism." *Black Scholar* 11 (8): 2–24.

Columbus, Christopher. 1989. *The Diario of Christopher Columbus's First Voyage to America, 1492–1493*. Norman: University of Oklahoma Press.

Conde, Yvonne M. 1999. *Operation Pedro Pan: The Untold Exodus of 14,048 Cuban Children*. New York: Routledge.

Corbett, Ben. 2002. *This is Cuba: An Outlaw Culture Survives*. Boulder CO: Westview Press.

Coronil, Fernando. 1997. *The Magical State: Nature, Money, and Modernity in Venezuela*. Chicago: The University of Chicago Press.

Corse, Theron E. 2007. *Protestants, Revolution, and the Cuba-U.S. Bond*. Gainesville: University Press of Florida.

Couceiro Rodríguez, Avelino. 2009. *Hacia una antropología urbana en Cuba*. Havana: Fundación Fernando Ortiz.

Cuban Grammy Winners. 2001. Richmond Hill, Ontario: GDN Records. CD.

Curet, L. Antonio, Shannon Lee Dawdy, and Gabino La Rosa Corzo. 2005. *Dialogues in Cuban Archaeology*. Tuscaloosa: University of Alabama Press.

Curtis, Debra. 2009. *Pleasures and Perils: Girls' Sexuality in a Caribbean Consumer Culture*. New Brunswick, NJ: Rutgers University Press.

Cushing, Lincoln. 2003. *Revolución!: Cuban Poster Art*. San Francisco: Chronicle Books.

Daigle, Megan. 2015. *From Cuba with Love: Sex and Money in the Twenty-First Century*. Oakland: University of California Press.

Dana, Richard H., Jr. 1859. *To Cuba and Back: A Vacation Voyage*. Boston: Ticknor and Fields.

Daniel, Yvonne. 1991. "Changing Values in Cuban Rumba, A Lower Class Black Dance Appropriated by the Cuban Revolution." *Dance Research Journal* 23 (2): 1–10.

———. 1995. *Rumba: Dance and Social Change in Contemporary Cuba*. Bloomington: Indiana University Press.

———. 2005. *Dancing Wisdom: Embodied Knowledge in Haitian Vodou, Cuban Yoruba, and Bahian Candomblé*. Urbana: University of Illinois Press.

———. 2011. *Caribbean and Atlantic Diaspora Dance: Igniting Citizenship*. Urbana: University of Illinois Press.

Daves, Delmar, dir. 1957. 1993. *3:10 to Yuma*. Culver City, CA: Columbia Pictures. VHS.

Davis, Angela. 1976. *Autobiografía*. Havana: Editorial de Ciencias Sociales.

Dawson, Barry. 2001. *Street Graphics Cuba*. New York: Thames and Hudson.

Del Real, Patricio, and Anna Cristina Pertierra. 2008. "Inventar: Recent Struggles and Inventions in Housing in Two Cuban Cities." *Buildings and Landscapes* 15: 78–92.

Deleuze, Gilles, and Felix Guattari. 1988. *A Thousand Plateaus: Capitalism and Schizophrenia*. London: Athlone Press.

Derby, Lauren H. 2009. *The Dictator's Seduction: Politics and the Popular Imagination in the Era of Trujillo*. Durham, NC: Duke University Press.

Desnoes, Edmundo, ed. 1967. *NOW: El movimiento negro en Estados Unidos*. Havana: Instituto del Libro.

Deutschmann, David, ed. 1989. *Changing the History of Africa: Angola and Namibia*. Melbourne: Ocean Press.

Díaz, Rolando, dir. 1998. *Si me comprendieras*. Mexico City, Mexico: Luna Llena Producciones. VHS.

Didion, Joan. 1987. *Miami*. New York: Vintage Books.

di Leo, Octavio. 2005. "It All Started in Madrid." In *Cuban Counterpoints: The Legacy of Fernando Ortiz*, edited by M. A. Font and A. W. Quiroz, 39–54. New York: Lexington Books.

Domínguez, Virginia R. 1989. *People as Subject, People as Object: Selfhood and Peoplehood in Contemporary Israel*. Madison: University of Wisconsin Press.

———. 1994. *White by Definition: Social Classification in Creole Louisiana*. New Brunswick, NJ: Rutgers University Press.

Dopico, Ana M. 2004. "The 3:10 to Yuma." In *Anti-Americanism*, edited by A. Ross and K. Ross, 47–68. New York: New York University Press.

Duany, Jorge. 1999. "Two Wings of the Same Bird? Contemporary Puerto Rican Attitudes toward Cuban Immigrants." *Cuban Studies* 30: 26–51.

Dunn, Marvin. 1997. *Black Miami in the Twentieth Century*. Gainesville: University Press of Florida.

Eastman, Benjamin. 2008. "Baseball in the Breach: Notes on Defection, Disaffection and Transition in Contemporary Cuba." In *America's Game(s): A Critical Anthropology of Sport*, edited by B. Eastman, M. Ralph and S. Porter, 126–57. New York: Routledge.

Eckstein, Susan. 2009. *The Immigrant Divide: How Cuban Americans Changed the US and Their Homeland*. New York: Routledge.

Eco, Umberto. 1986. *Travels in Hyperreality: Essays*. San Diego, CA: Harcourt Brace Jovanovich.

Editorial Pueblo y Educación. 1990. *Estudio y trabajo*. Havana: Editorial Pueblo y Educación.

Elejalde Villalón, Oscar. 2012. "Cubans Sharing Education: The Isle of Youth." In *The Capacity to Share: A Study of Cuba's International Cooperation in Educational Development*, edited by Anne Hickling-Hudson, Jorge Corona Gonzalez, and Rosemary Preston, 217–23. New York: Palgrave Macmillan.

Elkins, Stanley M. 1959. *Slavery: A Problem in American Institutional and Intellectual Life*. Chicago: University of Chicago Press.

Erisman, H. Michael, and John M. Kirk, eds. 1991. *Cuban Foreign Policy Confronts a New International Order*. Boulder, CO: Lynne Rienner Publishers.

Evans-Pritchard, E. E. 1940. *The Nuer: A Description of the Modes of Livelihood and Political Institutions of a Nilotic People*. New York: Oxford University Press.

Evenson, Debra. 1994. *Revolution in the Balance: Law and Society in Contemporary Cuba*. Boulder, CO: Westview Press.

Fedorak, Shirley A. 2009. *Pop Culture: The Culture of Everyday Life*. Toronto: University of Toronto Press.

Fehérváry, Krisztina. 2002. "American Kitchens, Luxury Bathrooms, and the Search for a 'Normal' Life in Postsocialist Hungary." *Ethnos* 67 (3): 369–400.

———. 2009. "Goods and States: The Political Logic of State-Socialist Material Culture." *Comparative Studies in Society and History* 51 (2): 426–59.

———. 2012. "From Socialist Modern to Super-Natural Organicism: Cosmological Transformations through Home Decor." *Cultural Anthropology* 27 (4): 615–40.

———. 2013. *Politics in Color and Concrete: Socialist Materialities and the Middle Class in Hungary*. Bloomington: Indiana University Press.

Ferguson, Ed. 1988. "African Studies in Cuba." *Cuba Update* IX (4–5): 30.

Fernandes, Sujatha. 2006. *Cuba Represent!: Cuban Arts, State Power, and the Making of New Revolutionary Cultures*. Durham, NC: Duke University Press.

Fernández, Damián J., ed. 2005. *Cuba Transnational*. Gainesville: University Press of Florida.

Fernandez, Nadine T. 1996. "Race, Romance, and Revolution: The Cultural Politics of Interracial Encounters in Cuba." PhD diss., University of California, Berkeley.

———. 2001. "The Changing Discourse of Race in Contemporary Cuba." *International Journal of Qualitative Studies in Education* 14 (2): 117–32.

———. 2006. "A Racial Geography: The Meanings of Blackness in a Havana Neighborhood." *Islas* 1 (2): 14–20.

———. 2010. *Revolutionizing Romance: Interracial Couples in Contemporary Cuba*. New Brunswick, NJ: Rutgers University Press.

Fernández de Juan, Adelaida. 1998. "The Egyptians." In *Cubana: Contemporary Fiction by Cuban Women*, edited by M. Yáúez, 175–79. Boston: Beacon Press.

Fernández Retamar, Roberto. 1989. *Caliban and Other Essays*. Minneapolis: University of Minnesota Press.

Fernández Robaina, Tómas. 2007. *Cuba racial: Personalidades en el debate (conferencias y ensayos)*. Havana: Editorial de Ciencias Sociales.

Ferrer, Ada. 1999. *Insurgent Cuba: Race, Nation, and Revolution, 1868–1898*. Chapel Hill: University of North Carolina Press.

Fiddian-Qasmiyeh, Elena. 2009. "Representing Sahrawi Refugees' 'Educational Displacement' to Cuba: Self-sufficient Agents or Manipulated Victims in Conflict?" *Journal of Refugee Studies* 22 (3): 323–50.

———. 2010. "Education, Migration and Internationalism: Situating Muslim Middle Eastern and North African Students in Cuba." *Journal of North African Studies* 15 (2): 137–55.

Figueroa Araujo, Max. 1976. "The Cuban School in the Countryside." *Prospects* 6 (1): 127–31.

Flores, Juan. 2009. *The Diaspora Strikes Back: Caribeño Tales of Learning and Turning*. New York: Routledge.

Follina. 2007. "Entrevista a Maima Mahamud" *Mujeres del Sahara* (blog). May 25. *mujeresdelsahara.blogspot.com/2007/05/entrevista-maima-mahamud.html*.

Forrest, David. 2002. "Lenin, the *Pinguero*, and Cuban Imaginings of Maleness in Times of Scarcity." In *Masculinities Matter! Men, Gender and Development*, edited by F. Cleaver, 84–111. London: Zed Books.

Foster, Robert J. 2008. *Coca-Globalization: Following Soft Drinks from New York to New Guinea*. New York: Palgrave Macmillan.

Frank, Andre G. 1970. *Latin America: Underdevelopment or Revolution; Essays on the Development of Underdevelopment and the Immediate Enemy*. New York: Monthly Review Press.

Frederik, Laurie A. 2012. *Trumpets in the Mountains: Theater and the Politics of National Culture in Cuba*. Durham, NC: Duke University Press.

Freeman, Carla. 2000. *High Tech and High Heels in the Global Economy: Women, Work, and Pink-Collar Identities in the Caribbean*. Durham, NC: Duke University Press.

Freyre, Gilberto. (1933) 1971. *The Masters and the Slaves: A Study in the Development of Brazilian Civilization*. New York: Alfred A. Knopf.

Fuente, Alejandro de la. 1990. "Los matrimonios de esclavos en La Habana, 1585–1645." *Ibero-Amerikanisches Archiv* 16 (4): 507–28.

———. 1995. "Race and Inequality in Cuba, 1899–1981." *Journal of Contemporary History* 30 (1995): 131–68.

———. 2001. *A Nation for All: Race, Inequality, and Politics in Twentieth-Century Cuba*. Chapel Hill: University of North Carolina Press.

Gal, Susan. 1994. "Gender in the Post-Socialist Transition: The Abortion Debate in Hungary." *East European Politics and Societies* 8 (2): 256–86.

García, Daniel., ed. 1995. *Cuba: Cultura e Identidad Nacional*. Havana: Ediciones Unión.

García, Juan A. 1999. *¿Quien le pone el cascabel al Oscar?* Santiago de Cuba: Editorial Oriente.

García, Nakord. 2011. "GENERACION 1979-ESBEC 53 'Carlos Fonseca Amador'.wmv." YouTube video, 14:27, posted December 19. *www.youtube.com/watch?v=sCeYCK3b-zw*.

García Alonso, Navgil. 2006. "Formados en la Isla más de 45 mil profesionales del Tercer Mundo." *Granma Internaciónal*, August 4.

García Canclini, Néstor. 1995. *Hybrid Cultures: Strategies for Entering and Leaving Modernity.* Minneapolis: University of Minnesota Press.

García Márquez, Gabriel. (1977) 1981. "Cuba in Angola: Operation Carlotta." In *Cuba's Internationalist Foreign Policy: Speeches, Vol. 1, 1975–80,* edited by Michael Tabor, 339–57. New York: Pathfinder Press.

———. 1989. "Operation Carlota." In *Changing the History of Africa: Angola and Namibia,* edited by David Deutschmann, 41. Melbourne: Ocean Press.

Garth, Hanna. 2012. "Things Become Scarce: Food Availability and Accessibility in Santiago de Cuba Then and Now." In *Taking Food Public: Redefining Foodways in a Changing World,* edited by Psyche Williams-Forson and Carole Counihan, 59–70. New York: Routledge.

———. 2013. *Food and Identity in the Caribbean.* London: Bloomsbury Academic.

Garton Ash, Timothy. 1997. *The File: A Personal History.* New York: Random House.

Gay-Calbó, Enrique. 2000. *Los símbolos de la nación cubana.* Havana: Ediciones Boloña.

Gébler, Carlo. 1988. *Driving through Cuba: Rare Encounters in the Land of Sugar Cane and Revolution.* New York: Simon and Schuster.

Geertz, Clifford. 1973. *The Interpretation of Cultures.* New York: Basic Books.

Geldof, Lynn. 1991. *Cubans: Voices of Change.* New York: St. Martin's Press.

Giuliano, Maurizio. 1998. *El caso CEA: Intelectuales e inquisidores en Cuba ¿Perestroika en la Isla?* Miami, FL: Ediciones Universal.

Gleijeses, Piero. 2002. *Conflicting Missions: Havana, Washington, and Africa, 1959–1976.* Chapel Hill: University of North Carolina Press.

Gleijeses, Piero, Jorge Risquet, and Fernando Remírez. 2007. *Cuba y África: Historia común de lucha y sangre.* Havana: Editorial de Ciencias Sociales.

Gmelch, George. 2003. *Behind the Smile: The Working Lives of Caribbean Tourism.* Bloomington: Indiana University Press.

Gmelch, George, and Sharon Gmelch. 2012. *The Parish behind God's Back: The Changing Culture of Rural Barbados.* Long Grove, IL: Waveland Press.

Gonçalves, João Felipe. 2012. "The Hero's Many Bodies: Monuments, Nationalism and Power in Havana and Miami." PhD diss., University of Chicago.

———. 2013. "Sputnick Premiers in Havana: A Historical Ethnography of the 1960 Soviet Exposition." In *The Socialist Sixties: The Global Moment in Eastern Europe, the Soviet Union, and Cuba,* edited by Anne E. Gorsuch and Diane P. Koenker, 84–117. Bloomington: University of Indiana Press.

———. 2014. "The Ajiaco in Cuba and Beyond: Preface to 'The Human Factors of Cubanidad' by Fernando Ortiz." *Hau: Journal of Ethnographic Theory* 4 (3): 445–54.

González, Héctor M. 1997. "Conciencia Socialista and Education in Cuba." Master's thesis, University of Alberta.

González, Juan. 2011. *Harvest of Empire: A History of Latinos in America.* New York: Penguin Books.

Gordon, Joy. 1997. "Cuba's Entrepreneurial Socialism." *Foreign Affairs* (January): 18, 20–22, 30.

Gordy, Katherine. 2006. "'Sales + Economy + Efficiency = Revolution'? Dollarization, Consumer Capitalism, and Popular Responses in Special Period Cuba." *Public Culture* 18 (2): 383–412.

Gregory, Steven. 2007. *The Devil behind the Mirror: Globalization and Politics in the Dominican Republic.* Berkeley: University of California Press.

Greising, David. 1998. *I'd Like the World to Buy a Coke: The Life and Leadership of Roberto Goizueta.* New York: Wiley.

Grenier, Guillermo J., and Corinna J. Moebius. 2015. *A History of Little Havana.* Charleston, SC: The History Press.

Gropas, Maria. 2006. "Landscape, Revolution and Property Regimes in Rural Havana." *Journal of Peasant Studies* 33 (2): 248–77.

———. 2007. "The Repatriotization of Revolutionary Ideology and Mnemonic Landscape in Present-Day Havana." *Current Anthropology* 48 (4): 531–49.

Guanche Pérez, Jesús. 1983. *Procesos etnoculturales de Cuba.* Havana: Editorial Letras Cubanas.

———. 1996. *Componentes etnicos de la nación cubana.* Havana: Fundación Fernando Ortiz.

Guevara, Ernesto. 2000. *The African Dream: The Diaries of the Revolutionary War in the Congo.* New York: Grove Press.

Gupta, Akhil, and James Ferguson. 2008. "Discipline and Practice: 'The Field' as Site, Method, and Location in Anthropology." In *The Transnational Studies Reader: Intersections and Innovations,* edited by Sanjeev Khagram and Peggy Levitt, 87–103. New York: Routledge.

Gutiérrez, Pedro J. 2001. *Dirty Havana Trilogy: A Novel in Stories.* Translated by Natasha Wimmer. New York: Farrar Straus and Giroux.

Gutiérrez Alea, Tomás. 1968. *Memories of Underdevelopment.* Instituto Cubano de Arte y Industria Cinematograficos.

Gutiérrez Alea, Tomás, and Juan Carlos Tabio. 1994a. *Guantanamera.* Instituto Cubano de Arte y Industria Cinematograficos.

———. 1994b. *Strawberry and Chocolate.* Instituto Cubano de Arte y Industria Cinematograficos.

Habermas, Jürgen. 1991. *The Structural Transformation of the Public Sphere: An Inquiry into a Category of Bourgeois Society.* Cambridge, MA: MIT Press.

Hagedorn, Katherine J. 2001. *Divine Utterances: The Performance of Afro-Cuban Santeria*. Washington, DC: Smithsonian Institution Press.

Hall, Stuart. 1995. "Negotiating Caribbean Identities." *New Left Review* 209 (January/February): 3–14.

Halperin, Maurice. 1978. "Oscar Lewis and the Cuban Revolution." *Queen's Quarterly* 85 (4): 677–85.

Hansing, Katrin. 2006. *Rasta, Race and Revolution: The Emergence and Development of the Rastafari Movement in Socialist Cuba*. Berlin: LIT/Transaction Publishers.

———. 2009. "South-South Migration and Transnational Ties between Cuba and Mozambique." In *Transnational Ties: Cities, Migrations, and Identities*, edited by Michael Peter Smith and John Eade, 77–90. New Brunswick, NJ: Transaction Publishers.

Hardt, Michael, and Antonio Negri. 2000. *Empire*. Cambridge, MA: Harvard University Press.

Härkönen, Heidi. 2014a. "Review Essay: Gender and Sexuality in Contemporary Cuba." *Suomen Antropologi: Journal of the Finnish Anthropological Society* 39 (4): 68–72.

———. 2014b. "'To Not Die Alone': Kinship, Love and Life Cycle in Contemporary Havana, Cuba." *Suomen Antropologi: Journal of the Finnish Anthropological Society* 39 (2): 83–88.

Harris, Daryl B. 1999. *The Logic of Black Urban Rebellions: Challenging the Dynamics of White Domination in Miami*. Westport, CT: Praeger.

Hearn, Adrian H. 2008. *Cuba: Religion, Social Capital, and Development*. Durham, NC: Duke University Press.

Hebdige, Dick. 1979. *Subculture, The Meaning of Style*. London: Methuen.

Helg, Aline. 1995. *Our Rightful Share: The Afro-Cuban Struggle for Equality, 1886–1912*. Chapel Hill: University of North Carolina Press.

———. 1997. "Race and Black Mobilization in Colonial and Early Independent Cuba: A Comparative Perspective." *Ethnohistory* 44 (1): 53–74.

Hemingway, Ernest. 1952. *The Old Man and the Sea*. New York: Scribner.

Hergesheimer, Joseph. 1927. *San Cristóbal de La Habana*. New York: Alfred A. Knopf.

Hermer, Consuelo, and Marjorie May. 1941. *Havana Mañana: A Guide to Cuba and the Cubans*. New York: Random House.

Hernández-Reguant, Ariana. 2002. "Radio Taino and the Globalization of the Cuban Culture Industries." PhD diss., University of Chicago.

———. 2004. "Blackness with a Cuban Beat." *NACLA Report on the Americas* September/October: 31–36.

————. 2005. "Cuba's Alternative Geographies." *Journal of Latin American Anthropology* 10 (2): 275–313.

————. 2006. "Havana's Timba: A Macho Sound for Black Sex." In *Globalization and Race: Transformations in the Cultural Production of Blackness*, edited by Kamari Maxine Clarke and Deborah A. Thomas, 249–78. Durham, NC: Duke University Press.

————. 2009. *Cuba in the Special Period: Culture and Ideology in the 1990s*. New York: Palgrave Macmillan.

————. 2012. "World Music Producers and the Cuban Frontier." In *Music and Globalization: Critical Encounters*, edited by Bob W. White, 111–34. Bloomington: Indiana University Press.

Hickling-Hudson, Anne, Jorge Corona Gonzalez, and Rosemary A. Preston. 2012. *The Capacity to Share: A Study of Cuba's International Cooperation in Educational Development*. New York: Palgrave Macmillan.

Hill, Matthew J. 2004. "Globalizing Havana: World Heritage and Urban Redevelopment in Late Socialist Cuba." PhD diss., University of Chicago.

————. 2007. "Reimagining Old Havana: World Heritage and the Production of Scale in Late Socialist Cuba." In *Deciphering the Global: Its Scales, Spaces and Subjects*, edited by Saskia Sassen, 59–77. New York: Routledge.

————. 2012. "The Future of the Past: World Heritage, National Identity, and Urban Centrality in Late Socialist Cuba." In *Global Downtowns*, edited by Marina Peterson and Gary McDonogh, 186–205. Philadelphia: University of Pennsylvania Press.

Hirschfeld, Katherine. 2007. *Health, Politics, and Revolution in Cuba since 1898*. New Brunswick, NJ: Transaction Publishers.

Hodge, G. Derrick. 2001. "Colonization of the Cuban Body: The Growth of Male Sex Work in Havana." *NACLA Report on the Americas* 34 (5): 20–28.

Hoetink, Hendrik. 1967. *The Two Variants in Caribbean Race Relations: A Contribution to the Sociology of Segmented Societies*. London: Oxford University Press. Published for the Institute of Race Relations.

Hofstadter, Richard. 1965. *The Paranoid Style in American Politics: And Other Essays*. New York: Knopf.

Holbraad, Martin. 2012a. "Truth beyond Doubt: Ifá Oracles in Havana." *HAU: Journal of Ethnographic Theory* 2 (1): 81–109.

————. 2012b. *Truth in Motion: The Recursive Anthropology of Cuban Divination*. Chicago: University of Chicago Press.

Hughes, Langston. 1993. *I Wonder as I Wander: An Autobiographical Journey*. New York: Hill and Wang.

Humboldt, Alexander von, Miguel Angel Puig-Samper, Consuelo Naranjo Orovio, and Armando García González. 1998. *Ensayo político sobre la Isla de Cuba*. Madrid: Ediciones Doce Calles.

Humboldt, Alexander von, and John S. Thrasher. 1856. *The Island of Cuba*. New York: Derby and Jackson.

Humphreys, Laura-Zoë. 2012. "Symptomologies of the State: Cuba's 'Email War' and the Paranoid Public Sphere." In *Digital Cultures and the Politics of Emotion: Feelings, Affect and Technological Change*, edited by Athina Karatzogianni and Adi Kuntsman, 197–213. New York: Palgrave McMillan.

Hunt, Christopher. 1998. *Waiting for Fidel*. New York: Houghton Mifflin.

Ibarra, Jorge. 1981. *Nacion y cultura nacional, 1868–1930*. Havana: Editorial Letras Cubanas.

Ichaso, Leon, dir. 1996. *Azúcar amarga [Bitter Sugar]*. Havana and Santo Domingo: Azúcar Films. VHS.

Jaffe, Rivke. 2010. "Tourism, Sexuality and Power in the Spanish Caribbean." *European Review of Latin American and Caribbean Studies* 88 (April): 111–16.

Jané, Pablo., ed. 1988. *La realidad de un sueño: Isla de juventud*. Havana: Ediciones Plaza Vieja.

Jatar-Hausmann, Ana J. 1999. *The Cuban Way: Capitalism, Communism and Confrontation*. West Hartford, CT: Kumarian Press.

Jenkins, John. 2010. *Travelers' Tales of Old Cuba*. Melbourne: Ocean Press.

Kaba Akoriyea, Samuel. 2012. "The Long Road to Neurosurgery: Reflections from Ghana on 18 Years of Studies in Cuba." In *The Capacity to Share: A Study of Cuba's International Cooperation in Educational Development*, edited by Anne Hickling-Hudson, Jorge Corona Gonzalez, and Rosemary Preston, 225–30. New York: Palgrave Macmillan.

Kearney, Michael. 1995. "The Local and the Global: The Anthropology of Globalization and Transnationalism." *Annual Review of Anthropology* 24: 547–65.

Kelly, John. 2006. *The American Game: Capitalism, Decolonization, Global Domination, and Baseball*. Chicago: Prickly Paradigm Press.

Kempadoo, Kamala. 1999. *Sun, Sex, and Gold: Tourism and Sex Work in the Caribbean*. Lanham, MD: Rowman and Littlefield.

Klein, Herbert S. 1989. *Slavery in the Americas: A Comparative Study of Virginia and Cuba*. Chicago: Ivan R. Dee, Inc.

Klein, Naomi. 2000. *No Logo: Taking Aim at the Brand Bullies*. New York: Picador.

Knauer, Lisa M. 2008. "Audiovisual Remittances and Transnational Subjectivities." In *Cuba in the Special Period: Culture and Ideology in the 1990s*, edited by Ariana Hernández Reguant, 159–78. New York: Palgrave Macmillan.

Knight, Franklin W. 1970. *Slave Society in Cuba during the Nineteenth Century.* Madison: University of Wisconsin Press.

Kornai, János. 1980. *Economics of Shortage.* New York: North-Holland.

Kutzinski, Vera M. 1993. *Sugar's Secrets: Race and the Erotics of Cuban Nationalism.* Charlottesville: University Press of Virginia.

Lachatañeré, Rómulo. 1992a. *El sistema religioso de los afrocubanos.* Havana: Editorial de Ciencias Sociales.

———. 1992b. *¡¡Oh, Mío Yemayá!! Cuentos y cantos negros.* Havana: Editorial de Ciencias Sociales.

Lampland, Martha. 1995. *The Object of Labor: Commodification in Socialist Hungary.* Chicago: University of Chicago Press.

Lehr, Sabine. 2008. "The Children of the Isle of Youth: Impact of a Cuban South-South Education Program on Ghanaian Graduates." PhD diss., University of Victoria.

LeoGrande, William M. 1980. *Cuba's Policy in Africa, 1959–1980.* Berkeley, CA: Institute for International Studies.

———. 1989. "Cuba's Policy in Africa." In *The Cuba Reader: The Making of a Revolutionary Society,* edited by Philip Brenner, William M. LeoGrande, Donna Rich, and Daniel Siegel, 375–95. New York: Grove Press.

León, Argeliers. 1991. "Of the Axle and the Hinge: Nationalism, Afro-Cubanism, and Music in Pre-Revolutionary Cuba." In *Essays on Cuban Music: North American and Cuban Perspectives,* edited by Peter Manuel, 267–82. Lanham, MD: University Press of America.

Levi, Vicki Gold, and Steven Heller. 2002. *Cuba Style: Graphics from the Golden Age of Design.* New York: Princeton Archetectural Press.

Levitt, Peggy. 2001. *The Transnational Villagers.* Berkeley: University of California Press.

Lewis, Oscar, Ruth M. Lewis, and Susan M. Rigdon. 1977. *Four Men: Living the Revolution: An Oral History of Contemporary Cuba.* Chicago: University of Illinois Press.

Lin, Yi-Chieh Jessica. 2011. *Fake Stuff: China and the Rise of Counterfeit Goods.* New York: Routledge.

López, Kathleen. 2013. *Chinese Cubans: A Transnational History.* Chapel Hill: University of North Carolina Press.

López Valdés, Rafael L. 1985. *Componentes africanos en el etnos cubano.* Havana: Editorial de Ciencias Sociales.

Loss, Jacqueline. 2011. "Topographies of Cosmonauts in Havana: Proyecto Vostok and Insausti's Existen." In *Havana beyond the Ruins: Cultural Mappings after 1989,* edited by Anke Birkenmaier and Esther Whitfield, 209–28. Durham NC, Duke University Press.

———. 2013. *Dreaming in Russian: The Cuban Soviet Imaginary*. Austin: University of Texas Press.

Loss, Jacqueline, and José Manuel Prieto González. 2012. *Caviar with Rum: Cuba-USSR and the Post-Soviet Experience*. New York: Palgrave Macmillan.

Loyola Moya, María A., ed. 2012. *Cuba etnografica*. Havana: Fundación Fernando Ortiz.

Luis, William. 2014. "Nota del Editor." *Afro-Hispanic Review* 33 (1): 7–12.

Lumsden, Ian. 1996. *Machos, Maricones, and Gays: Cuba and Homosexuality*. Philadelphia: Temple University Press.

Madrid, Alejandro L., and Robin D. Moore. 2013. *Danzón: Circum-Caribbean Dialogues in Music and Dance*. New York: Oxford University Press.

Marable, Manning. 1999. "Assata Shakur: 'The Continuity of Struggle'" *Souls: A Critical Journal of Black Politics, Culture, and Society* 1 (2): 93–100.

Marcus, George E., ed. 1999. *Paranoia within Reason: A Casebook on Conspiracy as Explanation*. Chicago: University of Chicago Press.

Márquez, Antonio. 2005. *Las cubarauis*. Sevilla: Azul Media.

Marshall, Peter H. 1987. *Cuba Libre: Breaking the Chains?* Boston: Faber and Faber.

Martí, José. 1959. *La cuestion agraria y la educacion del campesino*. Havana: Editorial Lex.

———. 1975. *Obras completas*. Havana: Editorial de Ciencias Sociales.

Martin, Laura. 1986. "'Eskimo Words for Snow': A Case Study in the Genesis and Decay of an Anthropological Example." *American Anthropologist* 88 (2): 419–23.

Martínez, Samuel. 2007. *Decency and Excess: Global Aspirations and Material Deprivation on a Caribbean Sugar Plantation*. Boulder, CO: Paradigm Publishers.

Martinez-Alier, Verena. 1974. *Marriage, Class, and Colour in Nineteenth-Century Cuba: A Study of Racial Attitudes and Sexual Values in a Slave Society*. London: Cambridge University Press.

Martínez Fernández, Luis. 1998. *Fighting Slavery in the Caribbean: The Life and Times of a British Family in Nineteenth-Century Havana*. Armonk, NY: M.E. Sharpe.

Marx, Karl. 1987. *Economic and Philosophic Manuscripts of 1844*. Buffalo, NY: Prometheus Books.

———. 1990. *Capital: A Critique of Political Economy*. London: Penguin Classics.

Marx, Karl, and Frederick Engels 1970. *The German Ideology: Part One, with Selections from Parts Two and Three, Together with Marx's "Introduction to a Critique of Political Economy."* New York: International Publishers.

Mason, Michael A. 2002. *Living Santería: Rituals and Experiences in an Afro-Cuban Religion*. Washington, DC: Smithsonian Institution Press.

Mazzarella, William. 2003. "'Very Bombay': Contending with the Global in an Indian Advertising Agency." *Cultural Anthropology* 18 (1): 33–71.

Mbembe, Achille. 2001. *On the Postcolony*. Berkeley: University of California Press.

McAlister, Elizabeth A. 2002. *Rara!: Vodou, Power, and Performance in Haiti and Its Diaspora*. Berkeley: University of California Press.

McLeod, Marc C. 2000. "Undesireable Aliens: Race, Ethnicity, and nationalism in the Comparison of Haitian and British West Indian Immigrant Workers in Cuba, 1898 to 1940." PhD diss., University of Texas.

McManus, Jane. 2000. *Cuba's Island of Dreams: Voices from the Isle of Pines and Youth*. Gainesville: University Press of Florida.

Medvedev, Katalin. 2007. "Dress, Hungarian Socialism, and Resistance." In *Dress Sense: Emotional and Sensory Experiences of the Body and Clothes*, edited by Donald Clay Johnson and Helen Bradley Foster, 23–35. New York: Berg.

Menéndez, Lázara. 1990. *Estudios afrocubanos: Selección de lecturas*. Havana: Universidad de la Habana.

Mesa-Lago, Carmelo., ed. 1971. *Revolutionary Change in Cuba*. Pittsburgh, PA: University of Pittsburgh Press.

Mesa-Lago, Carmelo, and June S. Belkin, eds. 1982. *Cuba in Africa*. Pittsburgh, PA: University of Pittsburgh.

Miller, Daniel. 1987. *Material Culture and Mass Consumption*. Oxford: B. Blackwell.

———. 1997. *Capitalism: An Ethnographic Approach*. Oxford: Berg.

———. 1998. "Coca-Cola: A Black Sweet Drink from Trinidad." In *Material Cultures: Why Some Things Matter*, edited by Daniel Miller, 169–87. Chicago: University of Chicago Press.

Miller, Daniel, and Sophie Woodward. 2011. *Blue Jeans: The Art of the Ordinary*. Berkeley: University of California Press.

Miller, Ivor. 1995. "Belief and Power in Contemporary Cuba: The Dialogue Between Santería Practitioners and Revolutionary Leaders." PhD diss., Northwestern University.

———. 2009. *Voice of the Leopard: African Secret Societies and Cuba*. Jackson: University Press of Mississippi.

Miller, Tom. 1996. *Trading with the Enemy: A Yankee Travels through Castro's Cuba*. New York: Basic Books.

Mintz, Sidney W. 1971. "The Caribbean as a Socio-Cultural Area." In *Peoples and Cultures of the Caribbean: An Anthropological Reader*, edited by Michael M. Horowitz, 17–46. Garden City, NY: Natural History Press.

———. 1986. *Sweetness and Power: The Place of Sugar in Modern History*. New York: Penguin Books.

———. 2010. *Three Ancient Colonies: Caribbean Themes and Variations.* Cambridge, MA: Harvard University Press.

Mintz, Sidney W., and Richard Price. 1992. *The Birth of African-American Culture: An Anthropological Perspective.* Boston: Beacon Press.

Moore, Carlos. 1988. *Castro, the Blacks, and Africa.* Los Angeles: University of California Press.

———. 2008. *Pichón: a Memoir: Race and Revolution in Castro's Cuba.* Chicago: Lawrence Hill Books.

Moore, Robin D. 1994. "Representations of Afrocuban Expressive Culture in the Writings of Fernando Ortiz." *Latin American Music Review* 15 (1): 32–54.

———. 1997. *Nationalizing Blackness: Afrocubanismo and Artistic Revolution in Havana, 1920–1940.* Pittsburgh, PA: University of Pittsburgh Press.

———. 2006. *Music and Revolution: Cultural Change in Socialist Cuba.* Berkeley: University of California Press.

———. 2010. *Music in the Hispanic Caribbean: Experiencing Music, Expressing Culture.* New York: Oxford University Press.

Morales Domínguez, Esteban, Gary Prevost, and August H. Nimtz. 2013. *Race in Cuba: Essays on the Revolution and Racial Inequality.* New York: Monthly Review Press.

Moreno Fraginals, Manuel. 1983. *La historia como arma: Y otros estudios sobre esclavos, ingenios y plantaciones.* Barcelona: Grupo Editorial Grijalbo.

———. 1995. *Economic and Social Factors in Cuba's Development.* New York: Research Institute for the Study of Man.

Moya, Eduardo, dir. 1984. *Algo más que soñar.* Havana: ECITV-FAR. VHS.

Mudimbe, V. Y. 1988. *The Invention of Africa: Gnosis, Philosophy, and the Order of Knowledge.* Bloomington: Indiana University Press.

Mueller, Tanja. 2010. "'Memories of Paradise': Legacies of Socialist Education in Mozambique." *African Affairs* 109 (436): 451–70.

Mujal-León, Eusebio. 2011. "Survival, Adaptation and Uncertainty: The Case of Cuba." *Journal of International Affairs* 65 (1): 149–68.

Muñiz, Mirta. 2003. *El cartel cubano.* Buenos Aires: Nuestra América.

Muñoz, Nicolás, dir. 2011. *El maestro saharaui: Océanos de exilio.* Spain: Toma24.

Nakassis, Constantine V. 2013. "Brands and Their Surfeits." *Cultural Anthropology* 28 (1): 111–26.

Naranjo, Luís. 2009. "Día de África en Camagüey respaldo cinco héroes." YouTube video, 0:47, posted May 29. *www.youtube.com/watch?v=m8h0LuvSNQ8.*

Nibbe, Ayesha. 2013. "Cuban Internacionalistas, Sports, and the Health of the 'Socialist Body' in Cuba and Africa. In *Health Travels: Cuban Health(care)*

On and Off the Island, edited by Nancy Burke, 178–201. San Francisco: UC Medical Humanities Consortium.

Novás Calvo, Lino. 1973. *Pedro Blanco, el negrero*. Madrid: Espasa-Calpe.

Núñez Jiménez, Antonio. 1976. *Isla de Pinos: Piratas, colonizadores, pebeldes*. Havana: Editorial Arte y Literatura.

———, ed. 1985. *Conferencia Internacional Presencia de Africa en América*. Havana: Comisión Cubana Conmemorativa del Encuentro de las Culturas del Viejo y del Nuevo Mundos.

Ochoa, Todd R. 2010. *Society of the Dead: Quita Manaquita and Palo Praise in Cuba*. Berkeley: University of California.

Oleschuk, Merin. 2011. "Engendering Food Meaning and Identity for Southern Sudanese Refugee Women in Brooks, Alberta." Master's thessis, University of Alberta.

Oliver, Regino, dir. 1990. *Caravana*. Havana: Instituto Cubano del Arte e Industria Cinematográficos. VHS.

Olwig, Karen F. 1990. "The Struggle for Respectability: Methodism and Afro-Caribbean Culture on Nineteenth-Century Nevis." *Nieuwe West-Indische Gids / New West Indian Guide* 64 (3/4): 93–114.

Ong, Aihwa. 1999. *Flexible Citizenship: The Cultural Logics of Transnationality*. Durham, NC: Duke University Press.

Oppenheimer, Andres. 1992. *Castro's Final Hour: The Secret Story Behind the Coming Downfall of Communist Cuba*. New York: Simon and Schuster.

O'Reilly, Richard. 1984. *El pueblo negro en Estados Unidos: Raices historicas de su lucha actual*. Havana: Editorial de Ciencias Sociales.

O'Reilly Herrera, Andrea. 2001. *ReMembering Cuba: Legacy of a Diaspora*. Austin: University of Texas Press.

Ortiz, Fernando. 1941. *Martí y las razas*. Havana: Publicaciones de la Comisión Nacional Organizadora de los Actos y Ediciones del Centario y del Monumento de Martí.

———. 1985. *Nuevo cataturo de cubanismos*. Havana: Editorial de Ciencias Sociales.

———. 1987. *Entre cubanos: Psicología tropical*. Havana: Editorial de Ciencias Sociales.

———. 1990. *Glosario de afronegrismos*. Havana: Editorial de Ciencias Sociales.

———. 1995a. *Cuban Counterpoint: Tobacco and Sugar*. Durham, NC: Duke University Press.

———. 1995b. *Los negros curros*. Havana: Editorial de Ciencias Sociales.

Ortiz, Fernando, and Isaac Barreal. 1993. *Etnia y sociedad*. Havana: Editorial de Ciencias Sociales.

Ossman, Susan. 2007. *Places We Share: Migration, Subjectivity, and Global Mobility.* Lanham, MD: Lexington Books.

———. 2013. *Moving Matters: Paths of Serial Migration.* Palo Alto, CA: Stanford University Press.

Padilla, Mark. 2007. *Caribbean Pleasure Industry: Tourism, Sexuality, and AIDS in the Dominican Republic.* Chicago: University of Chicago Press.

Padrón Hernández, Maria. 2012. "Beans and Roses: Everyday Economies and Morality in Contemporary Havana, Cuba." PhD diss., University of Gothenburg.

Palmié, Stephan. 2002. *Wizards and Scientists: Explorations in Afro-Cuban Modernity and Tradition.* Durham, NC: Duke University Press.

———. 2013. *The Cooking of History: How Not to Study Afro-Cuban Religion.* Chicago: University of Chicago Press.

Paquette, Robert L. 1988. *Sugar Is Made with Blood: The Conspiracy of La Escalera and the Conflict between Empires over Slavery in Cuba.* Middletown, CT: Wesleyan University Press.

Patico, Jennifer, and Melissa L. Caldwell. 2002. "Consumers Exiting Socialism: Ethnographic Perspectives on Daily Life in Post-Communist Europe." *Ethnos* 67 (3): 285–94.

Pérez, Gustavo, dir. 2006. *They Would All Be Queens / Todas iban a ser reinas.* Burlington, VT: Americas Media Initiative. DVD.

Pérez, Iratxe, dir. 2007. *Caribeños del Sáhara.* Navarre, Spain: Simetría Producciones.

Pérez, Iratxe, and Ricardo Galdeano, dirs. 2008. *Caribeños del desierto.* Navarre, Spain: Simetría Producciones.

Pérez, Luis A., Jr., ed. 1992. *Slaves, Sugar, and Colonial Society: Travel Accounts of Cuba, 1801–1899.* Wilmington, DE: Scholarly Resources.

———. 1994. "Between Baseball and Bullfighting: The Quest for Nationality in Cuba, 1868–1898." *Journal of American History* 81 (2): 493–517.

———., ed. 1998a. *Impressions of Cuba in the Nineteenth Century: The Travel Diary of Joseph J. Dimrock.* Wilmington, DE: Scholarly Resources.

———. 1998b. *The War of 1898: The United States and Cuba in History and Historiography.* Chapel Hill: University of North Carolina Press.

———. 1999. *On Becoming Cuban: Identity, Nationality, and Culture.* Chapel Hill: University of North Carolina Press.

Pérez-López, Jorge F. 1995. *Cuba's Second Economy: From Behind the Scenes to Center Stage.* New Brunswick, NJ: Transaction Publishers.

Pérez Firmat, Gustavo. 1994. *Life on the Hyphen: The Cuban-American Way.* Austin: University of Texas Press.

———. 1995. *Next Year in Cuba: A Cubano's Coming-of-Age in America.* New York: Doubleday.

————. 2012. *Life on the Hyphen: The Cuban-American Way*, rev. ed. Austin: University of Texas Press.

Pérez-Rey, Lisandro, dir. 2004. *La Fabri_K*. Miami, FL: Gato Films. DVD.

Pérez Sarduy, Pedro. 1990. "An Open Letter to Carlos Moore." *Cuba Update* Summer: 34–36.

Pérez Sarduy, Pedro, and Jean Stubbs, eds. 1993. *AfroCuba: An Anthology of Cuban Writing on Race, Politics and Culture*. Melbourne: Ocean Press.

————, eds. 2000. *Afro-Cuban Voices: On Race and Identity in Contemporary Cuba*. Gainsville: University Press of Florida.

Perry, Marc D. 2004. *Los Raperos: Rap, Race, and Social Transformation in Contemporary Cuba*. Austin: University of Texas at Austin.

————. 2008. "Global Black Self-Fashionings: Hip Hop as Diasporic Space." *Identities: Global Studies in Culture and Power* 15 (6): 635–64.

————. 2009. "Hip Hop's Diasporic Landscapes of Blackness." In *From Toussaint to Tupac: The Black International since the Age of Revolution*, edited by Michael O. West, William G. Martin, and Fanon Che Wilkins, 232–58. Chapel Hill: University of North Carolina Press.

————. 2016. *Negro Soy Yo: Hip Hop and Raced Citizenship in Neoliberal Cuba*. Chapel Hill: Duke University Press.

Pertierra, Anna C. 2008. "En Casa: Women and Households in Post-Soviet Cuba." *Journal of Latin American Studies* 40: 743–67.

————. 2009. "Private Pleasures: Watching Videos in Post-Soviet Cuba." *International Journal of Cultural Studies* 12 (2): 113–30.

————. 2011. *Cuba: The Struggle for Consumption*. Coconut Creek, FL: Caribbean Studies Press.

Peters, Christabelle. 2012. *Cuban Identity and the Angolan Experience*. New York: Palgrave Macmillan.

Porter, Amy L. 2008. "Fleeting Dreams and Flowing Goods: Citizenship and Consumption in Havana Cuba." *Political and Legal Anthropology Review* 31 (1): 134–49.

Porter, Bruce D., and Marvin Dunn. 1984. *The Miami Riot of 1980: Crossing the Bounds*. Lexington, MA: Lexington Books.

Portes, Alejandro, and Alex Stepick. 1993. *City on the Edge: The Transformation of Miami*. Berkeley: University of California Press.

Portuondo Zúñiga, Olga. 2001. *La Virgen de la Caridad: Símbolo de cubanía*. Santiago de Cuba: Editorial de Oriente.

Premat, Adriana. 2009. "State Power, Private Plots and the Greening of Havana's Urban Agriculture Movement." *City and Society* 21 (1): 28–57.

————. 2012. *Sowing Change: The Making of Havana's Urban Agriculture*. Nashville, TN: Vanderbilt University Press.

Pullum, Geoffrey K. 1991. *The Great Eskimo Vocabulary Hoax, and Other Irreverent Essays on the Study of Language*. Chicago: University of Chicago Press.

Queeley, Andrea. 2010a. "The Passing of a Black Yanqui: Field Notes from a Wannabe Santiaguera." In *Fieldwork Identities in the Caribbean*, edited by Erin B. Taylor, 77–104. Coconut Creek, FL: Caribbean Studies Press.

———. 2010b. "Somos Negros Finos: Anglophone Caribbean Cultural Citizenship in Revolutionary Cuba." In *Global Circuits of Blackness: Interrogating the African Diaspora*, edited by Jean Muteba Rahier, Percy C. Hintzen and Felipe Smith, 201–22. Chicago: University of Illinois Press.

Rahier, Jean, Percy C. Hintzen, and Felipe Smith. 2010. *Global Circuits of Blackness: Interrogating the African Diaspora*. Urbana: University of Illinois Press.

Rahier, Jean, ed. 1999. *Representations of Blackness and the Performance of Identities*. Westport CT: Bergin and Garvey.

Rangel Rivero, Armando. 2012. *Antropología en Cuba: Orígenes y desarrollo*. Havana: Fundación Fernando Ortiz.

Rather, Dan. 1996. "The Last Revolutionary." *CBS Evening News*, July 18. New York: CBS.

Rausing, Sigrid. 2004. *History, Memory, and Identity in Post-Soviet Estonia: The End of a Collective Farm*. Oxford: Oxford University Press.

Remesal, Agustín. 1998. *El enigma del* Maine*: 1898: El suceso que provocó la guerra de Cuba: accidente o sabotaje?* Barcelona: Plaza y Janés Editores.

Rich, Donna. 1989. "Cuban Internationalism: A Humanitarian Foreign Policy." In *The Cuba Reader: The Making of a Revolutionary Society*, edited by Philip Brenner, William M. LeoGrande, Donna Rich, and Daniel Siegel, 405–13. New York: Grove Press.

Richmond, Mark. 1991. "Exporting the Educational Revolution: The Cuban Project to Become a World Educational Power." In *Cuban Foreign Policy Confronts a New International Order*, edited by H. Michael Erisman and John M. Kirk, 167–79. Boulder, CO: Lynne Rienner Publishers.

Richmond, W. Kenneth. 1973. *La revolución de la enseñanza*. Havana: Instituto Cubano del Libro.

Rickover, Hyman G. 1976. *How the Battleship* Maine *Was Destroyed*. Washington, DC: Naval History Division Department of the Navy.

Rivero de la Calle, Manuel. 1984. *Antropologia de la poblacion adulta cubana*. Havana: Editorial Científico-Técnico.

Rojas, Marta. 1987. "Internacionalismo como una pequeña O.N.U." *Cuba Internacional* 19 (7): 16–21.

Roland, L. Kaifa. 2004. "El color no importa: Tourism and Race in Contemporary Cuba." PhD diss., Duke University.

————. 2006. "Tourism and the Negrificación of Cuban Identity." *Transforming Anthropology* 14 (2): 151–62.

————. 2011. *Cuban Color in Tourism and La Lucha: An Ethnography of Racial Meanings*. New York: Oxford University Press.

Rosendahl, Mona. 1997. *Inside the Revolution: Everyday Life in Socialist Cuba*. Ithaca, NY: Cornell University Press.

Rouse, Roger. 1991. "Mexican Migration and the Social Space of Postmodernism." *Diaspora* 1 (1): 8–23.

Routon, Kenneth. 2005. "Unimaginable Homelands? 'Africa' and the Abakuá Historical Imagination." *Journal of Latin American Anthropology* 10 (2): 370–400.

————. 2010. *Hidden Powers of State in the Cuban Imagination*. Gainesville: University Press of Florida.

Rumbaut, Rubén D., and Rubén G. Rumbaut. 2005. "Self and Circumstance: Journeys and Visions of Exile." In *The Dispossessed: An Anatomy of Exile*, edited by Peter I. Rose, 331–55. Amherst: University of Massachusetts Press.

Rumbaut, Rubén G. 1991. "The Agony of Exile: A Study of the Migration and Adaptation of Indochinese Refugee Adults and Children." In *Refugee Children: Theory, Research, and Services*, edited by Frederick L. Ahearn, Jr. and Jean L. Athey, 53–91. Baltimore, MD: The Johns Hopkins University Press.

————. 1997. "Assimilation and Its Discontents: Between Rhetoric and Reality." *International Migration Review* 31 (4): 923–60.

Ryer, Paul. 2000a. "Book Review: 'Inside The Revolution: Everyday Life in Socialist Cuba' by Mona Rosendahl." *American Ethnologist* 26 (4): 968–69.

————. 2000b. "Millenniums Past, Cuba's Future?" *Public Culture* 12 (2): 499.

————. 2006. "Between *La Yuma* and *África:* Locating the Color of Contemporary Cuba." PhD diss., University of Chicago.

————. 2010. "The Hyphen-Nation of Cuban-Educated Africans: Rethinking the '1.5 Generation' Paradigm." *International Journal of Cuban Studies* 2.1 and 2.2 (Spring/Summer): 74–87.

————. 2011. "Cars, Cigars and Cuban Coffee: Capitalism, Socialism and Mimetic Branding in Miami and Havana." Paper presented at Global Post/Socialisms? An Interdisciplinary Conversation on Asia, the Americas, and Europe. Riverside, CA, Oct. 20.

————. 2014. "The Seeing Eye is the Organ of Tradition." *EthnoCuba* (blog). October 10. etnocuba.ucr.edu/the-seeing-eye-is-the-organ-of-tradition.

————. 2015. "The *Maine*, the *Romney*, and the Threads of Conspiracy in Cuba." *International Journal of Cuban Studies* 7 (2): 200–11.

———. 2017. "The Rise and Decline of La Yuma: Global Symbols, Local Meanings, and Remittance Circuits in Post-Soviet Cuba." *Journal of Latin American and Caribbean Anthropology* 22 (2): 276–97.

Safa, Helen I. 1995. *The Myth of the Male Breadwinner: Women and Industrialization in the Caribbean*. Boulder, CO: Westview Press.

Sahlins, Marshall D. 1972. *Stone Age Economics*. New York: Aldine de Gruyter.

———. 2012. *What Kinship Is—And Is Not*. Chicago: University of Chicago Press.

Samuels, Peggy, and Harold Samuels. 1995. *Remembering the* Maine. Washington, DC: Smithsonian Institution Press.

Santa Cruz y Mallen, Francisco X. 1940. *Historia de las familias cubanas*. Havana: Editorial Hercules.

Santovenia y Echaide, Emeterio S. 1928. *Libro conmemorativo de la inauguración de la Plaza del* Maine *en la Habana*. Havana: Talleres del Sindicato de Artes Gráficas.

Sartorius, David A. 2013. *Ever Faithful: Race, Loyalty, and the Ends of Empire in Spanish Cuba*. Durham, NC: Duke University Press.

Sartre, Jean-Paul. 1961. *Sartre on Cuba*. New York: Ballantine Books.

Sawyer, Mark Q. 2006. *Racial Politics in Post-Revolutionary Cuba*. New York: Cambridge University Press.

Schiller, Nina Glick, and Thomas Faist. 2010. *Migration, Development, and Transnationalization: A Critical Stance*. New York: Berghahn Books.

Schiller, Nina Glick, and Ayse Simsek-Caglar. 2011. *Locating Migration: Rescaling Cities and Migrants*. Ithaca, NY: Cornell University Press.

Schlosser, Eric. 2002. *Fast Food Nation: The Dark Side of the All-American Meal*. New York: Harper Collins.

Schmidt, Jalane D. 2008. "Locked Together: The Culture and Politics of 'Blackness' in Cuba." *Transforming Anthropology* 16 (2): 160–64.

Schwartz, Rosalie. 1997. *Pleasure Island: Tourism and Temptation in Cuba*. Lincoln: University of Nebraska Press.

Schweid, Richard. 2004. *Che's Chevrolet, Fidel's Oldsmobile: On the Road in Cuba*. Chapel Hill: University of North Carolina Press.

Serpa, Enrique. 1982. *Contrabando*. Havana: Editorial Letras Cubanas.

Serviat, Pedro. 1986. *El problema negro en Cuba y su solución definitiva*. Havana: Editora Política.

Shakur, Assata. 1987. *Assata: An Autobiography*. Chicago: Lawrence Hill Books.

Simoni, Valerio. 2008. "'Riding' Diversity: Cubans'/Jineteros' Uses of 'Nationality-Talks' in the Realm of Their Informal Encounters with Tourists." In *Tourism Development: Growth, Myths and Inequalities*, edited by Peter M. Burns and Marina Novelli, 68–84. Oxfordshire, UK: CABI.

Simpson, Renate. 1984. *La educacion superior en Cuba bajo el colonialismo español*. Havana: Editorial de Ciencias Sociales.

Smith, Robert C. 2006. *Mexican New York: Transnational Lives of New Immigrants*. Berkeley: University of California Press.

Smith, Raymond T. 1988. *Kinship and Class in the West Indies: A Genealogical Study of Jamaica and Guyana*. Cambridge: Cambridge University Press.

———. 1996. *The Matrifocal Family: Power, Pluralism, and Politics*. New York: Routledge.

Sorín Zocolsky, Mónica. 1985. *Humanismo, patriotismo e internacionalismo en escolares cubanos*. Havana: Editorial de Ciencias Sociales.

Stepick, Alex, Terry Rey, and Sarah J. Mahler, eds. 2009. *Churches and Charity in the Immigrant City: Religion, Immigration, and Civic Engagement in Miami*. New Brunswick, NJ: Rutgers University Press.

Stolcke, Verena. (1974) 1989. *Marriage, Class, and Colour in Nineteenth-Century Cuba: A Study of Racial Attitudes and Sexual Values in a Slave Society*. Ann Arbor: University of Michigan Press.

Stout, Noelle M. 2008. "Feminists, Queers and Critics: Debating the Cuban Sex Trade." *Journal of Latin American Studies* 40 (4): 721–42.

———. 2014. *After Love: Queer Intimacy and Erotic Economies in Post-Soviet Cuba*. Durham, NC: Duke University Press.

Strachan, Ian G. 2002. *Paradise and Plantation: Tourism and Culture in the Anglophone Caribbean*. Charlottesville: University of Virginia Press.

Sublette, Ned. 2004. *Cuba and Its Music: From the First Drums to the Mambo*. Chicago: Chicago Press Review.

Sunderland, Patricia, and Rita M. Denny, eds. 2007. *Doing Anthropology in Consumer Research*. Walnut Creek, CA: Left Coast Press.

Sutton, Constance R., and Elsa Chaney. 1987. *Caribbean Life in New York City: Sociocultural Dimensions*. New York: Center for Migration Studies of New York.

Tanaka, Maki. 2011. "Heritage Modern: Cityscape of the Late Socialist Political Economy in Trinidad, Cuba." PhD diss., University of California, Berkeley.

Tannenbaum, Frank. (1940) 1992. *Slave and Citizen*. Boston: Beacon Press.

Tattlin, Isadora. 2002. *Cuba Diaries: An American Housewife in Havana*. Chapel Hill, NC: Algonquin Books.

Taussig, Michael T. 1980. *The Devil and Commodity Fetishism in South America*. Chapel Hill: University of North Carolina Press.

Taylor, Erin B. 2010. *Fieldwork Identities in the Caribbean*. Coconut Creek, FL: Caribbean Studies Press.

Thelen, Tatjana. 2011. "Shortage, Fuzzy Property and Other Dead Ends in the Anthropological Analysis of (Post)Socialism." *Critique of Anthropology* 31 (1): 43–61.

Torres-Cuevas, Eduardo. 1995. "En busca de la cubanidad." *Debates americanos* 1 (Jan.–June): 2–17.

———. 1996. "En busca de la cubanidad (II)." *Debates americanos* 2: 3–11.

Touré, Ousmanne M. 2004. "God is with Cuba and with Fidel." *Jeventud rebelde*, October 14.

Trouillot, Michel-Rolph. 1992. "The Caribbean Region: An Open Frontier in Anthropological Theory." *Annual Review of Anthropology* 21: 19–42.

———. 1995. *Silencing the Past: Power and the Production of History*. Boston: Beacon Press.

———. 2003. *Global Transformations: Anthropology and the Modern World*. New York: Palgrave Macmillan.

Tsing, Anna L. 2000. "The Global Situation." *Cultural Anthropology* 15 (3): 327–60.

———. 2005. *Friction: An Ethnography of Global Connection*. Princeton, NJ: Princeton University Press.

Tucker, Robert C., ed. 1978. *The Marx-Engels Reader*. New York: W.W. Norton.

Turner Martí, Lidia, Rolando Buenavilla Recio, Diego J. González Serra, Justo Chávez Rodríguez, and Alicia Obaya Martínez, eds. 1996. *Martí y la educación*. Havana: Editorial Pueblo y Educación.

Twine, France W. 1998. *Racism in a Racial Democracy: The Maintenance of White Supremacy in Brazil*. New Brunswick, NJ: Rutgers University Press.

Ubieta Gómez, Enrique. 1993. *Ensayos de identidad*. Havana: Editorial Letras Cubanas.

Vaughan, Umi. 2006. "Shades of Race in Contemporary Cuba." *Islas* 1 (2): 21–24.

Vazquez, Alexandra T. 2013. *Listening in Detail: Performances of Cuban Music*. Chapel Hill: Duke University Press.

Veenis, Milena. 1999. "Consumption in East Germany: The Seduction and Betrayal of Things." *Journal of Material Culture* 4 (1): 79–112.

Verdery, Katherine. 1992. "The 'Etatization' of Time in Ceausescu's Romania." In *The Politics of Time*, edited by Henry J. Rutz, 37–61. Washington, DC: American Ethnological Society.

———. 1996. *What Was Socialism, and What Comes Next?* Princeton, NJ: Princeton University Press.

———. 2014. *Secrets and Truths: Ethnography in the Archive of Romania's Secret Police*. Budapest: Central European University Press.

Verdery, Katherine, and Elizabeth Cullen Dunn 2011. "Dead Ends in the Critique of (Post)Socialist Anthropology: Reply to Thelen." *Critique of Anthropology* 31 (3): 251–55.

Vertovec, Steven. 2009. *Transnationalism*. London: Routledge.

Viddal, Grete. 2012. "Vodú Chic: Haitian Religion and the Folkloric Imaginary in Socialist Cuba." *New West Indian Guide* 86 (3–4): 205–36.

Wade, Peter. 1993. *Blackness and Race Mixture: The Dynamics of Racial Identity in Columbia*. Baltimore, MD: Johns Hopkins University Press.

———. 2010. *Race and Ethnicity in Latin America*. London: Pluto Press.

Wallerstein, Immanuel M. 1976. *The Modern World-System*. New York: Academic Press.

Watzlawick, Paul. 1977. *How Real is Real? Confusion, Disinformation, Communication*. New York: Vintage Books.

Weems, John E. 1958. *The Fate of the* Maine. New York: Holt.

Weinreb, Amelia R. 2009. *Cuba in the Shadow of Change: Daily Life in the Twilight of the Revolution*. Gainesville: University Press of Florida.

Wenders, Wim, dir. 1999. *Buena Vista Social Club*. Germany: Road Movies Fillmproduktion GmbH. VHS.

West-Durán, Alan. 2004. "Rap's Diasporic Dialogues: Cuba's Redefinition of Blackness." *Journal of Popular Music Studies* 16 (3): 4–39.

———. 2013. "Zurbano and 'The New York Times': Lost and Found in Translation." *AfroCubaWeb*, April 6, *www.afrocubaweb.com/alan-west-zurbano-nyt.html*.

Weston, Kath. 1997. *Families We Choose: Lesbians, Gays, Kinship*. New York: Columbia University Press.

Whiteford, Linda M., and Laurence G. Branch. 2008. *Primary Health Care in Cuba: The Other Revolution*. Lanham, MD: Rowman and Littlefield.

Whitten, Norman E., Jr., and Arlene Torres, eds. 1998. *Blackness in Latin America and the Caribbean: Social Dynamics and Cultural Transformations*. Bloomington: Indiana University Press.

Whorf, Benjamin L. 1956. *Language, Thought, and Reality*. Cambridge, MA: The MIT Press.

Williams, Robert Franklin, Martin Luther King, Jr., and Truman Nelson. 1962. *Negroes with Guns*. New York: Marzani and Munsell.

Wirtz, Kristina. 2004. "Santeria in Cuban National Consciousness: A Religious Case of the Doble Moral." *Journal of Latin American and Caribbean Anthropology* 9 (2): 409–38.

———. 2007. *Ritual, Discourse, and Community in Cuban Santería: Speaking a Sacred World*. Gainesville: University Press of Florida.

———. 2009. "Hazardous Waste: The Semiotics of Ritual Hygiene in Cuban Popular Religion." *Journal of the Royal Anthropological Institute* 15 (3): 476–501.

———. 2014. *Performing Afro-Cuba: Image, Voice, Spectacle in the Making of Race and History*. Chicago: University of Chicago Press.

Yang, Mayfair Mei-hui. 1994. *Gifts, Favors, and Banquets: The Art of Social Relationships in China*. Ithaca, NY: Cornell University Press.

Yazid, Chejdan M. 2009. "De la toronja y de la tormenta." Caribbean of the Sahara, accessed May 18, 2009. *www.caribbeanofthesahara.com/poemas.htm.*

Yglesias, Jose. 1968. *In the Fist of the Revolution: Life in a Cuban Country Town.* New York: Vintage Books.

Yurchak, Alexei. 2003. "Soviet Hegemony of Form: Everything Was Forever, Until It Was No More." *Comparative Studies in Society and History* 45 (3): 480–508.

———. 2006. *Everything Was Forever, Until It Was No More: The Last Soviet Generation.* Princeton, NJ: Princeton University Press.

Zatz, Marjorie S. 1994. *Producing Legality: Law and Socialism in Cuba.* New York: Routledge.

Zunes, Stephen, and Jacob Mundy. 2010. *Western Sahara: War, Nationalism, and Conflict Irresolution.* Syracuse, NY: Syracuse University Press.

Zurbano, Roberto. 2014. Cinco minutos de reflexión contra el racismo. *Negra cubana tenía que ser* (blog), October 10. *negracubanateniaqueser. com/2014/10/10/cinco-minutos-de-reflexion-contra-el-racismo.*

INDEX

Page numbers in *italic* indicate illustrations.